ALFRED WILLIAMS

ALFRED WILLIAMS

HIS LIFE AND WORK

By LEONARD CLARK

A Reprint with a new Introduction by the author

DAVID & CHARLES : NEWTON ABBOT

7153 4456 0

This book was first published by William George's Sons in 1945
This edition published 1969

© 1969 Leonard Clark

Printed in Great Britain by
Redwood Press Limited Trowbridge Wiltshire
for David & Charles (Publishers) Limited
South Devon House Railway Station
Newton Abbot Devon

INTRODUCTION TO THE 1969 EDITION

This book about Alfred Williams, hammerman and poet, was first published in a modest edition in 1945. It attracted a great deal of attention at the time and was favourably reviewed, largely because its readers were deeply moved by the story it had to tell of the life of this heroic man, and the support he received from his wife, Mary. Now that the book is to be reissued in a new format, I am given the opportunity to say something about it, for I would wish to correct some of my youthful exuberances. A quarter of a century later, I am able to see my subject in better perspective. If I were writing this book again, from scratch, I believe that I should do it rather better. Amongst other things, I should not only tone down some of my remarks but also be more economical of language. I should omit a great deal of what I wrote originally about Alfred Williams's books and about what the reviewers of his day had to say about them. Although he was a most gifted and accurate writer of topography, and a genuine poet, I should not now make the extravagant claims I once made for him, nor include so many clogging details. But what I wrote all those years ago cannot be corrected because of the method by which this book is now produced; I can only ask a generation of newer readers to forgive me for my earlier lack of proportion.

What remain unaltered are the facts of Alfred Williams's life. I would not wish to do anything about a single one of these. They shine out as clearly as they ever did. There were all those early struggles of childhood and adolescence, the desertion by an improvident father at so tender an age, the struggles of his mother with eight children under the age of twelve to feed and clothe, his all-too-short village school education and the gradual forming of his rugged character during the uncertain days of his adolescence. There were, also, all the efforts Alfred Williams made to teach himself and to widen his knowledge of books. He was a natural student, with an amazing memory and an outstanding capacity for hard work and self-discipline. And all this was to continue against the grim background of the Swindon railway factory with its continual grind and heavy manual work. Yet, such was the stature of this man, that he was acknowledged to be one of its best workmen. At the same time he was well versed in Latin and Greek, and in the history and natural phenomena of his immediate neighbourhood.

But Alfred Williams was something more than an indomitable workman-scholar. The poems and prose books he wrote, if not sufficient to establish him as a major writer, cannot be dismissed as the work of a well-meaning amateur. The poems were skilfully put together though sometimes many of them were too reminiscent of Alfred Williams's classical reading. The nature poems he wrote, though, especially *The Hills, The Testament,* and *Natural Thoughts and Surmises,* are passionate and personal statements, couched it is true in the poetic language of their times, but revealing the inner thoughts and feelings of a mature poet-philosopher. The prose books do not deserve to be forgotten. *Life in a Railway Factory* is a minor classic, a searing social document of labour conditions at the beginning of the present century; *A Wiltshire Village, Villages of the White Horse,* and *Round About the Upper Thames,* are valuable contributions to the history and folk lore of the English countryside, with their many vivid pictures of villagers, customs, and scenery. *Folksongs of the Upper Thames* has preserved many of the ancient pieces which might well have disappeared for ever.

But it is the later years of his life which highlight the final triumph and tragedy of Alfred Williams, as seen against the background of his enduring love for Mary, the grief of their childless marriage, and his slow decline into disillusionment. He experienced lack of recognition as well as of money. His horticultural efforts were also a miserable failure. The last few years were only relieved by the building of their own house with their own hands and with Alfred embarking on the learning of Sanskrit. And, finally, there was the death of Mary and his own sudden and sad farewell to life.

What a story it is, of dedication and unflinching courage, of positive accomplishment. It is no record of failure. Alfred Williams proved abundantly that the spirit of man is capable of the highest when associated with true endeavour and a belief in the value of things for themselves.

In my original preface I wrote,

The story of Alfred Williams is the tragedy of one who was a misfit in the social system of his day. He was like one born out of time, though his particular form of individualism and protest would have clashed with the system of any age. His unusual gifts of character, highly developed intelligence, his originality of outlook, his honesty of utterance, and his abhorrence of any kind of sham or regimentation, separated him from many members of his own class. Not that Alfred Williams was autocratic in his everyday contacts. On the contrary, this provincial proletarian had a wide knowledge and deep understanding of the needs and strivings of his fellowmen. What is more, he boldly espoused their cause during the whole of his life.

Yet, with one or two rare exceptions, he lived apart from the organised 'working men movements' which were a feature of his age and remained strangely unsympathetic in his attitude towards political socialism and the machinery of its reforms. And this is well understandable, for had it not been for the patronage and financial assistance of a benevolent aristocrat his early books would never have been published during his lifetime. Alfred Williams was indeed a true aristocrat, for all his wealth and power was of the mind and spirit.

I would not wish to change a single line of this. I am only amazed that Alfred Williams is not better known today by a generation which tends to take for granted some of the values and material benefits which lives like his have bequeathed to them.

The original list of acknowledgments thanked many who helped Alfred Williams during his lifetime and gave me great assistance when I embarked upon my task. There is no point in listing them again—all those faithful friends who believed in him and recognised him for what he was. They were under his spell as I have been for so many years. If they were here now, they would surely rejoice that he has not been entirely forgotten. It is my belief that the young of today, with their uncompromising honesty and directness, their struggles in a far more material and standardised age, will be captivated and humbled by this, almost incredible, story of a noble life.

LEONARD CLARK

"His achievement is an abiding spiritual example to the workmen of this country"—ROBERT BRIDGES.

"You can guess that nothing encourages a writer more than to get such letters, and I owe some friendships which I value very much to them, especially that of Alfred Williams, the Hammerman Poet, as someone named him, who is indeed a wonderful man, having taught himself English Literature, and much of French, Latin, and Greek in the scanty leisure—not leisure at all, I am afraid I should almost call it—of a worker at the Great Western forges at Swindon."—JOHN BAILEY to SAMUEL J. LOOKER, September, 1918.

"England is greater to-day because Alfred Williams lived a brief day in her life"—ALBERT MANSBRIDGE.

CONTENTS

ILLUSTRATIONS

PREFACE AND ACKNOWLEDGEMENTS

THE story of Alfred Williams is the tragedy of one who was a misfit in the social system of his day. He was like one born out of time, though his particular form of individualism and protest would have clashed with the system of any age. His unusual gifts of character, his highly developed intelligence, his originality of outlook, his honesty of utterance, and his abhorrence of any kind of sham or regimentation, separated him from many members of his own class. Not that Alfred Williams was autocratic in his everyday contacts. On the contrary, this provincial proletarian had a wide knowledge and deep understanding of the needs and strivings of his fellowmen. What is more, he boldly espoused their cause during the whole of his life.

Yet, with one or two rare exceptions, he lived apart from the organised "working men movements" which were a feature of his age and remained strangely unsympathetic in his attitude towards political socialism and the machinery of its reforms. And this is well understandable, for had it not been for the patronage and financial assistance of a benevolent aristocrat his early books would never have been published during his lifetime. Alfred Williams was indeed a true aristocrat, for all his wealth and power was of the mind and spirit.

But it is only the mosaic of his life, with its continual economic embarrassment and miserable ending, which bears the marks of tragedy. His final achievement, seen now and in perspective, was supreme, and certainly matched by few others in this century. His unshaken belief in the power of the spirit enabled him to emerge triumphant from the maelstrom, and this in spite of, perhaps, because of, the many disappointments and acute poverty which haunted his later years. The nature and immensity of this triumph has something in it of the positivity of the old Greek drama, for it is imbued with the eternal. It not only affords to those who come after, an abiding example of character painfully but surely forged through adversity, of suffering which, in the words of Sir Alfred Zimmern, led Alfred Williams to "the fullness of human existence", but also it has that quality of permanency which, when it turns from cruelty and ugliness, is all beauty and fulfilment.

Hence, a full-length biography of this truly remarkable figure is long overdue. It is now some fourteen years since Alfred Williams died in utter loneliness and unwarranted frustration in his self-made cottage in the village of South Marston, Wiltshire. And since this catastrophe for English letters, there has always loomed on the horizon the menacing possibility that much of the material necessary for the sincere biographer, who wished to produce a work which has something more than colourful journalism, might be scattered and lost. For letters, press-cuttings and manuscripts get burned or salvaged, memories fade, books go out of print and circulation, key people die.   Since his death, the number of people who knew Alfred Williams intimately and rejoiced in his comradeship, has grown steadily less.   Fortunately for the present biographer it has been possible for him to handle and read a very large number of Alfred Williams' letters, to have been given willing access to much published and unpublished material which dealt with the various aspects of his life and work, and, most valuable of all, to have received accurate and cross-checked witness from his sisters and oldest friends.   There have been those, too, so necessary to a biographer, who have kept his memory green by publishing articles and letters about him from time to time in a sympathetic local press, arranged regular pilgrimages to his birthplace and cottage, recommended his books, raised stones to his memory, and, in short, permitted no opportunity to slip by without passing on some of the magic and inspiration which they themselves had captured from their friend. They have treasured his memory well and tenderly nurtured it under the rolling South Country skies.

So, to all who have thus laboured, and who have given free advice, constant encouragement and material assistance, the biographer tends his sincere thanks and makes due acknowledgement.   For without them, this life could not have been written.   They include the following: Mr. A. E. Withy, the late Mr. Llewellyn Robins, Mr. and Mrs. Henry Byett, Mr. J. B. Jones, Mr. W. D. Bavin, Miss Elizabeth Ann Williams, Mrs. Laura Pill, Miss Ellen Williams, Mrs. Ada Mary Thorne, Mr. Stanley Hirst and the Swindon Education Committee, the Principal of the Swindon Technical College, the Curator of the Swindon Museum, the Swindon Workers' Educational Association, Mr. Stanley Jarman (photographs), Dr. and Mrs. Albert Mansbridge, Sir Alfred Zimmern, Canon Guy Rawlence, the late Mr. C. H. Hollick, Mr. A. E. Cole, Mr. E. R. Denwood, Mr. William Dowsing, Mrs. Miles, Mr. Percival Cackett, Mrs. Field, Miss Maisey, Mr. Stanley George (letters written to Mr. Reuben George), Mrs. Ireland, Mr. J. V. Campbell Hack (letters written to Mrs. Hack), Mr. Douglas Simmonds, Mr. George Milsted and Messrs. Gerald Duckworth, Ltd., Mr. Galloway Kyle and Messrs. Erskine Macdonald, Ltd., Mr. Basil Blackwell, Mr. John Murray, Miss J. Bailey (letters written to and by Mr. John Bailey), *The Wiltshire Times*, The Swindon Press, Ltd., *The Wilts and Gloucester Standard*, *The Highway*, *The G.W.R. Magazine*, *The Englishman* (India), *The Empress* (Calcutta), *Railways*, *The Cawnpore Reciter*, *The Indian Daily Telegraph*.

And finally, to the one who patiently and ungrudgingly watched the development of this work from its genesis, and typed the main of its chapters.

Every effort has been made to avoid infringement of copyright.   If, inadvertently, this has been committed, the biographer tenders his apologies.

PROLOGUE

THE Berkshire and Wiltshire Downs slumber like leopards couched in the evening sunlight. They are old in wisdom, in mystery, and in remembrance. They dream away their long secrets through the years, and time rolls over them.

If the traveller out from Swindon makes his way to Notgrove Long Barrow and lifts up his eyes to the southern hills, he will see in glory, thirty miles away on the imprisoning horizon, those very Wiltshire Downs. Behind him to the north flower the Gloster Cotswolds. The edges of the Downs break into the heaving prominences that are White Horse Hill, Liddington Castle and Burderop Down. The latter, more commonly known as Barbury Hill, reaches, with a crown of beeches, 900 feet into the sky to the right of his weathered sister of Liddington.

When the traveller stands in repose and security, either on Liddington or Barbury, he will see, far beneath him, the multi-coloured meadows and pastures of the Vale of the White Horse. If he knows the district well, he will realise, when he rests on Barbury, that it, and Coate and the village of South Marston lie in one straight line before him, and that the smoke which floats from the high woods of the Cotswolds to the north comes from the chimneys of the cottages in that poem which men call Painswick. This is indeed one of the serenest vistas in the Upper Thames basin.

But a stranger on Liddington will wonder why a simple Ordnance Survey Triangulation pyramid there bears a plaque with an inscription which reads:—

> Liddington Hill. The Hill beloved of Richard Jefferies and Alfred Williams.

Jefferies, yes. But Alfred Williams?

Let him tramp over to Barbury Hill; he will find on it a sarsen stone, a massive block of grey wether weighing over three tons, bearing two bronzes, each with an inscription. One reads:—

> Richard Jefferies, 1848—1887. It is eternity now. I am in the midst of it. It is about me in the sunshine.

The other, which faces north-east to Liddington, reads:—

> Alfred Williams, 1877—1930.
> > Still to find and still to follow
> > Joy in every hill and hollow
> > Company in solitude.

So on these cathedral hills there rest the proud memorials of two noble Wiltshire men, unknown to each other during their lifetime, but here linked beneath the clouds as an everlasting sign that they sang the same song and laboured for the same ideals of truth and beauty.

When the traveller leaves the heights behind him and descends to the plains, let him return to Swindon. In the stamping shop of the busy railway factory here, this same Alfred Williams worked as a hammerman for nearly twenty-five years of his life; it stands to-day in all its noise and thunderous fury, the most poignant reminder of this lover of Liddington and Barbury.

He knew the streets of Swindon all his life and on the walls of its Town Hall is now nailed a bronze tablet which says;—

In Memoriam. Alfred Owen Williams, 1877—1930. Lyrical Poet, Classical Scholar, Master of English Prose, Who, self-taught, self-inspired, while toiling at the forge, illumined all around him with

"The light that never was on sea or land,
The consecration and the Poet's dream."
Sunt hic etiam sua præmia laudi,
Sunt lacrimae rerum et mentem mortalia tangunt.

"His achievement is an abiding spiritual example to the workmen of this country."—Robert Bridges.

Alfred Williams? He must have been no mean man to be thus commemorated in the town which knew him so intimately, and for a Poet Laureate to feel it an honour to be associated with a Hammerman. Williams—the "classical scholar"—might well have translated the Virgil quotation on that tablet, "Even here doth virtue reap its just reward, and mortal chances touch the soul to tears".

But there are other witnesses to his genius elsewhere in this town. The majority of his library books, so hardly obtained, so eagerly studied, are in the Commonweal School. Many of his original manuscripts, written over the wearying years in his neat and bold handwriting, are in the Technical College. Relics of his are in the Museum, and his published works are on the shelves of the Public Library. Swindon's Institute for the Blind is dedicated to his memory and bears his name; the first £55 of its endowment fund came from the sale of a plot of land which once belonged to him.

From the hills to the town, from the town to the main Shrivenham road, and then through a canopy of trees along a country lane, the traveller is at South Marston, a sweet and rare village, where Williams lived for nearly all his life and which to-day is quick with his memory. The country people who quietly come and go are sealed for ever in the

words of his picturesque writing. Many of them knew him personally.
These thatched houses and shining meadows, that dignified little
church, the birds, flowers, and trees—all remember his name. He was
born in that house, lived for the greater part of his life in that one, while
the cottage opposite the village hall and War Memorial he and his wife
built with their own hands.

Open the little gate of this cottage, traveller, and walk up the path-
way that cuts the front garden into two flowering plots. Halt then in
reverence at the front door. Over its porch is another inscription;—

In memoriam. Alfred Williams, the Hammerman Poet, lived here.
Born 7 February, 1877; died 9 April, 1930.

This sturdy little house is "Ranikhet", the dream-child of his latter
days.

Only a few yards away, across the green, loud with the cries of home-
coming ducks and geese, is the churchyard. Here he and his wife are
buried. His grey, granite memorial is shaped like an open book and
has incised on the slab on which it rests, some words of his own:—

"I will sing my song triumphantly.
I will finish my race.
I will work my task."

This was a man, then, of many memorials and many friends. This
village and the countryside for miles around it, with its streams and
hills and downland were his continual inspiration.

Who was this man ?

CHAPTER ONE

ORIGINS

ALFRED WILLIAMS was born on 6th February, 1877, in the Wiltshire village of South Marston. There seems some doubt as to whether the birth took place on the 6th or the 7th. The birth certificate gives the 6th as the date, but the baptismal certificate gives it as the 7th; his mother was adamant that he was born on the 7th, and all his memorials record the latter date. The birth was registered on 10th March, 1877, in the Highworth sub-district, the certificate giving the name as Owen Alfred Williams; the name Owen was rarely used by him.

On the paternal side, he was descended from very good Welsh stock; on the maternal, there were ancient links with Herefordshire. His father's forbears had been lawyers, and three generations back there had been a judge. In the next generation, which included his grandfather, David Aust Williams, there were two members of the legal profession and one of the medical. David Williams, a young farmer, married Ann Roberts, the daughter of a neighbouring wealthy farmer; their thirteenth child and tenth son, Elias Lloyd Williams, born at Conway in 1849, was the father of Alfred Williams.

David Williams, later on in life, gave up his farming interests and learned the artistic side of woodwork. He soon found plenty of work, and his contracts took him to all parts of the country, where he used his special skill in constructing the decorative woodwork in mansions, churches, and public buildings. The son, Elias Lloyd, also took to the trade, and frequently travelled with his father. On one occasion they carried out some work for the Duke of Newcastle at his country seat in Nottinghamshire. As a result of this contract they met the Duke's solicitor, Alfred Bell, who had recently purchased the main of the property in South Marston. Bell was so pleased with the quality of the Williams' work for his client that he approached them with the suggestion that they should journey into Wiltshire and execute the whole of the woodwork for the model cottages and school which he proposed to build at Marston. The offer was accepted and the Welshmen moved south.

They were excellent craftsmen and would have resented strongly any reference to themselves as village carpenters. It is true that general carpentry was a necessary part of their structural work, but, in the main, their craft lay in the setting out, carving, joining, and setting in position of the various examples of their decorative work. Elias, beside being

a very good craftsman, was interested in the law, architecture, and
poetry. When on his travels he usually carried with him a pocket
edition of Pope's *Iliad*.

Alfred Williams' mother's ancestors had been farmers and builders.
His great-grandfather, Hughes by name, came from Herefordshire,
where he was a small farmer. In later years, he and his wife Elizabeth
rented a farm near Malmesbury, from the Earl of Suffolk and Berkshire.
Here they brought up seven children; Joshua, the youngest, was
Alfred Williams' grandfather.

The elder Hughes was eventually pressed for service in India,
leaving Elizabeth to manage the farm and rear her children single-
handed through the hungry years of the mid-nineteenth century.
Joshua was always ailing; on one occasion, white bread had to be
specially obtained for him in order to save his life. The father, returning from India, continued with his farming. When Joshua reached
manhood, a small house at South Marston, with tanning sheds attached,
was bought for him and his elder brother Cornelius. There was a small
farm available and here, as tanner and smallholder, Joshua Hughes
laboured for fifty years.

Shortly after the Hughes family took over the Marston farm, there
moved into the village, John and Elizabeth Hayden. Hayden was a
stonemason, with three children, the youngest of whom was a daughter,
Ann. In course of time, Ann Hayden married Joshua Hughes and the
couple occupied a part of the family residence. Ann Hughes was a
gifted woman, and so interested in the Marston children that she
opened a school for a number of them whose mothers were compelled
to work in the fields. The marriage was a happy one; four children
were born to them, the third being Elizabeth, who was Alfred Williams'
mother. Alfred Williams well remembered his grandfather and refers
to him in his book *A Wiltshire Village* as " . . . my old granddad, Josh
Hughes, a true old rustic gentleman, very unsophisticated, but hard-
working and thrifty".

As their children began to grow up, Joshua and Ann were obliged
to move into a larger house. As they could not discover a suitable
residence in the village they had a house built for them which they
named Rose Cottage. The old tannery residence has long since been
demolished, but a part of the tanning sheds still remains in crumbling
ruin.

Elizabeth Hughes was the younger daughter and because of this
and also because of her delicate state of health, she remained at home
with her parents. She was a lovely creature, with a keen eye for
natural beauty and a deep appreciation and understanding of country
customs and manners. She was the darling of Joshua's old age and
she in her turn was devoted to him, and all her life paid tribute to the

uprightness and resolution of his simple character. She had many admirers in Marston and district, and many of them were considered "good matches" by her parents, but she declined them all. While on a visit to her brother in Reading, however, she met a government official and fell deeply in love with him. He was a Devonian from the borders of Dartmoor and the admiration was mutual; unhappily for both he succumbed to tuberculosis. She went to his funeral and then returned in sorrow to her home, vowing that she would never marry anyone else. To her dying day she treasured his Valentines and even mentioned them in her will.

When she arrived back at Rose Cottage it was to find David and Elias Williams installed as lodgers. On reaching Marston, they had found it difficult to procure accommodation in the village and when Ann Hughes was appealed to, she suggested, in the goodness of her heart, that they should stay with her for the time being. The inevitable happened. The grieving Elizabeth, then fascinating with all the charm of her saddened eighteen years, entranced the young Welshman so that he, wooing her with persistent ardour for two years, eventually married her shortly after his coming of age. This was in March, 1870.

The match did not meet with the approval of her parents, who felt confident that she was making a great mistake by marrying beneath her and to one whom they considered to be a "foreigner". It was certainly not a very propitious time for a young couple to start out in life together for prices were high and work at times not easy to come by. The first quartern loaf of bread they ever bought cost them half-a-crown. In later years, when Elizabeth was questioned as to why she had married Elias Williams, she replied, "I did so in the bitterness of my heart and to divert my thoughts, if possible, from the dead. I determined I would please my eye, if I broke my heart, and Elias *was* a fine looking man".

What she did not know was that he was already betrothed to a young woman in North Wales. Many years later, one of her sons who was then living in Rhyl, was introduced to a spinster past middle age. When she learnt who he was, she remarked, "Your father was to have been my husband; I loved him".

Elizabeth's family decided it would be best to accept philosophically the situation created by their daughter's marriage, and, as a wedding gift, they gave her a corner of what was known as "The Hook". This was a meadow lying at the centre of the village near an old boundary stone, from which latter, according to Alfred Williams in *A Wiltshire Village*, the name of South Marston may have been derived. On this piece of land Elizabeth and Elias Williams built Cambria Cottage, which was to be their future home. While it was being erected they continued to live with her parents at Rose Cottage. A further portion of "The Hook" was presented to Elias in order that he might build a workshop and timber loft on it; the land was mortgaged in order to find the money for the building of the cottage and workshop which were completed by the end of 1871.

"The Hook" meadow originally consisted of the ground on which both Rose Cottage and Cambria Cottage were built; the by-road now divides the two plots of land. The original writings relating to "The Hook" states that Elizabeth Hayden bought it from a certain Crowdy-Crowdy, of Highworth. It was bequeathed by her to a daughter of her first marriage, named Sarah Bourton. This latter had presented the site of Rose Cottage, together with £500 for building expenses, to her half-sister Ann and her husband Joshua, when they had left the tannery residence. When Sarah Bourton died she left the remaining portion of "The Hook" to Ann and Joshua Hughes, who in turn presented the major portion of it to their daughter Elizabeth and her husband Elias Williams.

Some years afterwards, Elias Williams rented a timber yard in Swindon and set up in business as a building contractor, but his venture, largely owing to a disastrous fire, and some unwise speculation, was unsuccessful.

CHAPTER TWO

CHILDHOOD

ELIZABETH WILLIAMS was only to have ten years of married life and these were not of the happiest. When she was only thirty, Elias left her with eight children on her hands—four girls and four boys, all under twelve years of age, the youngest being a babe in arms. The family, all of whom had been born in Cambria Cottage, consisted of Ernest Lloyd, Edgar David, Elizabeth Ann, Henry Oliver, Owen Alfred, Laura, Ellen, and Ada Mary. Alfred was thus the fifth child and fourth son. He was born in the room of Cambria Cottage facing south-west.

The departure of her husband was a blow, but though she felt keenly the shame of her position, she faced up to her new difficulties with courage and great patience. She resolved to be completely independent and to support herself and her large family entirely by her own labours. She devised various ways by which she might earn a living. She took in needlework, she stocked her window with sweetmeats, she took over the distribution in the South Marston area, of the newly founded *Swindon Advertiser* and tramped around the district every Saturday evening selling copies of that newspaper. Then, when the *North Wilts*

Herald needed a local agent, she undertook the distribution of that paper also over the same area. She delivered her papers for a quarter of a century and for her pains received a commission of threepence per dozen for the *Swindon Advertiser* and fourpence per dozen for the *North Wilts Herald*. Over the years her average sales of the *Advertiser* were seven dozen weekly; those of the *Herald* were rather lower. Thus, in order to add about three and ninepence weekly to her income, she trudged many weary miles in every kind of downland weather. When the elder children could do so, they helped in the sales of the papers. Her income from this particular source was sufficient to pay for her children's education, since there was no free schooling at that time in the village.

When hay harvest was in progress, she offered her services to a local farmer and in the appropriate season, went gleaning, often accompanied by the elder children. Laura and Ada well remember gleaning with their mother in the Four Docks Field, and her son, referring to these years in *A Wiltshire Village*, wrote: "I was a small boy of eight years when I worked the first summer among them. I shall never forget those early days in the fields; that was my first experience of real work". Elizabeth Williams worked for thirty years in those Wiltshire fields.

She was beset with worries. Her own health was precarious, largely through lack of sleep, and two of the children were generally ailing. Once, when there was typhoid fever in the house, she was unable to undress for five weeks, but she did her household work just the same. Life was a succession of trials and mishaps. One child fell into the fire and was badly burned. Another fractured a thigh. A third also fractured a thigh, while Laura, when only six weeks old, was burned on the right hand and arm by Alfred as she lay in her cot. He was then fifteen and a half months old and was amusing himself playing with fire and paper. When nearly two years old, Alfred wandered out of the cottage one summer evening in his night clothes and fell into a disused well in "The Hook", from which he was rescued with difficulty, after narrowly escaping suffocation in the sewage. A few months later he was rescued from drowning in a pond where he was fishing for minnows. At the age of three he was knocked down by a market gardener's cart a few yards from the house, the wheels of the cart actually passing over his stomach.

Then Elizabeth Williams received news which almost made her give up hope. Ever since her husband's disappearance she had continued the repayment of the mortgage which had been raised on "The Hook" and which was at the rate of five shillings weekly. But when the repayments had been nearly completed, she discovered that Elias had, entirely without her knowledge, arranged a second mortgage on the land in order to finance his unsuccessful Swindon venture. The first intimation that she had of this was when bailiffs suddenly arrived to take possession of Cambria Cottage and its contents. Fortunately, the furniture was her own and she was able to prove this, but the fact remained that she and her family were now homeless and destitute. Grandmother Hughes, however, came to the rescue and received Mrs. Williams and her eight children in Rose Cottage.

Alfred Williams remained with the rest of the family at Rose Cottage until his marriage. It stands still, with its well made porch a fine specimen of the woodwork craftsmanship of Elias Williams. It was here that both Joshua and Ann Hughes died, and in later years, Alfred's mother. Rose Cottage is still occupied by his sister Ada and her family; Cambria Cottage was occupied by other people.

So slender was her weekly income that the disbursement of it called for much skill, but Elizabeth Williams was scrupulously careful and made a point of balancing her budget, even to the last farthing. She refused to incur in any week more expense than she could clear in that week. And this, in spite of the fact that she made a point of refusing to buy cheap food substitutes which she considered to be uneconomical in the long run.

As each harvest time came round she went gleaning and the results of this, after threshing, she took to the West Mill at Shrivenham. In the milling of the gleanings she saw to it that too much gluten was not removed from them, for it was from this that she made a nourishing pudding, with suet for fat, and home-made jam or fresh fruit for flavour. This formed the family's staple diet during the corn harvest period. She always had a pig in the sty and served plenty of vegetables grown by her in the garden at Rose Cottage. Every week a large cake was made.

Cheap, ill-fitting boots were not favoured, either, and all the children wore boots made to measure from the best leather. These, though costly, were found to be more durable, and gave greater comfort, avoiding the crippling of feet. To the end of his days, Alfred was an impressive figure by reason of the uprightness of his carriage and the firmness of his tread. He attributed these entirely to his mother's early care for their feet, and has written in *A Wiltshire Village*: "When we were small boys and went to school, ours (i.e., boots) cost 8/6, as I remember, and were securely watertight. This we soon ascertained because we made haste to try them in the first ditch or pool we came to!"

Every Saturday night before bathing, the children were methodically doctored, and Elizabeth Williams was commended for this by the family physician who repeatedly said that if more mothers managed their families as she did he would be needed less often in their homes. Every night she mended their clothes and if the work was not completed, she rose early the following morning and finished the garments before breakfast. When the children had been washed, she sent them off to the village school, always punctual, always with shining boots, with clean pinafores for the girls and clean collars for the boys and never a broken bootlace. Her parting words to them were generally the same. "Be sure you put your hand to your forehead and say 'Thank you', and mind you say 'Please' with a polite bow."

Her kindliness of heart extended beyond her immediate home circle to all those in the village who needed sympathy and help. She even dared to venture into and clean the cottage of old Mark Titcombe, a quaint and mysterious character mentioned by Alfred Williams in *A Wiltshire Village*. The other villagers feared to cross the ancient's threshhold.

Alfred Williams has told us something about the South Marston school in his books. He attended it regularly with his brothers and sisters until his eighth birthday. Miss Deacon, who was the school mistress at that time, often used to tell the other children that the Williams' children were the best and the most polite scholars.

Shortly after his eighth birthday, Alfred Williams became a "half-timer", attending school for a part of each day only and being employed for the remainder by a local farmer. He took his place in the fields amongst the men and women and other young children, and was first employed at crawling on his hands and knees between drills of peas and wheat nearly a foot high, and methodically pulling out charlock by the roots. He also went stone-picking and "bird-starving"—the local name for bird scaring. Of these days he has written, "Old Launcelot (Launcelot Whitfield, the farmer at Burton Grove) had sent down to the school for boys and girls to help with the haymaking. I was one of those chosen to go forth and put my shoulder to the wheel or my hand to the implement. About all I really did do though, was to lead the horses, carry the wooden bottles of ale to and from the farm, or rake up the hay with the girls; but I felt very important, especially when the time came round to receive my wages for the task—a bright 2/- piece every weekend." And again, "To me it was a period of much happiness, and when I consider the particular qualities of my own parents, of the farmer who employed us, and those of my companions at that time and afterwards, and compare them with the present produce, I am not at all convinced that, although we are better educated, there is the same amount of kindness, honesty, and determination."

He was a passionate-tempered, impulsive little boy, with an innate spirit of adventure. His brain was so active that the rest of the family often felt a desire for quiet, since it was trying to be near him. When he lost his temper, which was fairly often, his sisters ran away from him, but the fit was soon over. He was fond of climbing trees, and when Sunday school was over he used to go for a ramble in the fields. One day he came to a tree which seemed an easy one to climb, with the added attraction of a slide down a branch to the ground. His sister Bess, who was with him, reminded him that he was wearing a new suit, and of the certainty of punishment if he tore it. The advice fell on deaf ears. He scaled the tree, slid to the ground, and ripped a sleeve. Sister and brother wept bitterly in anticipation of what would surely follow, and, although Elizabeth Williams was not given to beatings, Alfred suffered for his disobedience.

On another occasion, three of the family went carol singing, which the independent-minded mother had forbidden. When she learned what had happened, all three paid the penalty; the evening's takings had not been worth while. Laura remembers how at Christmas, Alfred would fill their stockings with cinders, though there were always some presents as well for them, bought out of his small store of pennies. She was often fascinated, while he tried the effect of making a pair of iron fire tongs produce "music," which he did by tying string to them, fixing it to his ears, and gaily knocking the tongs against a shovel.

Out of what he earned while half-timing, he began to save up for a steam engine and eventually made a special journey into Swindon with his mother where he bought a model for half-a-crown. It was the joy of his heart. The floor of the cottage saw it puffing away at all hours of the day, to the high delight of Alfred and the admiring onlookers. He always insisted that he should have an audience of at least three.

He had an abiding passion for trains and machinery of all kinds. The main G.W.R. line to London ran near the village and he spent much of his time watching the expresses rush by. He made friends with several of the engine drivers and, contrary to the rules, was often given short rides by them. At the age of ten he dared all his sisters to lie down between the metals and let a train run over them. They refused, but he, nothing daunted, calmly lay down while a long luggage train rumbled over him. Then he rose, pale with fear and excitement, and walked quietly back to the village; the experiment was never repeated.

In his very early years he made few young friends outside the family circle and got his greatest pleasure from roaming alone through the meadows around the village. He loved them especially when the grass was long, and soon he began to study nature in all her moods with an appreciative and discerning eye. He was a good son to his mother, and his understanding and courteous nature found expression in a deep sympathy for the poor and suffering. He became indignant when he heard of other people's oppressions, and was peculiarly attached to elderly people. Mark Titcombe and Betsy Horton, the latter a strange villager, were particular favourites; he immortalised both of them in later years in *A Wiltshire Village*.

Yet he loved his sisters and liked going for walks with them, especially when there were wild flowers to gather. They rambled round the hedges and banks and it was almost his greatest delight to carry home large bunches for his mother. It was she who told him the names of many of them. Violets and primroses were his favourites. The wild creatures appealed to him, too, and when a boy killed a grass snake and hung its skin on a tree to dry, he was beside himself with grief. Birds were another passion. He was playful and whimsical too, and when he was about twelve years old, he tried to get Bess to eat a mole which he had caught in the fields at a nearby farm, but, much as she loved her brother, she refused to satisfy his grim curiosity.

He has made references to his childhood in *Villages of the White Horse*. One tells the story of a very memorable experience. "The openness and strategic position of the Downs between Russley and Lambourne make them an ideal ground for military manoeuvres; many brilliant spectacles have been witnessed here in modern times and many mimic battles fiercely waged along the slopes and plains, amid the wheat stubble and turnip fields. Here we small boys used to come, tramping ten miles from home in the happy harvest holidays and being inextricably mixed up and confused with 70,000 or 80,000 troops, driven this way and that, now in the firing line, exposed to the terrific fusilade of the infantrymen's rifles, now under the heels of the cavalry, nearly trodden to death, running mile after mile, thirsty and sweating in the hot sunshine; at one time scolded out of our wits by the testy corporal, at another chaffed and encouraged by the fat, jolly cavalry sergeant, loitering among the sweet smelling turnips, and singing a snatch of song by himself:

'The girl I love, and the horse I ride'.

The thin red line of the infantrymen, stretching as far as the eye could see, the glint of the sun on the helmets, and the flashing of sabres, with the boom, boom, of the cannon, and the continual crack, crack, crack of the rifles, formed a scene never to be forgotten, though we somehow managed to lose our tiny stock of pence, lying down on the beautiful short turf, studded with harebell and scabious, and had to perform the long journey home on empty stomachs, singing as we passed down the narrow lanes of the valley."

And so the boy grew up in an atmosphere of industry, delight in natural beauty, and an appreciation of the simple life. Though the family possessed few books, it had a culture all its own. Elizabeth Williams, indeed, had poetic leanings. Sometimes while working in her garden, or in the fields, she would begin to compose, though there was rarely an opportunity for her to commit her thoughts to writing. She was a born storyteller. Ada also had literary gifts and wrote a number of poems; in later life, Alfred declared that she could justly claim to be a poet and once recommended her to send a selection of her work to a publisher. Ernest, the eldest brother, composed humorous parodies which he used to sing to his own tunes.

It was a happy and united family, with Alfred, in his early teens, its most vivacious member.

CHAPTER THREE

ADOLESCENCE

ALFRED WILLIAMS left school at the age of eleven, to find immediate employment at Longleaze Farm, an ancient farmhouse which lay beside the disused Wilts & Berks Canal and the Oxford Road, at the point where the road to South Marston branches off. The railway runs parallel with both road and canal, less than a hundred yards away. His first employer was a Mr. Tull, mentioned later by him in *A Wiltshire Village*. As no maids were employed at the farm, Alfred acted as houseboy. One of his earliest experiences while working at Longleaze, was to hear the labourers and their wives singing folk-songs while going about their daily work. He was fascinated by them. During these years, too, he retained his love for railway engines and he often watched them as they raced by on the main line. He was enthralled by their strange names and made every attempt to learn something about the immortals whose names were used on them. "I remember how long and carefully I used to wait behind the hedge to catch the wonderful names and store them up in my memory. How inexpressibly and mysteriously great some of those titles seemed to be to my boyish mind, even at that early age—Agamemnon, Hyperion, Prometheus, Ajax, Achilles, Atalanta, Mameluke; they fired my imagination and filled me with strange feelings of pride and joy."

Towards the end of 1890, Longleaze Farm changed hands and he began to serve at Priory Farm under a new master whose name was Chapman. The latter was about thirty years old and was a very easygoing man who had little idea of how to make his holding pay. Alfred was paid three shillings weekly and out of this sum his mother gave him three pence a week which he saved methodically until he had accumulated eighteen shillings. Then he bought a secondhand telescope so that he could view the stars and the downland hills on the distant horizon. The spirit of enquiry and the thirst for knowledge continued to bloom in him.

At the age of twelve, Alfred had to seek another place, for Chapman failed and left the Priory; the incoming tenant did not wish to employ any of Chapman's men. But the boy soon found work with Farmer Ody, whose farm lay near the South Marston signal box, opposite an old canal lockhouse on the north side of the Oxford Road. Here he remained until he was fifteen years old. Of this period he has written: "I have driven the plough, milked the cows, made hay, and harvested the corn with the farmer and his men".

His love for the countryside and his boundless admiration for, and sympathy with, the folk who tilled the soil, harvested the crops, and tended the cattle, developed during these formative years. While working for Ody he was once sent to Wanborough, which nestled at the foot of Liddington Hill, to assist in cutting corn and conveying it back to the farm. It was this journey which brought him for the first time into direct contact with the hills which he had only previously seen from a distance.

The quest for wild flowers continued, and he found many new ones on the banks of the River Cole, while there was a whole wealth of pond life to investigate in the stagnant waters of the disused Wilts & Berks Canal which stretched its sluggish depths near the fields where he daily worked.

While working at Ody's farm, he nearly lost his life, for one starlit night in mid-winter he was returning to South Marston over the frozen canal. Suddenly he found himself struggling in water up to his shoulders and it was only with the greatest difficulty and presence of mind that he extricated himself. It later transpired that a neighbouring farmer had given orders for holes to be made in the ice in order to trap would-be skaters.

But Alfred was frequently restless and irked to travel beyond the confines of his immediate homeland. He even went to the lengths of attending Highworth Fair for the purpose of getting himself hired out to another farmer in that area, but he failed in the attempt and returned, rather disconsolately, to Ody. He tried several times to join the Navy, but his mother intervened on each occasion because he was under age. Yet, like most other boys, he delighted in games, expeditions and pranks.

When work was over for the day he played cricket and football, hunt the fox, hurdle duck, buck buck, hide-and-seek, and quoits, with other South Marston boys, for he was not so shy of their company now. He jumped brooks, slid down the grassy slopes of hills, fished in the canal and river, and went nutting and mushrooming. There was always a tree to climb, and in winter, skating and sliding on the frozen canal or flooded meadows. A favourite sport was to ascend the church tower, largely to annoy the sexton, and there with other boys to stand on his head, much to the dismay of the anxious watching villagers. The old "boneshaker" bicycles of the day were ever a delight; the village churchyard was full of promise for adventurous games. After burials they used to help old Billy the sexton fill graves and perform other small offices. "I have more than once helped to tread the earth down upon the unhappy corpse to earn an honest penny."

When he was fourteen years of age he met Mary Peck, who had recently left school. She had come to South Marston from Eddington in Berkshire to assist in nursing the children of her eldest sister, a Mrs. Westell whose husband was the tenant of a local farm. Since Alfred had occasionally to carry messages to the Westell's farm, a casual acquaintance with Mary Peck gradually developed into real affection, especially on his side.

At the age of fifteen he decided on his first parting of the ways. Attracted by the much higher wages that could be obtained at the G.W.R. Works in Swindon, he left farm work behind him to embark upon a new and strange adventure. It was not that he was unhappy on the land, but young though he was, he was already thinking in terms of marriage, and the wages of a farm labourer were so low and the prospects of promotion so remote that he realised that he must make his future position secure if he were to gain his desired ends. Yet in many ways it was an ill day when he left behind him the companionship of the Wiltshire meadows for the unsympathetic atmosphere of the railway sheds. His brothers, Edgar and Henry, were already working at the factory and the three boys used to walk together each day from South Marston to Swindon and back, a distance of about four miles each way.

Alfred first began as a rivet hotter, and after a few months at this he so impressed the foreman with his interest and industry that he was promoted to the stamping shop as a furnace boy and at a slightly higher wage. He worked well, but always yearned for the countryside and its peoples. On his return from Swindon each evening, when weather permitted, he walked out into the surrounding meadows. He wrote what was probably his first poem when he had been in the stamping shop for a few months. This was a satire which dealt with the stupidity of some of the Marston villagers who were perpetually quarrelling over their cats. Though the verses were crude, they are interesting in that it was extraordinary that under such daily conditions he should have written a poem at all. But the creative urge was glowing within him, and in 1893 he began to paint.

Whenever possible, he made a point of going to see the army man-œuvres at White Horse Hill. One display, given in honour of a recent royal marriage, so fired his imagination that he made a water-colour drawing of the scene. This revealed an astonishing capacity for accuracy, for every detail was included.

The manœuvres had another effect, too, for he made a further attempt to join the services. This time it was the Marine Artillery, but he failed the medical examination and was told that he must have an operation if his application was to be successful. The boy agreed to this and it was arranged for him to enter St. Mary's Hospital at Paddington. His mother was kept completely in the dark, since he knew what her attitude would be, until the Sunday before his journey to London. In spite of her protestations he entered the hospital, remained for five weeks, was operated upon, and then tried again for the Marines. Again he was rejected and he returned to the stamping shop.

Painting took a firm hold on him and he tried his hand at oils. One large picture of the village church, complete with cows in the meadow occupying the foreground, so took the fancy of the owner of the cattle that he offered £5 for it, but this was declined on the grounds that the painting was designed as a wedding present for his brother Henry. A copied portrait of Mr. Gladstone, which he completed when he was nineteen years old, attracted a great deal of local attention. He sold many of his paintings locally and some of them may still be seen on the walls of houses in the Marston district.

That active brain of his then turned from painting to shorthand, for he realised that without expert tuition, which he could not come by, he could get no further with the improvement of his drawing technique. Pitman's Shorthand interested him for a year and then, making limited progress with it on his own, he dropped it forever. There followed an attempt to join the Metropolitan Police Force, but severe varicose veins in his groin made his application unsuccessful. He again went into hospital to have the veins removed, but the doctor would still not pass him, and Alfred Williams never became a policeman.

He saw to it, however, that the materialism of the Swindon factory did not unduly colour the searchings of his country-bred mind. His delight in roaming and fishing grew as the years passed and his study of the locality was no idle whim; he was gaining local fame as an authority on country sites and customs. Of his adolescent years he said: "I was resting on the soul of a crystal flower, to pay homage to creation and the Creator."

His next interest was politics and he began to make his mark as an intelligent debater and persistent heckler. He favoured the Liberal cause. The story is told of how there was once a meeting in South Marston in support of the Conservative candidate for a Parliamentary Election then in progress. Alfred Williams was present at this and put a number of awkward and embarrassing questions to the candidate; at the termination of the meeting he continued his attack. His arguments were so prolonged that the party vainly endeavoured to move on to the next meeting at Highworth. But the candidate himself was so entranced with his young opponent that he refused to come, with the words: "Oh no, you may do as you like, but I'm remaining here; it isn't often that I get a chance for a talk with one who is so intelligent and well-informed". And there he remained debating with Alfred Williams while the rest of his party had to proceed to Highworth without him.

Now eighteen years old, Alfred Williams presented a very good picture of a healthy and vigorous young Englishman. He was something over medium height, slender and graceful, and possessed of much natural poise. His lips were almost colourless, his teeth were nearly perfect and showed the care given to them, and he had a particularly determined lower jaw. His blue-grey eyes had no hint of insincerity in them; he had, indeed, honesty written all over him. His complexion was on the light side, with his brown hair usually short-cropped; his head was particularly well carried. Though he was working under not very wholesome conditions in the factory, he took great care with his appearance and out of working hours was always clean and well-groomed. Nature had endowed him with a first-class brain and a physique capable of much endurance.

He was beloved by his family and villagers alike, though few at this time would have prophesied any great future for him. There were, however, some who watched his development with interest and of these, Canon Masters, the vicar of Stanton Fitzwarren, realising how enthusiastic were the strivings of Alfred Williams for knowledge and self-expression, often exchanged opinions with him and lent him books from his library. Whenever he had a spare moment, Alfred walked out to the secluded country vicarage and conversed with Canon Masters.

In the spring of 1897, Alfred Williams began reading and studying in earnest, and a deep passion for literature began to assert itself. He was reading *Reynolds Newspaper* at the time and in one edition of this he came across several extracts from *Sweetness and Light*, a book which had been written by W. M. Thompson, the editor of the paper. Alfred was so carried away with the style and sentiments of the quotations that he immediately bought the book, which became a continual source of delight to him. He was transported to a new and unthought-of world and it is not surprising to find that his next step was to buy several of Shakespeare's plays. He generally had one of these in his pocket and it became a common sight amongst his fellow workers for him to be discovered wrapt in study during his dinner hour. Blessed with a very retentive memory, he soon gained an extensive knowledge of the texts, with a penetrating insight into Elizabethan modes and manners. His familiarity with Shakespeare frequently surprised experienced scholars.

And so this country lad continued with growing fervour his unend-

ing quest for knowledge. He refused to be daunted by the hard conditions of the factory and looked bravely into the future when he, too,.
might add to the store of literature.

CHAPTER FOUR

EARLY MANHOOD

IN 1900, a Swindon friend suggested to Alfred Williams that he
should take a correspondence course with Ruskin Hall, Oxford.
Williams, interested in the proposal, wrote for particulars. He was
attracted by the course in English Literature, and, though earning a
comparatively low wage, enrolled as a student, embarking upon a
four-years' course. Arthur Hacking was appointed his tutor. When
Williams unsuccessfully applied for the librarianship of the Swindon
Mechanics' Institute two years later, Hacking wrote him a testimonial
in which he stated that the course which Williams had followed had
dealt with the major and minor poets and writers. Thirty of Alfred
Williams' essays that he had read showed thoughtfulness, careful study,
originality and an excellent literary style. He also showed an inclination for archæology and had made considerable progress in Latin.
The actual course followed in English Literature included a historical
survey from Bede to Wordsworth, with a special study of the Eliza-
bethans. Williams was particularly enamoured of Cowper and became
an ardent admirer of *The Task*.

Williams said of the course: "Some of the books which I had to study
contained many Latin quotations and this determined me to learn that
language. I had considerable difficulties to overcome at the outset, for
the simple reason that I did not thoroughly understand English
Grammar, but after about eighteen months I found myself making
good progress. Beginning with the books of Caesar, I afterwards
became bolder, and dipped with delight into the wonders of Cicero,
Ovid, Sallust, Horace and Virgil." In fact, in one year he read nearly
all the *Gallic War* and after two years' study was so far ahead that
he had ploughed through the *Aeneid* seven times and committed to
memory large portions of it. Yet Williams was working a full day
at the factory with the long walk each morning and evening during the
whole of this period.

Shortly after his twenty-fourth birthday he became engaged to Mary
Peck. Since his adolescent farming days he had not entirely lost
touch with her and she was continually in his mind, but the friendship
was frowned upon by her sister and brother-in-law. Alfred Williams
was not considered by them to be a good enough match; he was a

"black" man as local people dubbed all those who worked in the factory. The Westells were much more anxious that Mary should marry one of Farmer Ody's sons and did all in their power to persuade her to accept young Ody by offering to stock a farm for them when they were married. Under the insistent pressure of her sister, Mary succumbed and became engaged to the young farmer. She then made it clear that her friendly relations with Alfred must be discontinued. But he was determined to win her for his bride and continued his suit with such fervour that she eventually, and gladly, threw over Ody and decided to marry Alfred Williams.

They were married on 21st October, 1903, at St. Saviour's Church, Hungerford, by the Rev. James Brine, the curate of the parish. Alfred was then twenty-six years old and she twenty-three. Her brother Albert and his sister Ada, with a friend, were witnesses at the ceremony. The marriage certificate designates Alfred Williams as "a stamper in engineering works, son of Elias Lloyd Williams, deceased (in 1899), a carpenter, and Mary Maria Peck, the daughter of William Peck, a moulder".

The wedding very nearly did not materialise. At the end of that summer, Mary had left Marston and gone back home to Eddington. She was anxious to have the banns published in her parish only, so that she might spare the feelings of the jilted Ody, who, with his family, was a regular attender at South Marston church. The banns were, therefore, not called in both parishes, and, though Alfred spent the necessary week-ends in Eddington when the banns were being called there, the South Marston vicar was unwilling to marry them. Alfred appealed for advice to the vicar of Shrivenham, as rural dean, who stated emphatically that the arrangements were in order, but suggested that it would be better to obtain a licence. Accordingly, the vicar of Eddington agreed to marry them and so the wedding took place in Berkshire, instead of in Wiltshire, as Alfred Williams and his bride had always wished. Since the Eddington vicar did not wish to offend his colleague at Marston, and following the advice of the rural dean, the couple were married by licence.

The honeymoon was spent quietly at Torquay where they enjoyed their first experience of a seaside holiday. They then returned to South Marston to live at Dryden Cottage, which lay almost adjoining Cambria Cottage, and where they were to reside for fifteen years. Naturally, Alfred continued his work at the Swindon factory, where he had now graduated to a full-blown hammerman.

The correspondence course gave him much pleasure and relief from the shop, but now he was a married man he thought it was his duty to better his chances of promotion by reading for London Matriculation. He chose as his subjects for the examination, Latin, Greek,

French, English, and Mathematics. He learnt the languages simultaneously, for, as he said, "Language first, then if I fail to keep the pace, I shall have the more valuable part, since the riches of words endure to the end, but you cannot speak Arithmetic". His capacity for assimilating language was phenomenal and all the more remarkable when it is considered how short was the time for study at his disposal. Yet in one year he had mastered the elements of Greek grammar and had read much from Xenophon, Homer, Anacreon, Theocritus, Bion, Moschus, Lucan, and Plutarch, in addition to making acquaintance with the *Alcestis* and the *Hecuba*. He had also ploughed through several French books. He was so filled with the wonder of his new knowledge that he wrote in a few weeks an epic which he called *Aeneas in Sicily* modelled upon classic forms. His library, which had grown steadily since his marriage, now had a strong classical bias. There were books in every room of Dryden Cottage and he bought new ones whenever he could afford them. In 1904 he translated into very readable verse the whole of Ovid's *Ariadne*.

In order to get through the massive programme which he had boldly planned for himself, he rose at four in the morning and after a small meal, studied by oil light until it was time to go off to work. Then followed a cycle ride in all kinds of weather. At the factory there was further reading during the dinner hour, and on returning home he made a hasty meal, generally bolting his food, and went on poring over his books with avidity until midnight. Only his wife knew when he snatched the time for sleep.

But the wearisome hours he devoted to concentrated reading by artificial light soon took their toll of him and his eyes began to cause him concern. On the advice of his doctor he discontinued night study until such time as his eyes had had complete rest. But Alfred Williams was impatient and would not wait nor discontinue his studies any longer than possible. So he imposed upon himself the task of recounting clearly everything he had learnt the day previously, while cycling to work. The summary was repeated on his homeward journey; in this way he was able to cut down the time he was giving up to his books by night.

He did not sit for London Matriculation, however, as after some months of preparation he came to the conclusion that his methods of study were unsuitable for examination purposes. He was more concerned with retaining his hard-won knowledge as a permanency in life since he realised that the mere gaining of a certificate would in all probability result in his forgetting all that he had learned. And this was anathema to him. It was for this reason that he did not attend evening classes in Swindon for he distrusted traditional methods of tuition. "My object," he said, "is to acquire in such a way as to retain, so I never pass to the second word until I have thoroughly mastered the first."

His methods of learning were individual. Some of them have been made available through a letter which he once wrote to a friend who had asked him the best way to learn Latin. 'First of all learn nouns and adjectives; these are the principal things in the beginning. If you pay sufficient attention to them, everything else will follow easily and naturally in its proper time and place. There is a very good old Latin saw which runs 'Festina lente', i.e., 'Hasten slowly'. Take care you follow this rule, but hasten all the time. I took care to cram in as much as possible under all circumstances, but I shall not advise you to do likewise. If you use a slate, have a slate pencil and chalk at hand. For the less important points use pencil, for the more important use chalk. Printing the words will help you to commit them to memory. It is surprising how much more easily you retain the image of a thing if you print it in chalk on your slate. Write out lists of new words, and lose them if you can in order to necessitate new writing. A difficult word or root you should keep in view for a day or a week-end. If possible, print it where the eye may light upon it, it will certainly help retention. I used to print a troublesome Greek word on the toe of my boot in the morning, and allow it to remain till the evening. Never mind what your workmates think or say. They may deem you to be eccentric, but you know what you are doing, while they do not. Besides, if they are not interested it is no business of theirs.

"As you progress and come to reading, you will do well to learn whole passages or complete passages by heart, and recite them to yourself aloud. Reading aloud from a book is also a capital exercise and helps one to a vocabulary. I knew many of Horace's Odes by heart, chapters of Sallust, Virgil's *Orpheus and Eurydice* from the Georgics, and Greek poems such as the *Thyrsis* of Theocritus, passages from Homer, pieces from Meleager, Anacreon, and others. These I used to recite about the down and meadows, by day and by night, or sitting by the seashore, and I have no doubt that I frightened more than one solitary traveller who must have been at a loss to understand such extraordinary behaviour.

"One other piece of advice I would offer, which is this. Since you are not going in for a school exam., don't trouble to write Latin, but read all you can. I remember that I spent several months trying to translate into Greek with Sidgwick's writer, but to little purpose. Tired of the drudgery, I discontinued it, and in two months I read the *Anabasis* of Xenophon, the first books of the *Iliad* and *Odyssey*, a book or prose extracts, and the play *Hecuba* which was of far greater value to a beginner than merely writing a few pages of Greek. Of course if you wish to get a degree you would have to do this, but the chief

thing is to make an acquaintance with an author, to wrestle with him,
and find out what he has to tell, or to teach, and when you have done
with him, pass on to another and enrich yourself at his expense, but he
will be none the poorer for all the wealth you may extract from his
repository."

Alfred Williams' textbooks, now preserved in Swindon, show how
detailed and patient were his methods. The margins are crowded with
references and annotations while the bindings and pages are so soiled
and fingermarked that they give a realistic picture of the hammerman
as student.

And so he continued, month after month, increasing the wealth of
his classical knowledge in the quiet little cottage, until the early hours,
completely oblivious to the fact that he had to be at work, four miles
away, by six o'clock on the following morning. Though his eyesight
had improved, he gave it little rest. Time upon time, friends tried to
persuade him to ease up on his self-imposed task, but with little avail.
He was a hard taskmaster to himself. He had now made the acquain-
ance of Henry Byett, who was employed in the office of the Swindon
factory and who was to become his lifelong friend and counsellor and
later his first biographer. The men had much in common and valued
each other's opinions, but when Byett quietly suggested that such
continual study would undermine his constitution and eventually
shorten his life, Williams replied, characteristically, "I cannot help it.
Life would not be worth living without my literature; I love it."

Alfred Williams was very blest in the choice of his partner. From
the beginning, Mary Williams recognised the greatness in him and
ministered to his many needs accordingly. She guarded him jealously,
seeing to it that he was not disturbed when occupied with study. She
was no scholar herself, but was sympathetic to all he undertook; her
nature was so finely drawn that she understood the urge of all his
strivings. Hers was not an enviable existence, yet she looked upon her
task as a privilege. Of a shy and retiring disposition, she made few
friends in the early years of her marriage, which meant that she was
practically alone for the greater part of the day; in the evening when
Alfred returned, it was only to see him turn to his books until bed-time.
The brief companionship of their evening meal, when he poured forth
on all the happenings of the day, and dwelt upon his aims and desires,
was her greatest joy. He would have liked to have given more time
to her, but it was she who unselfishly pressed him on to his goal. This
was, as later events proved, a mistake, for he—a complete egoist—
learned to rely entirely upon her, and she tended to make of him a god.
Of her he said, "No matter how late it is when I go to bed, Mrs. Williams will not retire until I do so. She is indispensable to my pursuits.
While she knits I commune with my gods. We lead a simple and quiet

life and I could not endure the thought of disturbance unless it were
to bring me in closer touch with facilities for realising the passion
within me." No man was ever mated to a more faithful woman;
her gentle but resolute character was his main source of power and
inspiration to his dying day.

In the first year of their marriage, Alfred Williams heard about a
competition which was being run in connection with a popular penny
weekly comic paper of the day, called "Nuggets". A prize of £100
was offered by the proprietors to the individual, who, over a period of
three months, forwarded the largest number of coupons cut from
editions of the paper. Williams, who on this occasion displayed
shrewdness and business acumen, acquired in his childhood when
distributing the newspapers for his mother, determined to secure this
prize. He did so in an enterprising manner.

He bought thirty copies of "Nuggets" and, after cutting out the
coupons, distributed the paper among his workmates. The following
week they bought the papers from him, and with the money still more
papers were obtained, which he distributed to an ever-widening circle.
Many of the men bought extra copies which they sold to their friends
after removing the coupons, which latter they handed to Alfred Williams. When they realised what his aim was and saw that he was intent on securing the hundred pounds, they rallied round and did all
they could to further his ends. And so the procedure continued, week
by week, in a number of the outlying villages around Swindon. The
result was that he collected so many coupons that he was an easy
winner, and at very little cost to himself. The main of the proceeds
was used to furnish Dryden Cottage and to buy some of the books
necessary for the correspondence course.

His study of nature continued to be an absorbing passion. Every
Sunday, whatever the weather, Alfred and Mary Williams walked along
the country lanes and into the fields and woods near Dryden Cottage.
He was as excited as a child when the new birds and butterflies appeared;
his house, in season, was sweet with the scent of freshly gathered wild
flowers. As of old, he made few intimate friends, but he gave himself
wholeheartedly to the village children, going out of his way to be with
them and to talk about their hobbies. Their simple country manners
intrigued him and he acknowledged their greetings with the greatest of
warmth. He knew them all by name. Nothing pleased him better
than to teach them scraps of poetry and to hear them repeat the rhymes
to him a few days later. The children looked upon him as someone
different and rather apart from the other village men. "Mister Willums"
they called him. "Hello, Mister Willums". It was his custom to
bring back from his rambles anything that he thought would interest
them. To-day it would be some strange insect, or a bright egg;

to-morrow the newly-born young of a fox or rabbit would engage his attention. Then he would gather the children round him and talk to them quietly about the habits of the creatures of field and hedgerow. The lesson over, he would carefully take back the young animals to their haunts.

He found time to acquaint himself with the trend of local and national affairs and spent at least ten minutes daily in reading *The Daily Telegraph*, though he bought this paper chiefly because of its literary articles. He was still mildly interested in politics, but his former Liberal opinions were now more akin to a progressive Conservatism. Though he never became a member of any political party, he generally voted for the Tories.

He gave of his best in the factory where he was one of the most painstaking workmen. Nobody could accuse him of wasting the company's time. He was generally one of the last to leave the steam hammer shop, for when the hooter had sounded, he made a point of remaining behind for a short while, and after washing his hands, would sit down and pore over a book. The idea behind this was to efface from his mind all the trials of the day's work and to give it fresh matter to digest on his homeward journey. He received little encouragement in the factory, for many of his workmates did not understand the motive behind his quest for knowledge. Yet he was never anxious to change his lot. Over and over again, Henry Byett tried to persuade him to take up lighter work and to apply for promotion to the office staff, but the entreaties availed nothing; Williams stated that he wished for hard, manual work and embraced its demands as affording an antidote and perfect change to his mental exertions. He was, indeed, such a useful and conscientious hammerman that on two occasions he was offered promotion, each time as foreman of the shop, but in refusing, he said he was not anxious to give orders to others or to sacrifice one jot of his individuality. He was chargeman of his gang, but he laboured as hard as his fellows, neither seeking nor accepting favours.

Several of the coarser men persecuted him and encountered his endeavours with definite opposition. It had been his custom, since studying with Ruskin Hall, to inscribe Greek characters at the rear of his steam hammer and on the iron band which encircled the furnace, in order to imprint them the better on his memory. He chalked the characters up on arriving at work each morning. One pompous official, thinking that the display was pretentious, and being jealous and ignorant of the spirit they betokened, gave orders for the marks to be effaced. These were carried out, but Alfred Williams continued to draw his characters until the official had the hammer daubed over with thick grease. Nothing daunted, however, Williams, in his own time, carefully removed the grease and re-wrote the characters, this time in

white paint. He was commanded to obliterate them himself. He refused to do so and told the persecutor in no uncertain language that as
often as the characters were rubbed out, so often they would be done
again, since the scrawlings were doing no harm to anyone in the shop,
but were helping him in his difficult studies.

During these years while he was enriching his mind with the thoughts
of the past he followed a definite timetable of study. Before he went to
work he spent the time reading French; at midday he turned to Latin;
and after the evening meal he perused his Greek. The appallingly
unhealthy conditions in which he worked in the factory, enveloped in
an over-heated and fume-sodden atmosphere, together with the dogged
hours of concentrated reading, would have crippled the brain and
physique of an average man. But Alfred Williams not only brought
to his strivings a strong and enduring constitution, but also he was fired
with a consuming desire to improve his mind, to broaden his outlook,
and to find himself in the closest harmony with the scholars of all ages.
He had the will to learn and to live beautifully and it was this, with the
support and encouragement of his wife and a few close friends, which
sustained him and drove him, perhaps desperately, on to his goal.

CHAPTER FIVE.

SONGS IN WILTSHIRE

DURING the winter of 1903 and the spring of 1904, Alfred Williams
wrote a lyrical play called "Sardanapalus". This was traditional in form and concept, and followed closely the original story.
He thought it was worth publishing, and after some hesitation, sent
it to John Lane for his consideration. Lane returned the work but,
in an encouraging covering letter, said that two of his readers who had
seen the play expressed admiration for much of it but regretted its
lack of form. The next year, Lane asked Alfred Williams to let him
have the play again; this time he showed it to Sidney Colvin, Watts-
Dunton and Swinburne. They all praised the work and considered
it to be a remarkable achievement for a man in Alfred Williams'
position. The possibility of publication was further considered, but
first Lane fell ill and then, on recovery, visited America, so for some
time the matter lay in abeyance. On his return to England he told
Williams that he had finally decided not to publish "Sardanapalus"
since the book market at the time was unsuitable for a play of that
kind. Lane was, however, genuinely interested in Alfred Williams and
his work, and paid tribute to his determination and courage; he went
so far as to approach some of his friends in the hope that they would

contribute towards the cost of the publication of the drama. But nothing came of this. Williams was naturally disappointed but later said, "It was not written for the theatre, but later I intend to study the requirements of the modern stage and work to that end."

For the next few years he worked untiringly at Latin and Greek, reading widely from the literatures of both. He followed up his play with a number of poems and also tried his hand at journalism. As a matter of fact, in December, 1906, the editor of *Pearson's Magazine* invited him to contribute a series of short articles to that paper dealing with his career and experiences in the factory. Williams was flattered and excited at this request and sent the editor several pieces, but none of them was printed. But by the spring of the following year he had by him enough poems to make a slim volume, which he called *Gifts to Eros*. He had written his first book. Then he sought a publisher but none would publish without a guarantee. Hearing, however, that the Authors' Association was about to issue an anthology, Williams submitted four poems to its editor, Fred G. Bowles, himself a lyric writer of some reputation. Two of the poems were translations and two were original compositions. Bowles decided upon the inclusion of the two latter; these were "The Greek Peasant's Prayer for Rain" and "The Brook".

The anthology, *New Songs*, published by Chapman and Hall, appeared in July, 1907, and attracted some attention; among others it fell into the hands of Swinburne and Colvin. The latter, already knowing something of the work of Alfred Williams, singled out the "Prayer" as being the best poem in the book, and in a review of the anthology said of this poem, "There is no redundance; every well-chosen word tells. There is no violence of metaphor, but every line presents a picture like a cameo. There is no ambiguity; no striving after effect. But there is beauty, simplicity and strength. There is no smell of the lamp, no modern morbidity, no torturing of language in the vain effort to express the inexpressible. It is the work of a man who has a clear vision of the thing he writes about and not of one who looks at the world with half-closed eyes or through a distorting lens. It is the kind of writing that will live". Now this was extraordinary praise for a solitary poem, and from such a critic these encouraging and bold words convinced Alfred Williams that he was destined to be a poet. The long years of study and preparation promised now to repay themselves. But he still was unable to find a publisher who would risk "Sardanapalus" or "Gifts to Eros".

But in spite of his apparent failures, Alfred Williams was becoming known outside Wiltshire and several articles about him had been written in various periodicals. One of these, entitled "Hammerman and Poet: A Story of Self-help", written by Frederick Rockell, another working-man poet, appeared in *The Millgate Monthly* at the end of 1907. Williams thanked Rockell for his kindly notice and the two struck up a friendship. "I know all my faults", he wrote to Rockell, "and so I am not over anxious to be in print. I should prefer total oblivion to disgrace and there is no greater disgrace to the sensitive mind than to see one's name in connection with an unseemly print". Rockell introduced him to William Dowsing, a poet and musician working in the Vicker's factory at Sheffield. Dowsing, like Henry Byett, became a lifelong friend and admirer. He immediately sent Williams a copy of his *Sonnets Personal and Pastoral*, which had just been published by Kegan Paul. Williams praised the sonnets and especially Dowsing's essay on the construction of the sonnet which formed the preface of his work. "Your verses are very neat and full, fresh and poetic. I think, to judge from your sonnets, that you ought to do something, but publishing is such a wretched process or I should have said 'attempted publishing' since I have not yet been successful in getting my work accepted."

More disappointments were in store for him, however, for though his name was becoming known, he still was met with refusals by publishers who would not venture on an unknown poet. At the end of 1908 he nearly succeeded in getting Dowsing's publishers to accept *Gifts to Eros*, but they wished for a guarantee; at this juncture Williams knew of no one to whom he might turn, though he did play with the idea of approaching Canon Masters for his financial help; Dowsing himself had had to find a guarantor for *Sonnets Personal and Pastoral*. *Sardanapalus* was still going the rounds in London, but though it was backed up by the good opinion of Colvin, no publisher was attracted to the work. Williams told Dowsing that he had no more interest left in it than he had in the moon !

He was, in short, beginning to realise dimly that the profession of a literary man was a tedious and laborious one, especially for a working man. Thoughts were passing through his mind that he was too ambitious and was attempting work far beyond his capacity. He told himself, often bitterly, that the pursuit of classicism as exemplified in his poetry was rather more the concern of the university don than the hammerman. But he kept plodding on and composed a little almost every weekend when he had the leisure and the quiet of Dryden Cottage for meditation. He knew that his poems were unsuitable for newspapers or for the more popular type of magazine. He was wise enough, of course, not to regard his writing as a livelihood and though on several occasions he was tempted to leave the factory, he was forced to the opinion that it would be better for him to remain a labourer and to aim at establishing a small and unpretentious niche in literature. But he was always desperately anxious to make that niche sure and certain for posterity. So he wrote calmly with his eyes on the future; it would have been all too easy for him to have lowered his standards and capitalised his humble position as a factory worker. His attitude to life in general is well summed up in a poem which he wrote, in 1908, called "All Minds Love Not Sport". This was written on the occasion of a local football cup-tie and in true Kiplinglike vein he condemned the attitude of those who resorted for their pleasures to what he dubbed the "chasing of wind". His then philosophy is clearly expressed in the last two verses of this early poem:

> "While players in race
> Wing over the course
> With sickening pace,
> And others are hoarse
> With frivolous cries
> Of thwarting or cheer
> That trouble the skies
> And deafen the ear,
>
> With pleasure of book
> I wander at will
> To babble of brook,
> Or gaze from the hill,
> Or cherish the leaves
> And lovingly stroke
> The ivy that cleaves
> Fast on to the oak."

He had some success with his prose writings, for three articles were accepted for the *Young Men's Magazine*. These were called "Self Culture", "The Art of Study", and "How to Read"; they were largely concerned with his own methods of learning. He dealt with such topics as self-helps and self-educators, elementary textbooks, learning languages, dictionaries, and methods of reading. In introducing Alfred Williams to his readers, the editor wrote, "His story should serve as a splendid stimulus to all young men, and his readiness to place his experience at the service of others is a quality which cannot be too much admired." For the three articles Williams was paid at the rate of 7/6 per thousand words, receiving in all for what represented his first earnings as a writer, the total sum of 22/6.

The year 1909 brought Williams new and valuable contacts and some very real literary successes. In that year the Authors' Association published, through Chapman and Hall, a further anthology called *Garnered Grain*. The editor was again Fred G. Bowles and for the second time, poems by Williams were included. These were "The Devotee" and "Ere I was quickened in the Womb". Bowles did in fact intend to publish four poems, but two odes from Anacreon had to be omitted owing to shortage of space. Once again Williams' work was singled out by critics. The *Daily Telegraph* in particular made mention of his linguistic and classical attainments and referred to him as "one of the most remarkable men in Wiltshire, if not in England". Williams was amused at this reference and told Dowsing that a fuss was being made about him because he used high-sounding classical names and made mention of Horace and Virgil, which appealed to a certain type of reader and thus gave him publicity for his poems about which the same people really cared very little. When the *Daily Telegraph* reporter interviewed him, Williams said to him: "Some people have thought that I should begin to wear a collar and tie to my work now. But I can tell you that I am not in the least ambitious to make a name for myself and I am not attempting to play to the gallery. I think it is my duty to go on working as I am doing. If you do not do your accustomed work you become dormant; you are like a pool of stagnant water". Largely as a result of the publicity he was then receiving, many offers were made to him to write his life story, but he declined them all for he was fearful that, because he had done fairly well with his classical studies, he might become a much over-rated person. Although he considered that Latin and Greek had afforded him excellent training, he wished at this stage that he had put his time to better purpose in English, though he knew that if he had done so he would probably have received less notice from the press.

To his list of writer friends he now made the interesting addition of Jonathan Denwood, the Cumberland poet and author, his work having been brought to Denwood's notice by Frederick Rockell. In these infant years of the new century, Williams, Dowsing, Rockell, and Denwood presented a courageous picture of determined working-men writers struggling for recognition. All had sprung from lowly origins and all knew what odds they had to overcome. But they were bold and sincere and their prose and poetry breathed the very spirit of assurance and independence.

Then in January 1909, Alfred Williams became friendly with Lord Edmond Fitzmaurice, of Bradford-on-Avon, a member of the Government and a leading figure in Wiltshire public life. Fitzmaurice was to become one of the greatest influences in Williams' literary development; without his financial help, much of Williams' work would never have been published. He encouraged the poet and consoled him in his high-minded purposes for twenty-one years and suggested to whom he might write for assistance and advice. The contact had been made as a result of Williams sending Fitzmaurice two sonnets dedicated to him which the latter, greatly admiring, acknowledged by a sympathetic letter in which he congratulated Williams on his poems in *Garnered Grain*.

For some time Williams had been in touch with Galloway Kyle and had sent him a number of his poems. Kyle now suggested that *Gifts to Eros* should be published as a co-operative effort and as the first volume of the firm of Erskine Macdonald which was about to be constituted, but which was not then actually in existence. Kyle himself was a director of the new firm. He was also in touch with Lord Fitzmaurice and further interested him in Williams as one of his constituents. It was clear that the volume could not be done without a patron or guarantor, for whatever the quality of the poetry, the market for new verse by an unknown writer was most uncertain. Fitzmaurice then generously offered to cover any loss, and himself read through the poems and made a final selection. So, by June, Williams was able to furnish Denwood with the information that the collection had gone to the printers. "There will be about 170 pages of poems, and the price of the vol. will be, I expect, 3/6 before pub., 4/6 afterwards. Mr. Kyle says the printer's bill would not be covered by 2/6 and he feels that it will be a cheap book at 5/-, but I wrote asking 3/6—4/6." Kyle was thinking of producing a book bound in a style similar to the Stephen Phillips' volumes published by John Lane.

Williams' hope had at last, at the age of 32, been realised. The weary years of patient study, the painful attempts at self-expression, the squalor and disillusionment of the factory, were to be crowned with success and, perhaps, recognition. He believed he had proved himself.

While waiting for the appearance of his book he read Richard Jefferies' *The Story of my Heart*, not having heard of his fellow Wiltshireman until then. The book swept him off his feet, and deeply moved him, for, as he read, he knew that he had trodden the same path and thought the same things as Jefferies, "only humble I, had never the language or force at my disposal to define them as he had done". Williams told Denwood of the effect the book had had upon him and confessed that for some six or eight years he had been a confirmed agnostic, largely as a result of brooding over scientific matters. He had read widely from the works of Darwin, Huxley, Spencer, Haeckel, Tyndall and Collins. Rational explanations of man and his place in the universe had attracted him so much that he had suffered the same agonies of spirit as Jefferies. He had groaned in desperation after the higher life of the soul, convincing himself by what he thought was logical reasoning that it was possible to arrive at an almost perfect state, above the reach of circumstances and environment. "I shut myself off from man, and was content to live in an atmosphere of glorious indefinability. But I was never happy, never assured, never confident. I doubted everything, and most of all myself."

Slowly, however, he had come to know the power of Christianity, and fortified by his Latin and Greek scholarship, had been able to view the scriptures, especially the New Testament, not narrow-mindedly, but in the light both of a pagan and a modern. He knew how unhappy and disillusioned Jefferies had been in spite of his genius, large heart, and boundless spirit. "His deep craving after soul-life, is, of itself, a conscious and powerful witness of the *divinum aliquid* within him and which arose from and finally rested in his affinity with God—the God of Jesus Christ".

Williams was essentially a happy man and it was not for nothing that he had learnt the secret of balanced living and, over the years, to rise above "the mad-headed, hair-brained, freak of an age of ours". Nothing gave him greater joy than to dwell upon the fields and hills of his own lovely Wiltshire and in them he found the deepest communion. In his moments of depression and disappointment he sought and discovered true peace while striding along the Downs. One who has memories of him at the time of the publication of his book says, "I recall him passing by the windows of my home at Stratton St. Margaret village, from the railway works in which he worked for so many years, a tall spare figure with no redundancy of body, nothing extra, hardly enough maybe to challenge life; upright as a dart, active, cheery, kind, courteous of disposition, with a mind which took broad sweeps and sailed uncharted seas."

In May, after reading a great deal of poetry, Williams wrote to Dowsing, on the eve of the publication of his own book, "It is strange to you, perhaps, but I know nothing of Swinburne. Perhaps I've read not forty lines of him; perhaps I've read no modern poetry, or at least I can brave out, perhaps, and say I have read a little modern poetry, but not much, nor do I intend to, after the little I have seen of it. I leave out Tennyson and Browning (in part at least) and speak of modern poetry in general. And this I say of the moderns: I will not be guilty of copying from them. I am blamed, though really I have not had an opportunity for criticism because I have had nothing published, I am blamed, I say for adhering to the older forms. Well, Mr. Dowsing, if I ever do get through, they can say what they like of the older forms, but I would rather be blamed for this than be blamed for copying the moderns. This, of course, out of no respect for any, but out of a far greater love for the better work of a couple of centuries ago. I have lately been reading up a little of contemporary verse. Bridges, Yeats, Phillips, Binyon, Hardy, Gallienne, Maddox Brown, Norman Gale, etc., etc., and this has produced in me a veritable disgust of modern '*tack*'. FORTY LINES OF DRYDEN CONTAIN MORE POETRY THAN TWELVE LARGE VOLUMES OF THE MODERN MUDDLE. I cannot help it one bit, but I can get more pleasure out of a page of Ovid than out of a bundle of our moderns."

And so in the August his book of poems appeared, not under the title of *Gifts to Eros* but as *Songs in Wiltshire*. Kyle sold Williams the book for 3/9; a retail price of 5/- was decided upon. Williams was to be his own bookseller but was so high-minded that he would not sell to anyone except at the cost price. At this stage, Williams said of the publisher, "From the democratic point of view I must not despise a house because it is not so prominent."

Alfred Williams worked strenuously in order to sell *Songs* for he did not wish Lord Fitzmaurice to be called upon to meet the guarantee. He was eventually successful in this aim, but it cost him £30 out of his own meagre savings, the greater part of which sum was spent on railway fares in order to visit friends and booksellers. He sent many copies to likely buyers, but several of these had to be reminded that they had neither paid for their copies nor returned them; such correspondence was an embarrassment to him. He travelled the length and breadth of Wiltshire at the weekends seeking supporters, which arduous task was made even more difficult by the fact that he was suffering from rheumatism. He personally canvassed the majority of the Wiltshire booksellers, but got limited support from them. Perhaps, under the circumstances this method was the only feasible one, as no publisher could undertake to "travel" the country with a single volume, and public sales would normally be negligible, but it was hard going. The first imprint was one of five hundred, with type to stand. A month after the appearance of *Songs*, Williams had sold just over a hundred copies, though its high price had deterred several possible buyers. It has been suggested that he should have got a local printer to produce a small cheap edition in paper covers in the hope that the cheaper price would have resulted in larger local sales. But Alfred Williams would never have done this.

Most of his friends bought copies and one new one in particular did him outstanding service. This was Reuben George, an insurance agent from Swindon, and a leading figure in the educational, religious, and social life of the district. George was a keen bibliophile and an enthusiast for poetry. He was an ardent admirer of Williams and his work, and wherever he travelled, even into the smallest of the Wiltshire villages, he carried copies of *Songs* with him, his zeal almost pressing them on to likely customers. The proceeds were sent on to Williams monthly.

Williams' own endeavours to dispose of the edition greatly fagged him, though he was glad of the opportunity it gave him of becoming more acquainted with the countryside; in the second week of October he sold over a hundred copies. He was ever anxious that his friends should not expect too much from his poetry. He stressed its immaturity, but in a rather pathetic letter to Dowsing he wrote, when telling him of his selling adventures, "We both have this defence, we are not university men".

The book received an encouraging reception, several critics being of the opinion that a new poet of insight and power had risen in England. Williams was not, however, in danger of having his head easily turned and though he valued the praises he received, he continued his work as hammerman. He had, as a matter of fact, gone quietly on and written nearly enough poems for another volume.

By the end of the year it was clear that the sales would cover all expenses. Whereupon Kyle wrote to the *Swindon Advertiser* on 15th November: "I trust a larger edition will be called for, so that not only no house in Wiltshire in which books are cherished will be without a copy, but that Mr. Williams will obtain some measure of pecuniary reward which will enable him to pursue more comfortably and effectively his arduous intellectual work and studies to the further credit of his famous county." Kyle was anxious to issue the second edition at a slightly higher price, but nothing was said at this stage about the poet receiving any profits; and in fact the second edition was not called for. Williams expressed his disappointment at the results of this first publication, but it is nothing exceptional in poets to believe that their publishers might have done better for their earliest books, and Kyle's judgment and enterprise did for Williams more than any other publisher up to that time—it gave him his start.

As for the booksellers, Williams said: "They want some Chinese crackers let off near them".

It was now that he became friendly with John Bailey, then sub-editor of *The Quarterly Review*, who had heard something of Williams' career and was attracted to his poetry.

Songs in Wiltshire consisted of fifty six original poems and four translations; it included the four poems which had already been printed in the anthologies. The book was dedicated "To Lord Fitzmaurice, whose spontaneous interest occasioned the appearance of this volume." Williams wanted the dedication to be more glowing, but Fitzmaurice only accepted it on condition that it should read as simply as possible. Kyle wrote an introduction which sketched the main details of Williams' career. In it he said: "The remarkable poems in this volume may be left to the public judgment, which will recognise their merit and beauty without the adventitious aid of a preface".

Some twenty-five of the poems are love songs, and of the twenty or so purely nature poems, four deal specifically with Wiltshire. The first poem is, in fact, a Wiltshire song which displays in no uncertain manner the feelings Williams had for his homeland. The solitude of the Downs ever appealed to his shy spirit and the long poem which he calls "On the Downs" is full of the exaltation which must often have surged within him. He tells of how he rested on the Downs on a day when his heart had been full of bitterness.

"O my heart! the day has been
    Full of bitter. Here we rest,
Unobtruding and unseen;
Stretched upon the shaded green,
    Unpossessing, unpossest
With the burning scorn of anger,
Yielding to divinest languor
    Dream we on the magic West."

His loneliness in the remote hills made him feel as if soul and body had parted, thus allowing him to sing freely and ecstatically of the beauty which flowed into his brain. A true Wordsworthian, he wished to mingle in spirit and in mood "With the darling down and dingle" and to find "Company in solitude".

"Liddington Hill" is another tribute to his county. He was deeply influenced by the sight of Liddington's eternal plateau rising from the bosom of the plain into the blue, with the broom and heather burning on its windswept slopes.

"O thou bonny high hill!
    I covet no other;
Our secrets we tell,
    For we love one another."

This poem shows Williams at his best, for it is written straight from the heart without any attempt at forcing the verse. It is the voice of the authentic nature poet speaking in passionate and deliberate accents of a familiar and well-loved scene.

The other nature poems do not particularly mention Wiltshire but all of them have Wiltshire inspiration and background. Williams sings joyfully of the common people he had known all his life as they lived out their even days in the fields around South Marston. He dwells upon the changing face of the countryside, with the seasons rolling on through the year. Here are "The Reaper's Song", "The Shepherd's Song", "The Harvest Song", and "The Swain's Song", probably all written at the same period and following a definite plan of action. With this singer in Wiltshire, we meet "The Keeper's Daughter" and wander with them both through the dank grasses of the cool water meadows. With him we roam into the wide harvest fields to see the homely country folk at their tasks, or ramble at will by his side along the banks of the little River Cole, babbling her music over sand and gravel.

Several of the nature poems praise birds. In "The Blackbird's Song", "The Rook's Monody", "The Cuckoo's Song" and "Philip Sparrow", Williams makes successful use of onomatopoeia. "The Blackbird's Canticle", written at odd times on a small piece of cheap paper and carried about by him in his waistcoat pocket until completed, is the best poem in this group. It reveals the accuracy of his observations of the countryside while the verse is free and sparkling, with crystal lights that flash from the jewellery of his word-magic. There is the heavy springtime smell of hawthorn in the poem and the atmossphere of old woods steals over the liquid warbling of the godlike blackbird as he upmounts over all.

> "O how the bonny blackbird sung,
> On the twisted old thorn bough !
> Now the hollow meadow-valleys hung
> In a trance to listen, ' 'Tis young, young, young,
> The morning, morning', sung the blackbird."

And later on the bird sings:

> "All honour to the daisy, the daisy;
> The pale-green, yellow-hearted primrose;
> The blowing plumes of the crimson herb-sorrel;
> The green-robed fern, and mother hedge-parsley."

There is no more charming sight in England than that of the Wiltshire shepherd tending his flocks on the bold bluffs of the downs. He is the salt of the earth; lying so close to nature he has a deep store of country knowledge. His is a pastoral simplicity, reminiscent of Arcadia and the Golden Age; it was his shy and tender attributes which appealed so much to Williams. He knew many of these shepherds intimately and often talked with them, and in "The Shepherd's Song" he imprisons in words the secret of their rustic philosophy.

> "Sleep close, my pretty lambs, so warm and white,
> The breeze is gentle and the moon is light;
> The god of folds, my sheep, your peace ensure,
> The hill is vacant and the pen secure.
>
> .   .   .   .
>
> "The little river, where my lambkins stray
> To watch the timid water-herds at play
> With silver prattle in the nodding noon,
> Now whispers in its banks a sleepy tune."

"The Cuckoo Song", which was later set to music by Roger Quilter, owes something to Marlowe; it is full of life, freshness, and nobility. The bird flashes before our eyes.

> "Blow, blow, winds of May,
> Ruffle the bloomy spray,
> Blow all the balm away;
> Hark ! 'tis my roundelay.
> Cuckoo ! Cuckoo !

Alfred Williams, 1877-1930

Elias Lloyd Williams

Elizabeth Williams

Here's to the merry morn,
Another joy is born,
Hail to the huntsman's horn,
For the bluebell greets the corn.
Cuckoo! Cuckoo!

I am neither fond nor fair,
I am neither here nor there.
Others my feast prepare,
For song is my only care.
Cuckoo! Cuckoo!

The love poems have an air of rich detachment about them. The simple Wiltshire maidens rub shoulders with statelier classical beauties and are enhanced by the comparison. The delectable Elizabethan artificiality of these poems is matched on the one hand by an intriguing and playful atmosphere and by a wealth of genuine sincerity on the other. When Williams wrote of true love, his art knew no bounds and of his wife Mary he could say:

"Whom shall I liken to my love?
None! for none is. Our Nature-mother
Attempted, but n'eer made another,
In earth beneath or heaven above;
Nor sweet-eyed maid, nor wife, nor brother,
Strong Love incarnate, nay! no other
Were half so loving as my love."

An almost perfect love poem, "A Woman's Face", owes its strength to the concreteness of its emotion and the discipline and sweep of its language. "Leave me not ever" is Gallic in concept with a dark and painful beauty and a most effective burden.

The influence of his classical reading is most marked and one of the outstanding features of his work to date. Williams reveals a wide knowledge of traditional verse forms, with an unusual understanding of, and sympathy with, the age in which they were conceived. But it was the Renascence colouring of the poems which appealed to so many readers and which pleased Williams himself so much. Nevertheless, he said that in future work he would break away from this particular influence; to his sister Ellen he wrote, "Now my one thought is to write *myself*, to make myself felt, my *personality*. I am sure I have a full soul if I can have the happiness of getting it out. Nature has the first claim on me. I have experienced man for some years and am disappointed in him."

But this sixteenth century technique shines like a beacon through all his writing. It was as if there had arisen, in what were rather unimaginative and uninspiring times, another Thomas Nashe, or Drummond of Hawthornden. Now Williams did not possess the lyrical power of either, but he did succeed, almost unknown to himself, in catching the same freedom, purity, and breadth that were theirs. It was not merely escapism that drove this factory worker to sing the praises and refinements of a Stella, Rosalind, Sylvia, or Helen, or merely chance that he should draw from the mirror of his sensitive imagination the story of Paris and Oenone. His voice rang true.

Two of the four excellent translations are renderings from Horace's *Odes*. The little "Chloe" ode, John Bailey considered was the best yet done into the English language, even including Conington. Bailey himself told Williams this when *Songs* was published.

The remaining poems in the book are largely autobiographical and introspective. Williams states his then philosophy of life in such poems as "Futurity" and "The Voyager". Here he writes like a metaphysician as if he had travelled the same road as Traherne or Henry Vaughan. With courage and determination, and devoutly believing in his affirmed destiny as poet, he craves for his development to be slow and well ordered. He knew that at that period he had no resounding world message to give, but he pleads that he may be left alone to work out his own salvation, surrounded by his books and the attractions of the comforting countryside.

One poem, "Lines on a Suicide", can hardly be placed in any category. It is a moving memorial to a friend, a simple country fellow, who, losing his wits, had dashed down a steep railway embankment into the path of an oncoming train. The tragedy welled within Williams and he wrote:

> "In thy sails a tempest
> Blew with strange fury, but my bark swam on
> O'er sunlit stricken waters and strown calms,
> Slower but safe. Swift and sure thy fall was,
> Whereat the angels weep; but God, in mercy,
> For so He sent His Mediator down
> To sit in judgment upon men, will hold
> Uneven balance, counting evil weakness,
> And only mourning that the good He gave thee
> Were swallowed up in this mortality."

Songs in Wiltshire was, therefore, a promising first book. It was remarkable in any case that such poems were possible at all from a man whose days were spent amid the crash and smoke of the forge, yet hardly a line reveals that he had ever seen, let alone worked in, such a depressing place. The poems might well have been the work of a man of leisure whose days were spent on the downs and whose evenings were given up to study and composition. But Alfred Williams had succeeded in making a very real world for himself apart from that noisy existence in which he was forced to earn his daily bread. The music and fragrance of his nature poems in particular are the hallmarks of the true worshipper of the countryside, whose delight was in simple and homely things, and whose inspiration, like Wordsworth's, emanated from a belief that every creature of nature was linked indissolubly with the spirit of God. It was not for nothing that the majority of the reviewers felt at once the freshness of his writing and agreed with the wholesome philosophy which was the hammerman's lodestone.

It is not surprising, however, that this first book of his should have blemishes. Some of the writing is forced and the effects overdone. Williams relied so much upon traditional verse forms (not to be wondered at at this stage) that he sometimes silenced his natural tongue and became too imitative. This is not to say that he did not experiment; many of the poems are daring flights. When he spoke simply, he did so with the authority of a Burns, a Clare, or a Barnes. But when he continued to draw from the store of his accumulated classical knowledge he sometimes lost his way and the weight of the heavy jewellery of his word decoration overburdened the underlying and essential thought. He said himself that many of these early poems lacked that stern discipline which he practised in his daily life. It was clear that had he known less, he would have written with more enduring power; he certainly had something to say but it was in the saying of it that he occasionally fell short. His ear, like the downland shepherd's, was close to the earth and his verse should, therefore, have been earthy and more solidly hewn. Williams saw this as he continued to develop. It became a growing conviction with him that polish and form could be overdone.

CHAPTER SIX

POEMS IN WILTSHIRE

THE town of Swindon now realised that a remarkable figure was working in its railway factory. At the end of February, 1910, Alfred Williams was invited by the committee of the Mechanics' Institute to deliver a lecture there. Largely as a result of this lecture, which was a successful one, he became acquainted with Joseph Barnard Jones, a brilliant and scholarly teacher in the town, who thus joined that small circle of Williams' closest friends and admirers. Jones from the beginning championed the cause of Williams and after the latter's death, did all he could to perpetuate his memory.

After the lecture, Williams wrote to Jones about it in the following terms, "I must have impressed the company present as being a very prosaic individual. For I cannot claim to be a great lover of society . . . I beg you to remember that I am a rustic, and I hope, not at all a spoiled one . . . If I had written something extraordinary it might have been expected, but I am sure I have not." He was as anxious as ever that the success and publicity so far obtained should not go to his head, though there was actually little danger of this happening.

J. B. Jones well remembers their first contact, when Williams came to see his library, and has said of it, "He had just seen his first volume of poems favourably noticed in the press, and was as shy as a young girl about it, disclaiming any merit of his own. As he grew animated, his voice, always to be listened to with pleasure, developed that musical light and shade which struck one, on first hearing it, as a species of phenomenon."

The lecture was followed by a second invitation. This, from the Swindon Literary and Debating Society, asked Williams to meet the members at a conversazione to be convened in his honour. It was also suggested to him that Lord Fitzmaurice should be invited to meet him officially at this social function (the two had so far only corresponded) but Williams was unwilling. He was anxious that there should be no fuss about what he had done; in addition, he thought his patron might well be embarrassed. The conversazione took place; Williams attended and read some of his poems.

Songs continued to sell slowly during the early months of 1910 though some of the later reviews were more unfavourable. "Of course I deserve rough treatment", he wrote to Dowsing "we all require the lash, and what is well, we get it. Perhaps in the first book we aim too high. We are too ambitious perhaps, too enthusiastic. We have not yet formed an estimate of ourselves, and when we have done all this, we shall still be a long way off the goal."

During the whole of that spring Williams was in poor health and suffered acute pain from stomach trouble. His wages at the factory were never more than 30/- a week and he was working nine hours a day as a hammerman for them. Yet he had a library of nearly five hundred books in Dryden Cottage and could claim to have read *The Aeneid* in the original seven times. It is known that at this period of his development he was studying four hours each night after having arrived back from Swindon at about 7.30 p.m. Neither was his life in the factory too happy, where his treatment by some of the minor officials continued to be disgracefully lacking in sympathy. At times there was so much unpleasantness and obvious jealousy that he was half inclined to change the whole course of his life and seek other and more congenial employment. "What with being assailed with internal fatigue, with fag in the worst form, with poor health generally, with the worry of keeping myself together at all cost, with increasing duties at the forge, the utter lack of sympathy, and enmity of one and another, I very often feel most unhappy. My strength seems very often to be exhausted. But it is useless to feel faint. You must march forward or fall to the rear. There is no room to turn back." This to Dowsing, shortly after *Songs* had attracted so much attention in thoughtful and cultured circles. But he was to have his triumph still, in spite of everything.

In the April he was asked to attend a gathering of poets and descendants of poets at the Holborn Restaurant, London. Williams, flattered and humbled, accepted the invitation. He hired a dress suit and spent a whole evening softening his work-hardened hands. He finished at the forge a little earlier on the auspicious day and travelled to London by express train, arriving at the gathering, over which Lord Coleridge presided, nearly half an hour late. During the lengthy proceedings he sat at a small table by himself. He was requested by the chairman to read a few of the later stanzas from "The Poet", one of the poems in *Songs*, but he was unable to do so, since by 11.30 p.m. the programme was only half completed, and he was anxious to reach Swindon by the early morning mail in order to be back at his hammer the next morning. Accordingly, he left the assembly of three hundred poets and descendants of poets shortly before midnight but not before he had got into conversation with W. E. Henley's brother and Dr. Cust, who was representing Milton. Williams stated afterwards that he was disappointed at not meeting Ella Wheeler Wilcox and was sorry that she was not present. But he did meet a reporter from *The Daily Mail* who had much to say to him and strongly advised him to write a book about his experiences in the Swindon workshop. Williams made a note of this suggestion.

The press on the following morning made much of the Poets' Gathering and *The Daily Mail* pointed out that Alfred Williams "a young man who works a steam hammer in the locomotive shop at Swindon in the week and muses with nature on the 'Wiltshire Downs' on Sunday", was the only twentieth century poet present. Williams himself had been unaware of this.

That summer he read nearly all Richard Jefferies' books, while a chance contact with a fellow worker in the factory, whose name was Hollick, led to an introduction to the writings of Max Müller. In a letter to Hollick in the May, he referred to Müller as follows: "I am sorry to say that I do not know much of him or of his work. It is well known that his scholarship ranks him with the greatest of modern times. His knowledge of languages, especially strikes one as very remarkable. He was a born linguist."

Williams' old Ruskin Hall tutor, Arthur Hacking, who had been watching his development with interest, drew his attention to the fact that *Songs* had just been reviewed in Berlin, where mention had been made of his talent and tremendous energy. The reviewer had gone so far as to hail Williams as one of the greatest living poets. Now Williams had for some time been an admirer of Goethe and said of the Germans and their scholarship in general, "They have laboured to elucidate language and literature and they are probably the greatest critics and commentators of the world. They spend much time and pains with the English tongue and probably know more of our literary qualities and traditions than we do ourselves. And yet as is so often the case, the most critical are the least productive in creative work. Just as great scholarship is not often accredited with ranks of real genius, for there is a tremendous difference between knowledge and the genius which creates new and beautiful work."

In October, 1910, he had correspondence with Edward Slow, the Wiltshire dialect poet, then living at Wilton. Williams, who admired all who wrote poetry, had sent him six sonnets that he had written about Wilton. Slow suggested that it would be a good idea if Williams were to give a series of lectures in various Wiltshire towns on "Working Men Poets", but nothing came of this suggestion. Nevertheless, Williams visited Slow at a later date, and the two, finding much in common, talked a great deal about dialect, local history, and archaeology.

Williams had been writing steadily throughout the year and had already selected a number of poems which he thought would make a second volume. Many of these were sonnets, and, though unlike Dowsing, he was not keen on the sonnet form, he knew it to be popular with the better class readers. Naively, he believed he had to consider this section of his new public. He had also composed many local poems dealing with such places as Stonehenge, Salisbury, Amesbury, Avebury, Marlborough, Savernake, and Bemerton. In fact, he toyed with the idea of publishing a whole book of Wiltshire poems, but decided in the end that he did not know enough about his county yet awhile to embark fairly on such a project. But he had a new book ready by January, 1911. Now began the search for a publisher.

He knew that he would have to have a patron again, so he wrote to Fitzmaurice about the matter. He told him of the financial success of *Songs* and of how Kyle had assured him that all expenses on this had been well covered; Williams himself had sold £35 worth of books. He drew Fitzmaurice's attention to the new work, and in giving him an outline of its general plan wrote: "In it I hope to be stronger, more original, more personal, and I might say experimental. The pieces I have in view are autobiographical, some couplets, a few sonnets—but not my best—the Danaë Ode (Simonides of Ceos), experiments with

Horace, and also experiments with Pindar, in a manner I have not seen before, that is, in his own long majestic line." Referring to couplets, he observed that they were apt to become formal, like Dryden, or affected like Keats, but that he preferred those of Dryden and Pope because of their majesty, music, and general powerful effect. The translations from Horace were definitely experimental, for he hoped one day to do the Odes in their entirety, but was uncertain at that time as to the best manner in which to make such translations. He had two ideas regarding this. J. B. Jones had lately lent him Lytton's Horace translations and had given him valuable information about them. Williams, therefore, did not know whether it would be better to try his translations in the strict manner of Lytton, or attempt to popularise Horace by "striking" through him. He also quite simply informed Fitzmaurice that he had sufficient material at hand for two more books of verse besides the publication proposed. One of these was a volume of factory poems.

Besides Müller, Jefferies, and Lytton, he had read Frazer's *Golden Bough*, which he admitted was a mystery to him. He went further, and told Hollick that since it was merely a myth, the book was unworthy of serious notice !

Fitzmaurice was as impressed as ever with Williams' determined industry and said he was willing to guarantee the expenses of the second volume of poems. Then Williams heard, through Reuben George (as Secretary of the Swindon Branch of the Workers' Educational Association), that this organisation might also be willing to meet part of the publishing fees of the proposed new work. Williams had been a member of the Swindon branch of the W.E.A. for a number of years and his work and unique career had been brought to the interested notice of Alfred Zimmern and Albert Mansbridge. Zimmern was intimately connected with the W.E.A., while Mansbridge was its founder and general secretary. But Williams was anxious that Fitzmaurice should not be offended, nor his offer of help immediately refused, so he asked Reuben not to mention the W.E.A. project to him.

In the June, Williams discussed the whole position with Reuben on the occasion of the annual visit of the Swindon W.E.A. to Coate Water —where they were to visit Richard Jefferies' house. Nothing was definitely settled as to what action Zimmern and Mansbridge might be able to take, but Williams was enthralled with this particular day's outing, mainly because he had a long conversation with Edward Garnett who had heard about him from Reuben and was anxious to meet him.

Then a third offer was made to meet the expenses of the new book. This came from the Hon. Mrs. Agar, of Stanton Fitzwarren, who for some time had been an admirer of Williams' writing and had given him considerable support; she had heard about him from Canon Masters and had, as a matter of fact, bought ten copies of *Songs in Wiltshire*. But Williams, with his usual independence, finally decided to be his own guarantor and declined the generous offers made by Fitzmaurice and Mrs. Agar. By the August, too, it was clear that nothing was going to come of the W.E.A. plan, though Mansbridge was hopeful that a cheap edition of *Songs* or of the new book, might be possible in the future.

All that summer Williams endeavoured to arrange terms with older and better known publishers, but was unsuccessful because he could not agree to act as guarantor for the money which was required by each of them; both Elkin Mathews and John Lane, for instance, were willing to publish for £65 to £70. Thus Williams fell back upon Erskine Macdonald again, and he and Kyle at length came to an agreement, deciding upon publication on a co-operative basis. The plan was simply to divide an edition of five hundred copies, each taking half, with Williams to pay his share from the sales he would personally make. The book, which was to be called *Poems in Wiltshire*, was to cost 3/6 and was to be of the same size and form as *Songs*, though with rather fewer pages. Williams' expenses would be covered if he sold some 200 copies. Now Kyle, possibly remembering the good sales of *Songs*, wished the retail price of the book to be 5/-, but Williams was unwilling because he knew how difficult it was to sell poetry at that price, and, as he wrote to Reuben in the September, "I am greatly dependent on my old Swindon friends for support".

Alfred Williams was confident that *Poems* was a better collection than *Songs*, but his experiences of the sales of the latter had convinced him that he would have to do most of the bookselling himself and that it would be inadvisable to expect much from the booksellers local or general. Accordingly, he set himself the patient task of writing to his friends and relations and appealing for their support. He was most anxious that the book should stand on its own merits, though he told his sister Ellen in the October that he thought some of the poems might not be "flash" enough for some readers, "though I believe that there are some good lines and thoughts; a great deal of it has gone over London as it is, and obtained high opinion. But good opinions do not buy books. The people do this, and though a book might be reviewed extraordinarily well, it might not on that account sell very well. The worst of reviews is that instead of 'whetting' the appetite, they very often 'satiate' it."

Night after night he applied himself to his task and eventually wrote to nearly all his Wiltshire friends. He felt keenly the general apathetic attitude of the reading public to poetry. "It is a regrettable truth, but it has to be admitted" he told Fitzmaurice, "that poetry is going out of the lives of most people; it seems almost a hopeless task to fix any interest in it."

His health was again giving rise to concern and Mary begged him to ease up. She might have pleaded with the wall. Yet, the daily and incessant grind at the forge, with the self-imposed strain of night study were beginning to take their toll of his iron constitution. Very rarely could he afford the time for social visits, even to his closest friends, for he knew that if he accepted the many invitations which were now being showered on him from all quarters, he would have less opportunities for carrying out his desired plans. He was always glad, nevertheless, to welcome to Dryden Cottage such intimates as Henry Byett and J. B. Jones, but he had to tell one persistent enquirer who wished to visit him that "Sunday is always my private day, but I am free for a little while in the late afternoon. You will understand how we literary people are placed with regard to time."

Whenever possible he escaped to the Downs because "that suits my complaint and helps me to see things." He much preferred making these excursions alone and he would be away for hours on end, only returning to his cottage when he was renewed and at peace. He was, however, fond of picnics and he and Mary made several blackberrying excursions with close friends.

The period prior to the publication of *Poems* was often depressing for him, but he was cheered by comforting letters from Fitzmaurice, who offered to buy copies of the new book, and from John Bailey, now literary editor of *The Times*, who sent him his new book on the study of poetry. He was uplifted, too, by reading a letter which appeared over the name of his sister Ellen in the local press, in defence of domestic servants. From early years she had been in service, which she believed was a high calling, but one too often misunderstood and generally ill-paid. Alfred applauded his sister's courage—and it needed some in 1911—in stating publicly that servants were over-worked, especially on Sundays. He told her that he hoped his new book would prove that he also had grit and determination and was not afraid of expressing *his* opinion.

Poems in Wiltshire duly appeared in the last week of November, 1911. The first copy was a present to his wife, who saw that it was dedicated to her; she had been quite unaware of Alfred's intention. Further presentation copies went to Fitzmaurice, "a small token of my esteem for, and indebtedness to you for your various helps and encourage-ments", Garnett, Bailey, Dowsing, Rockell and Denwood. And, on the eve of the publication of *Poems*, Williams heard that two of his recent poems, "The Smith" and "The Forge Man" had been printed in *The Nation*.

The 1911 volume differed in several essentials from *Songs*. Though a large number of the new poems were reflections on Wiltshire in particular and nature in general, many others were addressed to persons. There were also poems of a philosophical and autobiographical nature, with a group of translations from Greek, Latin, and French.

In a prefatory note, Williams thanked subscribers for their reception of *Songs* and wrote at some length about his conception of translating in general. Forty-eight of the sixty-seven poems were original compositions, eleven were translations from Greek, seven, translations from Latin, one, a translation from French, with one original Latin poem. Sixteen of the poems, of which eleven were sonnets, made direct mention of Wiltshire.

"About Wilts" is a successful piece of work, its metre reminiscent of Longfellow. Here is deep adoration of the county, coupled with the same wide knowledge of its history and beauty spots as before. There are several fine sounding lines, but owing to the continual use of adjectives, the colour is at times so overlaid that the general effect of power is diminished. But it is hard to resist the ease and sonority of such a passage as:—

"Can you trace a fairer garden, truer-trimmed or better-ordered ?
Here the Channel of the Avon, there the Valley of the Horse,
North the flowing Thames arises flowery-banked and jewel-bordered,
East the shallow silvery Kennet chimes along its reedy course;
Meadows here and blooming orchards, groves of poplar, walls of willow,
Spreading oak and elm and chestnut, arms and branches interlaced
With the honey bean and clover, and the coltsfoot sweet and yellow,
Like the letters on a girdle twined about a maiden's waist."

"Under the Hawthorn", which Williams dubbed "a review of all sorts of things, dealing largely with Swindon and its types of education, religion and life," is written in heroic couplets in the manner of Pope. Its theme is false education and town life. It states that the important thing in life is the application of acquired knowledge, and that the best school is experience, which with true education, should guide the intellect and exercise the will. This is true eighteenth century philosophising, with echoes of Crabbe and Bloomfield and here and there a gentle reminder of Thomson's "Seasons". Williams is ever faithful to the river Cole, "dear companion of my boyish years" and, throughout the poem he turns his thoughts from under the hawthorn to soliloquise on the passing of time and the decay of old customs. Without definitely mentioning the town by name, he roundly condemns Swindon, where "divine religion is mocked", and has little also to say in favour of the bookish learning it patronises. There is no mistaking his dislike for the town where he daily works; he was out of sympathy with all that it represented. "Under the Hawthorn" has many exquisite moments and a certain rugged and attractive beauty when its sentiments are confined to simple description, but considering it as a whole, the poem is long-winded and over-moralising. The argument put forward was well worth making, but verbosity marred much of the writing. He had still to explore the possibilities of disciplined technique.

"Music in Salisbury Cathedral" is an interesting and fairly successful effort at blank verse which attracted local attention. It has a nicely balanced sense of contrast and climax and its pictures of the sweetness, sorrow, joy, and solemnity of organ music, are drawn in an original manner. Williams enjoyed writing this particular poem, which, though not without a certain cloying effect, well illustrates his command of the written word.

"Homeland", written in couplets, deals with a battle unrecorded in history which may have taken place on Barbury Hill between the Britons and invading Romans. Mention is made of the River Cole and Liddington Hill, with a tribute to the memory of Richard Jefferies who also loved and wrote of Wiltshire scenes. The poem has many wistful thoughts and is a major example of Williams' unassailable regard for the White Horse district. It also, though indirectly, shows the influence of his classical studies.

"On the Druidical remains at Avebury", a sonnet-sequence, and "On the Roman Ruins at Chedworth", the latter place on the Gloucestershire border, are attempts to express archaeology in terms of poetry, and they show to a marked degree how keen was Williams' interest in local history. The last sonnet of the sequence, "On the Roman Remains at Chedworth", is one of the best pieces of writing in the whole book. The octet is dignified and entirely unforced.

> "Here once the Roman minstrel piped and sung;
> The dexterous blacksmith plied his iron trade;
> The busy looms their warp and woof displayed;
> The old centurion's sword and buckler hung;
> War's horrid implements aside were flung;
> Now tuned the midnight songstress in the glade;
> The fluttering eagle cast a peaceful shade;
> The timid maiden to her lover clung."

The sonnet, "To Hinton Parva" is nearly a gem. Williams is here in all his glory as the sweet singer of the Wiltshire villages as they were in their days of innocence and unspoiled beauty.

It is difficult all the same to separate the Wiltshire poems from those which deal in more general terms with nature. Both groups are complements and foils to each other. The poet extols the glories of woods, fields, birds, flowers, Dryden Cottage garden, and the returning seasons.

"There's a Sweet Little Flower", with an effective and delicate dance rhythm, is the nature lover writing verse, but his praise of the Herb Robert is sincere and realistic. It betokens a fine eye and ear. "Come into the Woods" is a clarion call to mankind to enjoy the beauties of the countryside.

The book has one poem, "Natural Thoughts and Surmises", which reaches a very high level. "This", he wrote to Denwood in December, 1910, "comprises my native and also my spiritual philosophy." With its nine massive stanzas, it was the longest poem he had written. It is introspective, deeply religious, and philosophical, dealing as it does, with great intensity, with life, death, truth, fate, the universe, the pride of the rich and powerful, and the adulation of the poor. Williams' own strongly personal philosophy is outlined in such lines as:—

"If the serial sun shines over the blue of the hills, I am content;
And if the wind roars through the trees and the swelling raindrops
    with it, I am content;
I do not run into ecstasies over nothing, nor figure ills for myself,
Being naturally mortal we shall learn the future soon enough."

His lofty argument states, with all the authority of Coleridge or Wordsworth, that divine law knows no bounds or fetters, and that death deprives man of everything in the end, except his eternal spirit. Towns and cities, riches and poverty, are all one in the ever-rushing stream of life, the same spirit that moves nature moves man also, for man is but a part of the wide universe. He owes nothing to heredity and whatever may befall the earth, he will continue majestically, for his deathless divinity will triumph over all. Williams had indeed shown himself to be "more powerful and more original". He is seen here as a shrewd thinker and student of human nature, clearly seeing the world beyond to which he was moving, through the eyes of nature which he worshipped. The curious free metre of the poem, with its subtle rhythms, is daring and original. One thinks naturally of Whitman, but the beautifully balanced cadences, alliterations, assonances and dissonances, might well have emanated from Gerard Manley Hopkins or John Donne. But the thoughts and surmises were peculiarly the hammerman's; their all-inspiring solemnity and masterly range of expression and feeling stamped him as a writer of immense possibilities. "Natural Thoughts and Surmises" has few false notes and the craftsmanship is a supreme effort.

A dozen poems, mainly sonnets. are tributes to friends, and these are sturdy and honest, clearly displaying his fine independent spirit. There are two sonnets dedicated to Fitzmaurice, poems addressed to his wife on her birthday, to Edward Slow, Canon Masters, and some of his old playmates. One of the latter is a poignant reminder of a boyhood friend, Charles Ockwell, whose passing had strangely troubled Williams. "The Earth Lover", in praise of Richard Jefferies, is probably the best poem in this group; it has much feeling for natural beauty and a theme that deals with the everlastingness of nature, and the passing of its great lover, Jefferies. The eighth verse of this poem is one of the most appealing quatrains Williams had written to date:—

"These woods of iron heart and strength,
The sun's warm beam that shoots and thrills,
The stream that winds its sinuous length
For ever downward from the hills ?"

The autobiographical poems make quite clear what Williams' philosophy was at this time. "Aspirations", on the immortality of the soul, can be considered as a cartoon for "Natural Thoughts and Surmises", with such lines as, "Through ill we rise to better" and "Death freeth, not enthralleth". "The Bells", owing nothing to Poe, was a favourite poem of Alfred Williams, for in it he writes very movingly of his indebtedness to Elizabeth Williams. Writing about this poem to Ellen, he had said, "There is one, 'The Bells', in which I have had the opportunity of mentioning mother and her battle. I hope it will not be overlooked among the others." He soliloquises on his own end with introspection, realising that he must one day also leave behind the things which his mother had loved. "My soul is free as ambient air" is in praise of poetry itself. He asserts that though his body is shackled, his spirit is free; he is in the company of the great ones when he walks in solitude.

The translations which had concerned Williams most of all, cover a wide field; some might consider them the most astonishing feature of the book. It is still difficult to realise that they were composed either in odd moments in the railway works, or at the dead of night in Dryden Cottage. In them, he keeps as far as possible to the original metres, but at the same time, gives, as he himself expressed, "the poems an English cast". As evidences of the scale of his reading and scholarship, we find translations from Pindar, Simonides of Ceos, Archilochus, Theognis, Sappho, Alcman, Plato, Timocreon, Menander, Philemon, and Horace. The seven translations from the latter's "Odes" are rendered most felicitously, with the third and fourth odes well above the average for this type of work. Though Williams considered all the translations as adventures with language, he was confident of their fitness and grace. Indeed, before the publication of the book, they had been seen and praised by Garnett and Bailey, while the advice and guiding hands of Fitzmaurice and J. B. Jones had always been available when called upon. Finally, though Williams was no great student or admirer of French, there is a rich and colourful translation from

Ronsard in which he almost completely succeeded in capturing the Gallic idiom.

Poems in Wiltshire was, with new and developed characteristics, an advance on *Songs*, though it had not the same unity; it was a different book. Williams is seen as the poet of varying lights, but with rather more of the individual poet finding personal expression. Nevertheless, there is still too great a reliance upon classical idioms and the tenets of ancient philosophy. But there is more depth in the book and one is struck by the religious note of many of the poems. The writing, often brooding and contemplative, has less of the sparkle and renascent freshness of the earlier book; and sustained and somewhat ponderous longer poems are apt, at times, to be wearisome.

But *Poems* was indeed a thoughtful and heart-searching expression; tinged with pain and acute melancholy, it is but a reflection of the hazardous spiritual experiences through which Williams had passed. But he remained the devout worshipper of simple beauty, with his love for his home county knowing no wane, but blossoming with added fervour. The book was well worth publishing if only for the inclusion of "Natural Thoughts and Surmises" which was the poem *The Times* singled out as being so full of life and vigour.

Poems was as well received as *Songs*, though in many quarters there was more than a tendency to overpraise Williams' poetic gifts because of the immensity of his triumph over general circumstances. No review gave him greater pleasure than that which appeared in the *Amsterdam Telegraph* and which simply said "Would one believe that these dainty verses were written by a workman, hard pressed by daily toil? This humble forgeman would put to shame many a lord. That in itself stamps him a remarkable man."

The humble forgeman had already proved himself to be a remarkable man.

CHAPTER SEVEN

PROSE AND MORE POETRY

THE same year was to bring another achievement and a vital decision. Williams had never forgotten the advice given to him by the reporter at the Poets' Dinner about the writing of his factory experiences. During 1911 he embarked upon such a venture.

Only Reuben George, Fitzmaurice and his sister Ellen first knew that he was turning his mind from poetry to prose. On 28th February, he told Fitzmaurice that he had compiled "a record of my experience in the workshop, strong, faithful pictures of the industrial life, rough and vigorous". The decision to write prose was, in fact, largely forced upon him by circumstances. He was perfectly well aware that sooner or later his health would break down and compel him to leave the railway works; then there would arise a distinct possibility that he might have to write for his livelihood. His poetry had brought little financial reward.

At the end of September, 1911, he was able to write to Fitzmaurice, "I have written a prose book this summer entitled *Life in the Factory*, about 250 pp., which greatly pleases me. I have the confidence to hope that it will be of interest to a great many when I have the opportunity of printing it, which will not be yet, however. There is no need to describe its character, that is set out in the title. I have endeavoured to give a faithful picture of the *life* of the place. Not of localities and machinery. Neither is it of an aggressive kind, but moderate in tone, though sufficiently sympathetic with the people, I hope." When informing Dowsing that October of his intention to occupy himself with a factory book, he said that he believed that what he had so far written would go as far, if not further, than any of his poetry—when he had the liberty to print it. Neither was the time yet ripe for the appearance of the factory poems.

Now Fitzmaurice, to whom Williams again turned for advice and encouragement, was a little worried about some of the sentiments expressed in the factory book and entered into a lengthy correspondence with its author about politics in general. Williams said that he realised the question of Capital and Labour was a delicate one, and though a working man and a victim of both systems himself, he had to acknowledge that there were considerations on each side. He believed that workmen as a body were not nearly so badly done by as they imagined, but it was true that they had many justifiable grievances. With particular reference to his own workshop he wrote: "There is a total lack of tact in dealing with the workmen; it is the haughty and autocratic spirit of the staff generally which drives men to extreme views. This is altogether deplorable, because the staff cannot, or will not see, that the very end they so much affect, they themselves render quite impossible of attainment. My own position, I confess, is somewhat illogical. Frankly, I cannot subscribe to the extreme views held by the Socialist-Labour people. Of late years I have inclined to the moderate view, though this again is not compatible with true progress."

For some years Williams was of the opinion that there was a dangerous spirit abroad in the ranks of the Socialist party which was determined to bring all the old institutions to the ground. He admitted that many Socialists were hard-headed and keen-witted. "They have no historical knowledge, no 'large' knowledge; they are bitterly anti-Christian, they are Republican to a man, they want the nationalisation of everything:

an eight hour day is their present demand, immediately after obtaining it they aver that they would commence an agitation for seven hours, and so on.   They are without sympathies, without scruples, and without a decent sense of justice at all; they are very materialist."   It is not difficult to see whence had sprung some of the ideas for "Under the Hawthorn" and "Natural Thoughts and Surmises".   Williams was sorry to see the old Liberalism dying out and true Conservatism becoming rare.

He franky told Fitzmaurice that it was his belief that the only thing to save the situation would be a judicious granting of concessions, a real desire to mediate, and to legislate for the good of the people, with a strong firm policy on the part of the administration.

In November, following upon the political correspondence, he informed Fitzmaurice, not unsurprisingly, that he hoped to write "a prose 'Life in the Village' next, making use of my own early experience on the farm, and portraying local character."   It was evident that Alfred Williams, through his prose and poetry, was determined to make his voice heard and his opinions felt.   In the very last week of 1911 he wrote to Dowsing, who was forlorn and depressed, "There is much heartaching work attached to literature, especially in the case of folk like ourselves, but don't despair ever, but nerve up.   God knows I have had cause enough to faint.   But I will 'swipe' those who try to grind me down yet".

Though Williams gleaned considerable satisfaction from the reception accorded *Poems in Wiltshire*, and had ready a number of other poems which he thought worth while publishing, he decided that for the time being it would be in his best interests to concentrate upon prose.   Knowing that he could not yet publish his factory book without losing his job at the works, he began, in the spring of 1912, to write the *Village Life* book.   By May, after just ten weeks' writing, and that, of course, in his spare time, he had completed the first draft of what he called *A Wiltshire Village*, and had sent the MS. to Fitzmaurice.   No composition had ever given him greater release or pleasure than this honest and unadorned story of the life that went on daily in South Marston.   He seemed to find a new strength and purpose during the early months of this year.

Fitzmaurice praised the new book and gave Williams some valuable information about Wiltshire; he also suggested that he was running a risk in covering much the same ground as Richard Jefferies had done before him.   "The motif of the work" wrote Williams to Fitzmaurice, "is to give a picture of rural life—an unvarnished one—as I have lived it, and also, to "contrast it with the towns, and beside this to sketch the locality—an unknown corner of north Wilts—and call attention to the farm labourer's lot.   I have tried, too, to dispel a little

Mark Titcombe

Alfred Williams
at the age of eleven years

Ann Hughes

of the glamour that, to the eyes of many, attaches to the factory condition. I want to show that higher wages is not the greatest *desideratum*
in life, for these are not obtained in the factories without terrific effort,
or corresponding inconveniences. At the same time, I should never
advise the farm labourer to 'lie down' and be quiet, though, as his
position is, he is nearly bound to do so. The farm labourer's position
is an extremely difficult one to remedy, as all know, but his case is not
hopeless, and I believe that the day will come when it will be possible
to do something for him." Williams hoped that *A Wiltshire Village*
would pave the way for his factory prose and poems.

Fitzmaurice, as a member of a landowning family, was naturally
interested in the references made to the life and lot of the agricultural
labourer. He knew, too, that his position was "an extremely difficult
one to remedy". He sent Williams a copy of the Wiltshire County
Medical Officer's Report for 1911 as he thought he would benefit
from a study of its statistics. Nevertheless, Fitzmaurice freely admitted
that he was not a skilled student of rustic conditions in general, but
had had some experience of them in a few Wiltshire villages.

In July, Williams offered *A Wiltshire Village* to Duckworth, who
accepted the book for publication without hesitation. Alfred Williams
considered this acceptance to be his first real score, but fully expected
considerable criticism of many of the opinions which he had expressed.
To J. B. Jones in September he wrote: "The pages go to 305 of matter,
with a four page preface, containing the 'argument' or the point of
view. I like it, on the whole, but I expect that I shall offend very many,
for there is a great amount of frank statement concerning many matters.
Generally speaking, however, it is a book of 'Nature and Life' and not
of opinion."

And to Dowsing in the same month, when he told him about the
village book, "Literature is a hard battle to fight for those who are
wound round with the chains of labour and get more 'kicks than
ha'pence', everywhere. But I suppose it is *in the blood* with us two
and we must push forward." Williams had heard from Kyle that there
were no more copies left of either of his poetry books; largely as a
result of the review in the *Amsterdam Telegraph* several copies of the
last book had found buyers in Holland. This news cheered him, but
immediately he had finished *A Wiltshire Village*, Williams fell ill again.
This time a severe bronchial cold, coupled with depression, kept him
out of Swindon for nearly a month.

But with the village book off his mind and already being printed, he
thought he would try his hand with a new volume of poems, the idea
being that any possible losses on it might be balanced by the profits
almost certainly to be made by the prose work; both books would help
to sell one another. Accordingly, he offered his third volume of poems,

entitled *Nature and Other Poems* to Erskine Macdonald in July, publication to be on a similar co-operative basis to *Poems in Wiltshire*. Kyle
was pleased to accept the work and the terms. "The poems contain",
wrote Williams to Jones, "what I think to be about my best on Nature,
but I do not *go in* for pretty speech much, but try to express feeling and
my deep love of the hills, trees, and flowers. I have two translations
from Horace—made some years ago—I have not had the time for
translating this year. I also have two extracts from an early poem
"Aeneas in Sicily", viz., the Story of Alcestis and The Cyclops, which
I like very well. The chief poems are "The Hills" of nine pages,
"The Testament" twenty odd pages, and the "Ode to Morning".
"The Testament" is my longest poem, and what I think to be the best
for thought and nature feeling". Williams also confided in Edward
Garnett that he considered "The Testament" to be his best poem.
"It is in *vers libres* which I think suits nature work very well . . . I can-
not twist my mind into the shapes required by the modern standards;
try how I will, I must 'enter in straight by the gate'."

Nature and other Poems was published by Erskine Macdonald in the
first week of October, 1912, dedicated, with a quotation from Moreau,
to the Hon. Mrs. Agar. An introductory sonnet stated that it was the
poet's wish for his work always to be straightforward, simple, and
natural. Including this sonnet, there are twenty-two original poems in
the book, with two translations from Horace. Though shorter than
the earlier books, *Nature and other Poems* contained "The Hills", "The
Testament" and the "Ode to Morning", all lengthy poems. Williams'
interpretation of and reaction to nature is the theme of the book, with
Wiltshire as his canvas.

Though not so marked as in *Songs* and *Poems*, the varied results of
his classical learning are in abundant evidence throughout this volume.
And Williams again shows himself as the experimenter with sounds
and rhythms. He strikes an even deeper note of serenity and reaches
higher peaks of sublime exaltation. It is clear that the contents of the
book had been more carefully chosen; the poems are more individual
and less imitative as though Williams had at last discovered what
exactly was his poetic message and what the best garment in which to
clothe it.

"Ode to Morning" recaptures the sensitive atmosphere and sparkling
imagery of the early romantics. Not that his zeal for nature has so
ecstatic a range as the German romantics; there is certainly rather less
of Heine and Schiller and the early dawns of *volkkultur* than of Wordsworth and the young Keats. We stand with the poet at the gate of a
summer dawn, in the midst of English Wiltshire, and see Liddington
Hill throwing "his still summit upwards plain and clear", and the pretty
villages of Stanton Fitzwarren and Sevenhampton slumbering in the

far shadows. Across this waking panorama move rapturous skylarks, meadows and dim woodlands. The poet yearns for the approach of dawn when the whole ring of countryside will light up with purity and strength; he wishes, too, for his dawning to come so that he may patiently await "the opening of a mightier day".

One expects to find a poem about the River Cole and is not disappointed. Williams' description of its waters in torrent is both lively and resounding. One is attracted to the line:—

"To whose impulsive stream the mill wheel clanks."

His joy at the sight of homely folk living graciously in the peace of their own simple surroundings, is aroused by a recollection of evening in a Wiltshire cottage. "The Cottager's Evening" instantly recalls Burns but it really owes little to him. It bears its own individual and wistful mark.

"The Re-Awakening", a stylish and concrete piece of poetic imagery, might well have been written by one of the more venturesome eighteenth century lyrists. It revolves round Williams' favourite theme— the coming of spring to a waiting earth after "storm-racked" winter, and the renewal of the poet's spirit and sources of inspiration.

"Living, from Sorrow's bed I rise
And drink the medicine of the skies;"

"The Hills" is one of the corner stones of this book, and indeed, the key to the fullest understanding of Williams' own development as prophet and poet. Its eight sweeping stanzas express, with all the passion and authority of a Shelley, a most positive and reassuring philosophy of life. There are tremendous surges of power here and breathtaking climaxes, too. We move with him in the very heart of nature, singing in unabated rejoicing the praise of celestial hills. The pattern of the poem could hardly have been better woven; such a rhapsody called for the discipline of rhyming couplets. Wiltshire to Williams is the seat of "beautiful hills", "quiet contemplative hills", "tender compassionate hills", and "ultimate hills". The whole beautifully balanced conception echoes, too, to the burden of "The Hills and my soul shall be one". Identifying himself with the spirit and breath of nature, Williams, in the fourth stanza, bears us aloft with:—

"I have come, O you hills ! with the tremulous heart of a fawn,
Quivering with passionate fear, in the grey-winged hours of the dawn,
Ere the high, adorable East has unveiled, and unfurled
Her broad blue ensign above the boundless tracts of the world;
I have come at your call, and fear lent wings to my feet,
With a cry in my soul, and the drum of my heart a-beat,
And the streaming blood of the sweat slid down from my brow,
As I clambered and came from the slumbering valley below;"

And in the fifth, he appeals to the wandering winds to reveal their secrets as they blow over the hills, while in the seventh stanza, shot through with a strange nostalgic beauty, he declares that he is not afraid of his "invisible fate" for throughout his life he will cling steadfastly to the loving and hopeful comradeship of his hills.

This is the essential Alfred Williams, with a genuine message born of contempt and mistrust of all materialism; devoid of all worldliness, he is both challenging and rich in promise. At no time in this psalm of the downland does he permit himself to be chained by the form which he had chosen as the mould of his thoughts; many a poet has fallen foul upon the rock of rhyming couplets. "The Hills", like all great works of art, carries one away into distant and unexplored realms of the mind, but does not forget to return us safely to the earth at the end of the journey.

Yet the monumental and documentary "Testament" is the peak poem of this collection, and probably the greatest single effort of Williams' poetic career. By it alone he will find a place amongst the immortals. Henry Byett has told of its genesis. "The Testament" was conceived by Williams "while seated meditating in the forked branches of a willow tree which hangs over a hatchway in the River Cole". The exact spot is in a field near and north-west of Acorn Bridge, on the main Swindon-Shrivenham road. Williams found it necessary, in order to find inspiration, to make frequent journeys to the river bank and to sit for hours, cramped and uncomfortable, in that willow tree. Such an expedition was only possible at weekends. When the spirit had moved him sufficiently he would dash back to Dryden Cottage, almost frozen to the marrow, in order to continue with the writing.

The free metre and the strongly emphasised rhythms of the poem were deliberately chosen so that he might the better able convey his thoughts without the stranglehold of a set and regular technique. That he was successful in his aim to a large extent is evident by the smoothness of the reading.

"The Testament" opens with a spirited, impassioned appeal to Nature. There is an invocation to the spirits of trees, pools, and summer perfumes. These are to be the poet's guerdons. We are invited to "listen to the distant world beyond us". Wearied and mazed by the depression of servile cities, the poet longs for escape to the refreshment of the countryside and the friendship of the familiar spot about his rural home, to "the old forked willow" and "the long sloping hill". None dare refuse the challenge and ready invitation of this opening stanza. Williams tells Nature "There is nothing very delectable in that I would sing to you". In linking himself with her, as if for solace, he refers to the unkindness of men in general and to the particu-

lar hatred, greed, and callousness of some of his workmates. One is
moved by the ache in such a line as "How they scorn the breath of my
mouth, and very nearly laid hands upon me". What a comment on
the treatment which he had so often received in the factory! One is
not surprised that in desperation Williams should turn to field and
hedgerow for other food and balm. So he expounds a way of life:—

"I have no desire of riches, nor of honour, I enjoy all naturally;
    I am the heir of all that I see, that is my possession;
    And the things that are invisible and eternal are mine also."

He follows Nature with watchful eye and ready ear, finding continual movement and colour, with growing delight, in all her aspects.
When he writes of "the rich grass up to his knees", "the little stream
very nearly dried up", "the pear tree by the chimney" and "the late
plum waiting to be delivered", Williams the nature lover treads in
paradise. This verse is grandiloquent, yet earthy and vital.

The fourth, fifth, and sixth stanzas are hewn out of a sheer delight
in living. Again he turns to trees, "O dear-loving trees, my comrades,
artistic and natural". Proudly he marches on to a tenth stanza, which,
singing of Art and Knowledge, finds "The God of Nature, my hope,
knowledge, my faculty." If he had the opportunity he believes he
could lift humanity up from pits of despair and teach it the secrets of
complete happiness, and create for it a religion of hope and comfort.
He would "Draw all the earth into one bond, all differences of people"
by bringing men into direct contact with "the green walks of life" and
"the sweetness of woods".

The poem moves to inevitability, and Alfred Williams has become
the trumpeter of deliverance—

"I am the apostle of hope, I am the proof of destiny,
    I am the finger of faith, the prophet of deliverance,
    The strong prison of pride, the death of hypocrisy,
    The scorner of artifice, the bold wrecker of convention.
    All life has its recompense, I am not unrewarded;
    I am full of strong rumour, I am great with futurity."

We have entered through the door of the deep silences of eternity to
find ourselves, with the poet, completely fused as partners of earth
and heaven.

Both "The Hills" and "The Testament" are thus logical continua-
tions of Williams' natural philosophy and feeling. His simple aim
had been to express himself in his own voice. When it was pointed
out to him that "The Testament" was reminiscent of the ideas and
technique of Whitman, he emphasised in his own forcible manner that
he owed nothing to him but the form, "and not much of that, for the
hexameter is the *base* of the line".

So *Nature and other poems* was safely launched. Just after the event, Williams addressed a rather remarkable letter to one who, after watching his development from afar with admiration, had become a friend and counsellor. This was William D. Bavin, a Swindon schoolmaster and a colleague of J. B. Jones. Williams wrote, with "The Testament" very much in his mind, of his doubts about the generally accepted view of immortality. "I do not believe in the Golden City altogether, and a passive sort of existence. Rather I think of a future of great activity—spiritual activity—and I believe in the boundless power of the spirit, its power to perceive and understand, a marvellous nobility, in fact, a total universality of power, but only for those who desire and aspire to such in this life." He felt that the future so very much depended upon one's present actions and that they who yearned for future life would have it, and abundantly. It was his belief that after death the soul was first received into the universal congregation of spirits and then finally into the full knowledge, presence, and nature of God and the mysteries of things. Those who had lived intensely on earth, burning for this or that endeavour, or filled with a true and noble love for individual knowledge, would be permitted the satisfaction of continuing in that worship and of deriving an even more intense joy and existence from it. Obedient to the will of heaven, Williams accepted unhesitatingly the divine promises of immortality.

"As to Pantheism pure and simple", he continued to Bavin, "I do not accept that, it is insufficient, as you have seen, in my case. When I say 'I shall flow with the rivers and tides' I mean not that I shall be a *watery part of them*, but that I shall flow with them *in knowledge, in spirit, in essence*, that I shall enter into everything—not materially, but by a subtle intelligence—the intelligence of the soul. That is my philosophy, though I fear it is not a very clear belief, or that it would not appear so to many people, though something in me compels me to hold on to the view."

Williams was here stating a similar faith to Shelley's, especially when he emphasised that he was a portion of the eternal

> ". . . which must glow
> Through time and change,
> Unquenchably the same."

And Victor Hugo, who was certainly no agnostic, had put forward a similar viewpoint when he wrote "Il faut dans le grand tout tôt ou tard s'absorber".

The book was even more enthusiastically received than the two previous publications. "The Testament" was singled out for greatest praise. John Bailey in *The Times* spoke of the purpose and sincerity of Williams and said that there were occasions when he achieved a rare beauty. Others considered his poetry an ideal marriage of fine taste and culture with rugged simplicity. They admired the fragrance of his writing which obviously sprang from a strong mind in the closest touch with nature. The detachment and essentiality of his poetry was remarked upon; *The Athenaeum* compared Williams and Cowper. Most enlightened readers saw at a glance that, like Jefferies, Williams had instilled into his nature work the real stuff of the country-side and parallel with this had delivered an originally conceived human testimony. Williams was no longer patronisingly dubbed "The Hammer-man Poet" or "The Harmonious Blacksmith". He was no longer praised, as W. H. Davies was in his early days, because being a poor working man he had been able to create such beauty. The wonder and astonishment had passed. He was now judged purely on the quality of his work. Fitzmaurice and Bailey sent him congratulatory letters, as did Lord Crewe, who had been sent a copy of the book by Fitzmaurice.

The sales of *Nature and other poems* were so good during the first few weeks that Erskine Macdonald announced an increase in the price of the remaining copies of the first two books by fifty per cent. The financial position of Williams was so desperate at the end of 1912 that he told Henry Byett that all his life savings had gone on the publication of his three books. He was seriously thinking of emigrating to Canada. He was bitterly disappointed at the small sales among his fellow work-men, though he was willing to make purchase easier by offering to accept contributions of threepence per week. It is very difficult at the present time to procure even a secondhand copy of any of these early works. When the Swindon Museum in later years was thinking of having an Alfred Williams' Corner where some of his books and MSS. could be shown, it was no easy task that the authorities set themselves to obtain original copies of these volumes.

But in the midst of all his troubles, Williams still had the comfort of his inner circle. Friends like Fitzmaurice, Bavin, Byett, Jones and Reuben George must have often lightened his load of worry. And there were always Dowsing and Denwood to turn to as fellow poets. To this company had been added another friend, Llewellyn Robins, introduced to him by Reuben, who was to become the dearest of them all, and to the end of his life, cut short by the cruellest tragedy, the staunchest of any of Williams' supporters. "Lou" Robins—he never went by any other name—had been completely blind since 1900; he kept a small general shop in Swindon where Williams might often be found chatting with him and his wife after leaving the factory.

Bavin, who was always ready with advice for Williams, had written an excellent review of the book in the local press. Williams was especially pleased that his friend had shown such insight into "The Testament", and in November wrote, "I heartily thank you for your kind and sympathetic treatment.   You know me well enough to know that I am no seeker after floppy praise, or worship of the vulgar. I do not care twopence what the crowd thinks of me, or my work either.   But the careful regard of the earnest few I certainly covet, knowing full well that they will make allowances for my errors and esteem my work for what it is worth." Reuben George remained faithful, too, in these early days and sold copies of *Nature and other poems* whenever he saw his chance.   That month Williams was thanking him for two guineas; Reuben had "persuaded" some of his insurance clients and fellow members of the W.E.A. to buy the book.

But in the midst of financial and health worries, Williams found time to read a paper, dealing with Greek poetry, to the Swindon Literary and Debating Society, which created some interest and afforded Swindonians a further example of the brilliance of his scholarship. He was often, however, disconsolate and disillusioned and was beginning to wonder whether all his efforts were really worth while.   He was irritated by some of the less favourable notices of the book.   He considered that the reviewer in one local paper had used the "language of a chemist" when dealing with "The Testament".   To Dowsing he said with some bitterness that one of the few rewards they had both got had been the friendships they had been able to make as a result of their writings.   "I suppose we have received little beside.   For my part, I have not sought money rewards, so I have not been disappointed." This latter remark was not strictly true for he had always felt that he at least should never have been out of pocket because of his publications.

He depended so much upon intelligent encouragement, and followed the development of his friends with very real delight and practical interest.   When, for instance, he could not hear J. B. Jones deliver a lecture in Swindon on Hardy, he was disappointed, as he admired both the work of his friend and the subject of the lecture.

We can thus view Alfred Williams in perspective at the age of 35, still patiently climbing, still struggling bravely to see the light and to keep his head above water, and his mind and spirit fresh and eager. He had already made his mark and had his triumphs.   He was hailed outside Wiltshire as a genuine poet with unusual power of insight. Many had paid tribute to his quest for knowledge and his victory over circumstances.   The world lay before him.   He had but to continue, to blossom further, to develop.   Only Mary Williams and those intimate friends knew what the fight was costing him.   For it certainly was a fight.   Only they realised, perhaps dimly, the gradual cumulative effect on his bodily and spiritual health.   Only they could realise what stature the man had and how colossal and noble was his personal character.   They knew that his courage, tenacity, and idealism was something transcending even his writings—astonishing though these were

CHAPTER EIGHT

A WILTSHIRE VILLAGE AND COR CORDIUM

"A WILTSHIRE VILLAGE" was published on Trafalgar Day, 1912. Williams considered that Duckworth's terms of a fifteen per cent royalty on all sales were excellent. It was like the realisation of a dream; he had not previously been used to such generous treatment. "I am having a hundred copies of the prose" he wrote to Bavin, "as we cannot rely much on Swindon booksellers. I should be very glad to supply anyone. Wyman's will not put it on their bookstalls at the station. Humbug!" The published price was five shillings.

Though he could ill afford it, Williams sent presentation copies, as was his custom, to some of the members of his family; there were also gifts to Fitzmaurice, Bailey, Reuben, and Mrs. Agar. To Ellen he said: "I hope you will like it. It is very unconventional. As I told you before, I do not expect to please all. I have aimed at the truth. There is no fiction at all about it, that I am aware of. Write and tell me all you think. . . ." He fully expected that his outspoken views on education, rustic life, and factory conditions would be adversely criticised and challenged in some quarters. "There is bound to be a little divergence of view with regard to certain lines I have taken up, and some of the opinions I have expressed," he said to Bavin. "Do you know, I do not think I am very ideal, though I may be enthusiastic? Yet, after all, the rustic life *is* the ideal life. I have tried to emphasize the fact that the greatest *serfdom* exists in the towns and about the factories, and not in the villages. You will see, at the same time, that when I sum up at the close, I have a few pointed things to say to the farmers and landlords; I do not give them an ounce of indulgence. I have tried to draw the line between the two representations, and to strike out the false for the true. Whatever I have written I have seen, though, what I have described is chiefly the immediate past. Yet the happy life is lived here now, exactly under my nose I might say."

Here spoke the true rustic. *A Wiltshire Village* is indeed a straightforward and ungarnished account of the daily life of South Marston. The vignettes Williams drew with such artistry were acclaimed with delight beyond the bounds of South Marston, but in the village itself there was little praise or surprise. When Henry Byett remarked to Williams that his comments would in all probability annoy some of the local people, Williams quickly retorted, "Not a bit, the boot is on the other foot, there are those who complain because they have been overlooked and consider they have equal right with those noticed, to have been included." There was, however, definite opposition, though many of the farmers who were trounced by Williams publicly stated that his judgments were sound and his information accurate. But it was the Vicar of Marston, the Rev. Angus Macdonald, who created the greatest stir. He had bought two copies of the book, and had placed one of them in the village Reading Room. After having pronounced on all sides that *A Wiltshire Village* was "too disgusting to read" and forbidden his parishioners to buy it or read it, Macdonald burned not only his own copy of the book, but also the one deposited in the village reading room. The latter was destroyed at 11 p.m. one autumn night. All this was done without any reference to Alfred Williams, though the Vicar had daily opportunities of meeting and speaking to him personally. Then, as if even after all this he could not conquer his ire, he attacked Williams on successive Sundays from the pulpit, without, of course, actually mentioning him by name. Williams was naturally taken aback and very hurt—this was the second time the same clergyman had made things difficult for him—but he showed a generous spirit and ignored the affair. He knew in any case that in the long run it would be Macdonald's reputation that would suffer and not his. Had the press been given particulars of the incidents, there is no doubt that the sales of *A Wiltshire Village* would have soared and Williams himself received excellent publicity.

The dedication of the book was a difficult matter for him to decide. "I thought of doing it to mother for some time," he wrote to his sister Ada "but Mr. Garnett gave me such help I was forced to acknowledge it somehow. I may be able to dedicate something to her yet. Never mind what the Marston folks say of the book . . . I am told that the work may rank as a classic in time to come." Consequently, the book was inscribed to Edward Garnett.

A closely packed and brilliantly laid out preface stated the broad aims of *A Wiltshire Village*. "I have endeavoured . . . to sketch out an old-fashioned, agricultural village . . ." Alfred Williams stressed the fact that high wages were not the be-all and end-all of existence; he could certainly speak with some authority on this matter. On several occasions opportunities occurred when he could have earned more money in the factory, but he felt that by doing so he would be bound to sacrifice something that was essential to his spiritual welfare. He believed that the aims of all working people should be directed to "more leisure, more rest, more time for study and thought, more time to 'live', a greater freedom, good health, a clear conception of themselves and things, and a truer sense of the real independence with it."

He made a short reference to a recent remark by Mr. Lloyd George who had asserted that he would prefer the "monotony" of village life for six months. Now Williams thought that this was a deplorable personal expression. "As for monotony" the preface continued, "let anyone come and toil in the dreary forge for a generation, and drag himself home night after night, and year after year, sick and weary, with aching limbs and heart, and not a gleam of hope in the future, simply a world without end of dull monotonous drudgery; that is far more painful than a quiet day on the farm and a long night's rest at the end of it. I have lived it, and wrought it, and felt it, and know what I say to be true."

Nevertheless, Alfred Williams' opinions are somewhat singular and contradictory, for, after his factory experiences one might have expected him to have had definite leanings towards Socialism. But he had always strongly criticised the type of leader the Socialists seemed to produce in the workshops; in *A Wiltshire Village* he argues like a true Tory—"a bigoted Tory" said the *Nation*.

The whole point of the book, as in *Natural Thoughts and Surmises*, revolves around his oft stated contention that the countryside is superior to the town. This claim, which was ever in his thoughts, is made over and over again in *A Wiltshire Village*. The non-political reader, however, is first attracted by the delicate nature writing contained in chapter after chapter. What could be more soothing and musical, for instance, than his description of the hatches on the River Cole, that gay stream which continually ran through the whole of his being? "There is a hole in the bed of the stream behind the hatch, six feet deep or more. The water, after passing through the gates, glides down to this over a floor of iron, and falls below with a melodious sound, quite untranslatable into the human language. There is no word, poetical or otherwise, capable of expressing the rich gurgling noise of water flowing over an uneven bed, and dividing against the smooth, mossy stones; it is neither a prattling nor a murmuring, a sound not of laughter nor of tears, but midway between the two, wonderfully rich, and thrilling, and suggestive; it is the language of eternity."

Then there is that lively picture of the coverts by the river, which reads, "A little way off in the meadows in either direction are two large coverts of open fir. These swarm with all kinds of wild birds, especially thrushes and blackbirds, magpies and wood pigeons. The busy squirrel leaps nimbly from tree to tree, the large gold brown hares spring through the tall grasses and the cock pheasant crows shrilly through the shadows. The tender 'coo coo' of the pigeons adds an air of exquisite peaceableness to the scene."

Williams deals in some detail with most of the scenery of South Marston and its immediate neighbourhood, and in so doing tells us much about himself and his boyhood. There are quaint country stories and customs, while a host of novel and colourful rustic characters who had made South Marston their home, suddenly spring to life and confront us with their histories. As he said in his preface, " . . . the characters that figure in these pages are not imaginary ones, but are, or were, real persons." We follow with quickening interest the lives of Betsy Horton, and Patsy the Watercress Man; we meet Jackie Bridges and Uncle Dicky, pass the time of day with Barley Nuggin or Launcelot Whitfield, or crack a whip with Jimmy the Carter. Mark Titcombe, Nellie Kempster, Dudley Sansum, and Granny Bowles—country folk with the beautiful Wiltshire names—are not puppets, or imaginary creatures, but people who were born, and who lived, worked, slept, and died in South Marston, and then were buried in its churchyard.

In his first prose work, Williams had revealed a new power. He was a genius at describing ordinary people. His characters are as frankly drawn as any in Shakespeare or Dickens. The disciplines of his language are as economical and telling as the Netsukes of Hottara Sonja. The cameo of Patsy the Watercress Man is an exquisite piece of relief. "Patsy was a familiar figure about the village, and in the town, too. He had been the local watercress man for many years, and had grown old in the occupation; he was well over seventy when he was forced to retire from it. Patsy was short and slight in stature, bent and stooping; his clothes were ragged and rough, his coat sleeves long, and his trousers short; his boots were very old and full of holes; his feet were naked within them; his hair was long and grey; his weather-beaten old face was clean-shaven and sharpish looking. He wore an old cloth cap and carried a large, flat-shaped open basket at his back, slung with cord over the shoulders." The imagery of this is as concrete as any picture by Hogarth or Pieter Breughel.

And what of this irresistible, elf-like creature, child of neither earth nor heaven? "Betsy Horton was very tiny and insignificant in stature; she was not more than four feet high. Her face was very wrinkled and sunburnt, like leather almost, for all her life had been spent in the open fields, and chiefly upon the cornland, summer and winter, too. At one time she picked couch, or pulled docks and thistles, hoed the young roots, made hay, tied the corn after the reapers, fed the threshing machine, cleaned and pitted the swedes in autumn and helped the shepherd all the winter. Her nose was straight; she had large brown eyes, strong features. Her general expression was most quaint; she was an old-fashioned little body. Her grey hair was parted in the middle and tied up in a little wisp behind, or contained in a net. She wore a blue print sunbonnet and a coarse brown apron to work, with thick boots."

Throughout the book there are a myriad signs of Williams' joy in all living things, with an overwhelming passion for pools, streams, rivers, and waterfalls. He states his forthright opinions about many topics. He writes with first-hand knowledge about village life, workhouse conditions, folk-lore, depopulation. Chapter Seven, which is concerned with Education, is a very valuable contribution.

It is interesting to compare Williams with Jefferies, in general terms. Both writers were well informed about nature, though Jefferies had wandered farther afield and approached the study of her more scientifically. But Williams knew nature not only as an inspiration but used her as a backcloth against which he could place the living characters of actual drama. This is easily understandable. Jefferies was fortunately able to live closer to the heart of nature and farther from the noise and rush of busy streets for many years. For the greater part of *his* life, Williams rubbed shoulders with all sorts of men and women and only escaped to nature when they disappointed him.

A Wiltshire Village, if anything, is a little long and packed with too much detail, but the purity and sincerity of the style are maintained throughout its pages. Williams certainly succeeded in making the countryside articulate and realistic. *The Times,* at the conclusion of its notice, said: "It is because Mr. Williams . . . knows and loves the woods and waters, the plants and the beasts, that he makes a countryside live for us again as it still is here and there, as it will not be anywhere for long." Indeed, even at the time when Williams was writing, many of the old-fashioned people and country things had already passed into history.

The year 1912 was truly a wonder year for Williams. Two books were published, two were in manuscript, another was planned, and the daily grind at hammer and textbook continued. He was overloaded with work, but was as unselfish and keenly interested as ever in the well being and activities of his friends. When Dowsing published a book of poems at the end of the year he was full of generous praise for his successful treatment of the sonnet. Poor Dowsing received few really congratulatory notices on the quality of his work; early in 1913 Williams was cheering him with the words: ". . . . they do not give much encouragement to the *likes of us* who are not in the ring. I was glad they did recognise your impeccable 'verse' though. I still maintain that certain sonnets in this book are pretty well unsurpassed by the best of our moderns. You have no need to fear for your future credit."

As it deserved, *A Wiltshire Village* sold well; 700 copies had been disposed of by the first week in February, 1913. Williams himself—with the ever-ready assistance of Reuben—got rid of 80 of his 100 in a little over a fortnight after receiving his batch from Duckworth. Then on 20th January he informed Fitzmaurice that he was writing another prose book and that during the late summer of 1912 he had been visiting many villages in the neighbourhood at the weekends in order to collect

suitable material for it. "I am now on another book of countryside
life. I am 'doing' the life of a dozen villages from Wroughton to the
Blowing Stone all along the downside, writing in dialect, folklore and
all sorts of quaint stuff, but especially attempting to depict the life and
characteristics of the agricultural classes in that region. It will not be
stylish literature but I hope to preserve a lot of interesting matter, and
to prove there are some good folk still about these parts." To his
sister Ada he wrote that he was rapidly preparing ". . . . for a book
round Highworth, Lechlade, Fairford, Kempsford, and the Upper Thames
villages generally. . . . I have spent a good deal of time there already."

But in spite of his occupation with prose, and gladdened by the
knowledge that *A Wiltshire Village* had already earned him some £28
in royalties, Williams could not resist the call of his first love. A fourth
book of poems was with Erskine Macdonald by the middle of 1913.
This was to be called *Cor Cordium* and the same terms of publication
on a co-operative basis were decided upon. He told Ada something
about this book, how many of the pieces were autobiographical, and
how many were confessional. "Half the work shows my evolution
from a *doubting* to a *trusting* state in religious belief, and the other half
are love poems . . ."

Cor Cordium was published on 25th October, 1913. Gift copies
went to the usual patrons and friends. That to Dowsing had the
enclosure ". . . . hoping that you will find it in your heart to accept the
book, with its many shortcomings, and do not be too severe with the
poor author, who, at best, will get but little for his pains and trouble,
except, perhaps, a few strokes from the critics' pen, and a gibe or two
from his shop mates . . ."

And to John Bailey, to whom *Cor Cordium* was dedicated, Williams
said, "I would the contents were worthier, though it is useless to offer
any apologies for poor stuff, and I shall not expect or require any
mercy to be shown me in respect of my position as a workman, and the
difficulties with which I have laboured." He feared that some critics
would be disappointed ". . . . at not finding some terrible, battering,
blasphemous stuff such as seems to delight a good many at the present
time." He told Fitzmaurice that the new poems were quiet and quite
unlike those being penned by some modern poets, much of whose work
was often "vulgar, violent slang".

Williams' health was better that year and the improvement allowed
him to continue his research on the new prose book. Nevertheless,
he told J. B. Jones in the October that the worry of his books was
great and he had to redouble his efforts to keep active. He was especially grateful to Reuben for his assistance with sales but was sorry
to have to depend on old friends time after time. "I despair of getting
any local support except among those who know me personally."

Cor Cordium has affinity with *Songs in Wiltshire,* for it displays much of the Renascence spirit and colour of his first book. Apart from the longer poems it is a collection of love lyrics, with a free translation, "Ariadne to Theseus" from Ovid, thirty-six poems in all. Two of the poems, "Leave me not ever" and "A Kiss", had already appeared in *Songs in Wiltshire,* but since they were love poems Williams seemed to think it more fitting to place them in the more correct context of *Cor Cordium.*

This fourth book of verse marks the end of a chapter in Williams' well-defined literary development. It is his last really worth-while poetic contribution and lies at the top of that crescendo which had begun four years earlier with *Songs in Wiltshire.* During this short period, both his technique and attitude to ultimate realities had matured and undergone changes; though there were still two more books of verse to come and poetry to be written in Ireland and India, *Cor Cordium* must be considered to be the peak of his achievement. After 1913 there is little else which reaches the same intensity or power.

If the bulk of his output is reviewed at this stage and his poetry examined in cold perspective, one immediately realises that Williams was primarily a natural philosopher expressing himself through the medium of poetry. He had thought out the problems of life for himself as he knew them to exist in town and country, and strengthened by his knowledge and reading of the past, had formulated an individual and sustaining creed. These ideas he expounded in poetry. Apart from a handful of tender love and nature lyrics, his best work which embodies this natural philosophy, arrived at after years of mental and spiritual conflict, is to be found in six poems. These are "Natural Thoughts and Surmises", "Under the Hawthorn", "The Hills", and "The Testament" of the three earlier books, with "Retrospection" and "Historia Cordis" of *Cor Cordium.* Williams' niche in literature, at least as far as his poetry is concerned, is secure and significant but it is a small one. There were occasions when he reached the sublime heights of the major poets, but much of his writing was uneven. To some extent he was a mystic, though not of the *genre* of Blake or Christopher Smart, but there are certainly traces of Henry Vaughan and other of the metaphysicians in the longer poems. Crabbe and Whitman were the spiritual godfathers of his technique. The six poems mentioned were all interlinked and represent a body of work which will always uplift because of the ardour of their conception, the sincerity of their expression, and the realism of their message. The spirit of Wiltshire, was, of course, in every poem Williams wrote.

Cor Cordium strikes a very personal and spontaneous note; it has a wealth of inspired nature writing. The selection of the poems is again careful and the planning and arrangement of the poems rather different from earlier books.

"Retrospection" and "Historia Cordis" are the two longest and most dramatic poems in the book. Each, divided into two parts, has the same introspection which characterises "The Testament" and "Natural Thoughts and Surmises".

"Historia Cordis" is a full-blooded manifestation of Williams' inner self. A vast revelation of altruistic philosophy, it is indeed the story of his heart and holds nothing back. He begins by sighing for the days that are gone, for in those days there was

> "a deathless love
> For all that is noble, and good, and true."

As a simple country lad, he yearned for freedom;

> "And a fever came into my youthful blood."

He longed to fathom the ocean of time; daringly and gloriously he soared

> "to the topmost pillars of Heaven."

As a young man, new out of adolescence, all stark and groping in the fastnesses of his Wiltshire village, lost in the inexplicable mysteries of a fire so strangely chained within him, he struggled like a chrysalis to burst imprisoning bonds. He first sought for the meaning of truth in Nature. Unfulfilled and unsatisfied, he turned to books:

> "To the hoary pride of the schools,
> To the Roman seer, and the Grecian sage."

So the fight went on, for victory was not yet won. True Elizabethan that he was, and sure in the knowledge that all life must pass, he asked of himself

> "Then what am I more than a mist or a shade,
> Or a breath of air, or a drop of dew,
> Constant, and changing, and fickle, and true,
> And light as a promise or vow ill-made?"

Still the years rolled by into manhood and the wheels of his fate hastened on. Everything he had faith in passed, like formless shadows, with time ever restless and ever mocking at the evil and the just—

> "Gone! as an idle vision or dream,
> Or a little cry in the stillness of night,
> Or a breath of wind, or a glimmer of light,
> Or the ripple that stirs on the face of the stream.
>
> Gone! as the vapour that lifts o'er the sea,
> Gone! as a rolling cloud o'er the plain,
> Gone! as the tempest, or thunder, or rain,
> Or the quail's shrill pipe, or note of the bee."

And so to the second part of the poem which prays

> ". . . that our restless spirits might be
> . . . consoled and soothed by a sure-born power."

There came a consuming desire for "the breath of philosophy" and "a safe repose from our fears". He looked for a sign. He sought the end of man's journey, though he knew that if he had the answer to his questionings it would profit him but little. He is therefore resigned to the unknown future and is thankful that joy and beauty remained for him to sing their delights in the present. There is no need for worry. Striving "for impossible things" has vanished; instead, he turns full faced and with courage to "the region of Man". Now is the time. Neither past nor future are worth fretting over.

And so there finally emerged a solid conviction, for, by the time he had reached middle age, he knew deep in his soul that the only balm and lasting comfort lay in the heart of Nature herself. He had returned to his first quest. This is the voice of Wordsworth and of Cowper and of Shelley. Williams joins company with Gray, Collins, and Burns. Like them, he found reality and truth in the springing world about him. His religion, which was very much theirs, is summed up in these words—

> "But my heart will turn again to the wood,
>   And my ebbing thoughts will tire of their theme,
>   And my mind will back to the wandering stream,
> And my fingers will dally with berry and bud;
>
> And I long to walk unseen with the herds,
>   And feel the gentle wave of the breeze,
>   As it bends the tender tops of the trees,
> Or watch the wheeling flights of the birds;
>
> Or stretch my weary limbs in the shade,
>   And turn my careless eyes to the east,
>   Till the daylight dims and drops in the west,
> And a silence falls on thicket and glade,
>
> That is only broke with the night-bird's cry,
>   Or the ploughboy whistling his homeward tune,
>   Or the hounds that bound and bay to the moon
> Shaping her tireless course in the sky.
>
> For there is the greatest bliss to be found,
>   And there are the joys which never can tire,
>   And the end of all my earthly desire,
> For a mingled sweet is in every sound."

"Retrospection" was much admired by John Bailey who told Williams that he was the only one to write the couplet well in that style since Crabbe. The poem was conceived at a time when Williams was feeling particularly despondent. He was far from happy in his contacts with some of the workmen and foremen in the factory, while at South Marston he found that a section of the villagers, who had known him all his life, if not directly hostile, belittled his endeavours. His friends in Swindon and elsewhere who acknowledged the courage and integrity of his character—and also bought his books—helped to sustain him when his spirit was at its lowest. And he could always turn for refreshment to the countryside; wandering in the meadows around the village, he entered into comradeship with the downlands. There was always Mary, too, to whom he could cleave, and in whom he could find repose when the blackest depression was upon him.

Just after the publication of *Songs in Wiltshire* he was in some doubt as to what course he should follow regarding the future of his own education. He sought new fields of learning and study, and turned for advice to a high official in the works, one who had been responsible for many advances in the provision of educational opportunities in Swindon. Williams thought he would be the very man to guide his footsteps. He called on the official in Swindon, but the advice Alfred Williams was given came as an unbelievable shock and nearly shattered him. Completely out of harmony with the delicate and scholarly mind he had been asked to counsel, the man held out little hope of Williams' ultimate success in the world of letters and scholarship and said that a man in his lowly position was doomed to failure. He told Williams to concentrate his future energies on his daily work at the forge and to leave the writing of prose and poetry to others. Williams was broken-hearted at these crushing suggestions. In agony of mind and spirit he stumbled back to Marston to pour out the whole bitter experience to Mary Williams. She, gentle and understanding, gave him what comfort she could, but he had been so discouraged that for a long time he felt he could never lift his head again or write another word. But on the day following the disastrous meeting he wrote "The Greek Peasant's Prayer for Rain" and later "On the Downs" both of which poems appeared in *Songs in Wiltshire* and bear evidences of the bruising he had received. Williams never forgot the unhappy incident.

Alfred Williams then began to write "Retrospection" and steadily worked at the poem until its completion in 1913. Written in rhyming couplets with skilful variation, it is almost entirely autobiographical. The poet begins by saying that he had lately been reading many books of a diverse nature; some of these had been written by minor authors. He then tells of his meeting with a "lettered wight" and of the advice given by him:—

> "Too many private singers of thy kind—
> Blind unavailing leaders of the blind—
> Assail the public ear, and cry for fame,
> Dim with the brightness of poetic flame."

He is told that there is no place in literature for the minor poet whose "homely verse no critic would endure". This damning lack of encouragement and palpable ignorance of the function of the poet greatly wounded Williams' pride so that "Awhile the Muse's temple I forsook". Turning instinctively for solace to nature, the poet soon discovered that there was a place in the scheme of things for linnets, doves, and skylarks as well as for nightingales.

> "What . . . one master of the lute,
> And needs be every other minstrel mute ?"

For days he roamed the woods in the depths of despair where even natural beauties seemed to hold no delight for him.

The poem continues with an enquiry into the purposes of nature and the reason for man's sojourn on the earth. Williams knows that since he is mortal, all his fears and loves are mortal, too, but he likewise feels that

> "Bound with an earthly clod, we cannot rise,
> And casting off the clod, the spirit flies."

Man is only born to fulfil the follies of his ancestors; only in his heart's desires is he immortal.

So, shot through with the ache of his material experiences, the poet calls upon earth and heaven to witness that his fault must be in his pedigree.

> "I had no influence upon my birth."

But hope shines through, with the conviction that nothing is in vain. Williams praises all learning, for instance, and the study of the classics in particular and relates how, after the comradeship of books, there followed delight in nature.

> "Filled with the majesty of page and line,
> And soaring from the human to divine,
> Abundant Nature was his next resort—
> The living paradise, and Beauty's court,
> The healer of the heart, the doom of grief,
> Strong with the medicine of flower and leaf."

Nature to him became a necessity—a "general physician". And so, having traversed the twin roads of learning and nature, he is able to acclaim

> "Henceforward now, no longer 'Whence I came ?'
> But 'Whither going?' Not 'I was', but 'Am'."

His retrospection reaches its climax on a high religious note.   Since all inspiration comes from the Maker, He alone is sufficient to lift man up in triumph from the black pit of despair.   The doubts and questionings vanish once the poet is sure that he possesses within him great potentialities and much of positive and permanent value.   There is an all-seeing God always about and around him, who beautifies his heart and mind, he has the joy of his books and friends and the bounty and diversity of nature.   Though he may find only a low place on the roll of the great ones, yet he had a definite place and his contribution to mankind is necessary.

"Retrospection" is thus a complete answer to the thoughtless blundering counsellors of this world.   But it is more than this.   It burns with the assurance of victory, and of idealism, and of triumph over sheer materialism.   Courage of the highest order is the text of this poem and though much of its matter could have been condensed, without any loss of power, it has the seal of sincerity.   That he knew his Maker's purpose for him was Alfred Williams' life discovery.   He had lighted on his lodestar.

"The poet's ready heart resolved to song,
And shouted with the seasons as they swept along."

The other poems in *Cor Cordium* are the love songs which Williams had written over a number of years.   They were not addressed to any person in particular, though many of them were certainly inspired by Mary Williams.   Alfred Williams had had no love affairs, but was in point of fact shy of women's company, being by temperament a solitary. These poems must therefore—unless we attribute some deep psychological significance to them—be of rather an artificial nature and are of the type which were fashionable in the fifteenth and sixteenth centuries. They are all charming, elegant and well turned, but they lack passion and freedom.   At times their imagery and the use of nature symbols remind one of Tennyson, but their emphasis is upon form rather than content.   The verse patterns, often French in origin, are varied and interesting in themselves.

"If Love prove not unkind" is the best in this group.   Its quiet pastoral character and clever conceits are in juxtaposition to the realism of "Retrospection".

The first two verses of "All things delight in sleep" are so lovely that they are worth quoting:

" All things delight in sleep,
    Morning to eve inclines
Slowly the purple-woven shadows creep,
    And heaven moves onwards with its myriad signs
Above the watery deep.

> At noon among the hills,
> The shepherd makes complaint,
> At even, to the murmur of soft bells,
> Leads his flocks downward to the valleys faint
> With blowing daffodils."

The love poems and shorter lyrics generally, afford several examples of Williams' ability at writing a memorable single line. One hazards the suggestion that one line was often pure inspiration, that he would note this down while he was about his daily work, and then construct a poem around it. This is a genuine method of craftsmanship. Such lines as "Drinking the dazzled dew" and "Long as this winding river bends through the bearded plain", which, with others leap to the eye from the pages of *Cor Cordium*, are gems of first brilliance. On the other hand, the constant use of such clichés as "sweet sprite", "love locked out", "love and his arrows", etc., tend to spoil the final effect of several of the poems. It is strange to observe that the man who could write such telling and powerful prose and find such dignity of line in his longer poems, should find it necessary to rely upon such artificiality of sentiment when writing a love poem.

Cor Cordium sold well and was greatly admired as a work of art. "Retrospection" and "Historia Cordis", as the natural developments of "The Testament" and "The Hills", attracted most attention. By the close of 1913 Alfred Williams had established himself as a poet whose voice could not be ignored. What the critics did not know then was that he had delivered his message and that he had little more to say of consequence in poetry. He was now to travel along other paths and to make other discoveries.

CHAPTER NINE

CROSS ROADS

THE second prose work was finished by the end of April, and accepted by Duckworth in July for inclusion in the autumn catalogue. Williams had worked at it, on and off, for about eight months, the greater part of this time being devoted to obtaining and classifying its matter. The actual writing took barely three months. He thought it to be of greater interest than *A Wiltshire Village* in that it provided a readable record of a fascinating and wider piece of country. "I have an idea of continuing this plan a little further, and attempting a work around and behind Highworth, depicting life in the Upper Thames valley, in the villages and small towns there; the conditions are different from those of the Downside, and the population different from those who dwell on our uplands, so that it might be interesting to be able to make the comparison; though I have not attempted to introduce too much of the economic, but to have pages that may be pleasantly read by any." This to Fitzmaurice in July, 1913.

Williams was nothing if not logical; *Villages of the White Horse*, as the new book was named, was the obvious extension of *A Wiltshire Village*. Yet, though the two books naturally have a great deal in common, in that they contain the same type of matter, they have some striking differences. As far as *A Wiltshire Village* was concerned, Williams had only to range over a small area which he knew intimately, and which lay at his doorstep. When, however, he conceived the idea of *Villages of the White Horse* in 1912, he knew that it would be necessary for him to travel over and systematically explore the country he intended to describe, since much of it was new to him. Again, *A Wiltshire Village* had South Marston and its immediate neighbourhood as a focal point and set out to compare its charms with the drabnesses of town life in general and Swindon in particular. Now there is not the same insistence on such comparison in *Villages of the White Horse* and there are only one or two passing references to Swindon and its railway factory. It is more than probable that this was a deliberate piece of strategy, since Williams had in hand and ready for publication, *Life in a Railway Factory*. He did not want to run the risk of repeating himself and so weakening the effect of what he intended to tell the world in his factory book.

He was very anxious that *Villages of the White Horse* should contain the minimum of controversy, though it was not his intention to hide anything from the public concerning the daily lives of poor village folk. He hoped that the time would come when he would be free to advance his own opinions and make unfettered comments concerning the changes which had taken place and were taking place in the villages. He anticipated that he would again receive criticism when *Villages of the White Horse* was published, but in some ways he preferred this to fulsome praise and, as he told a friend in the November, "a few blows will do me more good".

Villages of the White Horse was inscribed to Mrs. Story Maskelyne, of Bassett Down, Wroughton. Since 1906 she had been an admirer of Williams and a practical supporter of his endeavours. She had always bought copies of his books as they appeared; he had been her guest on several occasions when they had discussed his aims and ideals. She was fervent for the Wiltshire countryside and it may have been the knowledge of this, which determined Williams to dedicate the book to her. As in *A Wiltshire Village*, there is a preface which begins: "In a previous work I endeavoured to sketch out a single village;

Here I have attempted to present a whole locality, as I see it, and as
I have known it." This locality, twenty miles in extent, and within
reasonable cycling distance of Marston, had within its perimeter some
of the most ancient villages in England, all with traditions and customs
stretching back to the prehistoric peoples. And in each of the villages
Williams discovered the same kind of lively and attractive folk as
figured in the pages of *A Wiltshire Village*, exactly "as I found them,
rough and plain, frank and hearty, honest and homely." Williams
concludes the introduction by referring to the ecomonic conditions of
the countryside, and calls upon the reader to judge for himself as to the
truth of his statements. As ever it was his earnest desire to enlist
sympathy on behalf of village folk because of their "patience, courage,
simplicity and modesty."

Twenty villages receive comprehensive treatment and there are
references to as many more. Their names are enchanting in themselves,
so that even before we delve deeply into the book, we are fascinated
by the mere mention of them. These villages remain as memorials
to, and witnesses of, Williams' industry on their behalf; they were of
his spirit and he of theirs. This White Horse area is typically and
undeniably English. It breathes so much poetry that the future
traveller through it must share the joy of Williams in lighting upon
such loveliness. The villages and hamlets to which he introduces us
are Bassett Down, Wroughton, Hodson, Chiseldon, Badbury, Med-
bourne, Liddington, Wanborough, Aldbourne, Baydon, Hinton Parva,
Bourton, Bishopstone, Idstone, Ashbury, Kingston Winslow, Knighton,
Woolstone, Uffington, and Kingston Lisle.

He tells us many things about their dialect, customs, history, and
people. The latter pass before us in all the quaintness of their medieval
pageantry, a goodly company of sturdy folk. We follow, with Williams,
the calendar of the year, with its flowers, birds, animals and trees, all
taking their place in the pattern of the downland landscape, the whole
making a composition as serene as a painting by Constable or Corot.
Cottages, mansions, churches, mills, inns, tracks and ruins are all here
for the imagination to feed upon. We learn of old village industries.
We are taken into the homes of the carters, shepherds, blacksmiths,
farmers, thatchers, and breeches makers, who live at peace under the
blue sky of the Downs. As a travel book alone, *Villages of the White
Horse* is a work of art.

What of these inhabitants of the White Horse villages? So well
defined are their characters that it is as if we were meeting them in
the flesh and greeting old and familiar friends. There are people as
diverse as William Breakspear, Granny and Farmer Ferris, Dickie
Austin the old church clerk, Benny Haylock the gamekeeper (who had
tutored Richard Jefferies), Uriah Partridge and Sawyer John. And

odd little Betsy Horton bobs up once again to quiz us from under the
shade of her blue print sunbonnet.

Would you like to see the milking and the milling? Or go down
into the valley to see the water threshing? Let Williams take you.
In these villages, too, you may find soap making, brewing, boot
making, weaving, hurdle making, watercress growing and flint digging,
or at least evidences of their having gone on in the past. Woodman,
cowman, ballad singer, schoolmaster, poacher, and constable, ply
their trades and go their ways through the tapestry of these pages.
We behold forgotten battles and election riots, handle strange cottage
ornaments, eat Wiltshire bacon under Wiltshire thatch, wander by
church and mill, and feel our blood run a little cold at the eerie stories
of witches and goblins. We are initiated into the mysteries of Clerk's
Ale and Lot Mead; it is our privilege to join the merry revels of Cow-
fair, Dobbin Sunday, and Hock Tide.

The dignified and unaffected language of *A Wiltshire Village* is also
the chief characteristic of *Villages of the White Horse*. There is a Bunyan-
like quality about this picture of the Downs.

"The huge, whale-backed downs roll away—looking suddenly at
them you seem to catch their motion visibly, like that of a sleek,
round-bellied monster turning in the deep green waters; line after
line and curve after curve run into each other, and are intermingled.
To the east is the impregnable fortress of Liddington; here are the
mysterious-looking woods and hangars that mock and tantalise you
with their deeply-felt silence; there the frowning, rigid earthworks,
overlooking the wide red and gold cornfields stretching to the north-
east."

There is a sketch of an English shire as telling as anything written
in similar accents by Jefferies or Edward Thomas.

"In the distance lie the downs, ranged along with graceful and
exquisite ease, green and golden, or faint blue, rising and falling in
a series of lovely lines, softly blending and intermingling, while below
is a panorama of fertile cornfields, studded with farms and ricks, and
numerous clumps of beeches dotted about, and the long white road
winding through the middle of the hollow towards Liddington Castle,
visible on the sky-line, four or five miles away."

Meet Jonas Goddard. He was an eighty-year old carter living in
a tiny cottage at Badbury Bottom.

"He was short in stature, sturdily built, and a little corpulent. His
features were strong and square, hair grey, short grey beard, pleasant
mouth, and merry sparkling eyes. His trousers, much too small
around the waist, were drawn together and held with a bootlace;
he wore a corduroy jacket, and a waistcoat of the same material, with
big brass buttons, each stamped with the head of an animal; a dog,

a fox, a horse, a bull, a camel, and a dromedary; a small billycock hat was perched upon his head. He was born at Winterbourne Basset and came of the old stock. His grandparents had a family of eighteen, he was one of twelve, and his own family numbered half a score."

Benny Haylock, the old gamekeeper was "a most eccentric person. He would not allow people in the woods under any pretext whatever, but ordered them all unceremoniously away, frightening the timid with his gruff voice and threatening language and behaviour."

What an exhilarating and original idea it was to use the Vale of the White Horse as a stage, and for the villagers to act their living dramas on it to the accompaniment of bubbling waters, singing birds, and the sound of soft country voices! This book has the hush of old woods in it and the mellowness of summer twilight falling on stable and stack. Its pages are fragrant with the perfume of wild flowers recollected in tranquillity; soft-eyed animals steal timidly into its chapters from their secret haunts in field and hedgerow. In short, *Villages of the White Horse* is a masterpiece. It is individual and unique, and Williams must have loved both the assembling and the writing of it. Perhaps the essence of the whole book is found in the opening paragraph of Chapter Thirteen which deals with the villages of Ashbury and Kingston Winslow. Williams views the Downs in all their beauty. "Though all the villages of the downside have many things in common, the same physical characteristics, and general scenery, the same type of cottages and farmhouses, there is still a delightful variation all along the line in their altitude, disposition, and aspect, and in the individual features and detailed beauty of each separate place. The slopes of the downs, if they have general forms, are continually changing and interchanging in localities, assuming new and strange shapes, charming and surprising with their grace and exquisiteness, at one time standing out bold and abrupt as a mountain ledge, at another, sweeping, curving, and winding round in a serpentine, or blending and interfusing, full of sweetness, of a delicate green, or rich brown, golden, purple, or faint blue, or indigo, or robed in pearly mist; for ever reflecting the mood of the heavens, and sympathetic to the heart and feelings of man."

Was it prophetic that *Villages of the White Horse* should have been published in 1913? By the time the Great War had finished it would have been nearly impossible to have written a book of this type. Landmarks and villages remain; people die. Indeed, by 1913 many of the ancients had already gone, customs and manners were changing with the fashion; rural industries had almost vanished. By the end of 1918, though the tiny Cole still made its placid and uninterrupted way through downland valleys, though Wiltshire horses and ploughmen, as grave as ever, strode across the skyline, and the patchwork of shining acres, golden cottages and farmsteads slept in the sunlight, much more had changed. Much more had gone. Bacon Jack had quietly slipped away without a word, and Granny Ferris had smiled and said a last farewell. Abraham Ashton no longer day-dreamed with face cupped in hands over a sea of sheep at Wroughton; young John the Hinton blacksmith had looked for the last time on his hammers, "Dragon", "Useful" and "Slogger". Uriah Partridge's hurdles still withstood the blast over at Ashbury, but Uriah Partridge himself was keeping a last tryst with Ruth Westell, his neighbour, whom Alfred Williams had once compared to Canidia, because she had her gown tucked up.

And the village band at Uffington blew only into ghostly silences. And the dancers had put away their bells and ribbons.

Williams knew in 1913 that the final decay of true rural life was imminent, but with eyes on Liddington for inspiration, he recaptured the spirit and poetry of the old things, and his heart leaped within him when he considered how the Downs themselves would never disappear from man's vision so long as there was a Wiltshire poet to sing about them. Wayland Smith would lurk in his cave for ever, and Acorn Bridge stride the Cole like an unbroken tune long after Williams was dust.

By the time 1913 had ended Alfred Williams had barely seventeen more years to live; and war was in the air. Yet, before he was forty years of age he had shown his worth both as a poet and writer of prose. How many outside his own intimate circle had any idea at this time that he was a poor workman who spent more than a third of his day at the mercy of an oily forge, with ears shocked by the crash of steel hammers, rather than enslaved by the song of downland birds?

The new year began very badly for Williams. He was again to arrive at a crossroads and to make a far-reaching decision. His health, never really satisfactory, now gave him cause for serious concern. On 16th February, 1914, he was writing to a new acquaintance, Guy Rawlence of Wilton: "I have been very poorly this last month and have been in bed all day with something that troubles me much: violent pains below the heart, and I've not been able either to read to write. I have been over-exerting myself, I expect, I shall have to lie up for a week or two."

This was all very troublesome because he had already begun work on a new book about the Upper Thames valley, "and the villages and small towns there". About a half of it had been set out in its first draft by the end of February.

As the pains below the heart did not subside, he was obliged to consult his doctor who diagnosed the trouble as acute dyspepsia and frankly told him that he must resign from the factory. Smoke from the furnaces had, over the years, destroyed his whole digestive system. Further, the doctor said he must immediately give up. There was no time to lose. Williams heard the verdict calmly. If it had been at all possible he would have forsaken heavy manual work years before, for, though in his early days he had welcomed the contrast to literary work, he had eventually grown to hate everything connected with the factory. In March he writes to Henry Byett: "I have been at home for three weeks with acute dyspepsia, but I shall start again next week, I hope. I have not been feeling well since that very cold fortnight, but I kept moving until I was forced to give up. A complete rest was what I needed most of all. . . . Dr. Muir says I must be more careful of myself, or else be content to become a confirmed invalid. I have for many years suffered from indigestion, especially at Swindon."

During his enforced rest he worked in the fields as he hâd done when a boy, but, as he told Alfred Zimmern, he was "surprised to find I was very easily knocked up, though the work was not hard. I cannot endure much physical effort." And while at home he heard that *Villages of the White Horse*, in spite of its very good reviews, had sold slowly and as for *Cor Cordium*, "poetry does not touch the hearts of people and you cannot blink the fact".

A fortnight later, entirely against Muir's orders, Williams was back at the forge but finding the going very heavy. Though he had returned, he knew better than anybody else that he would be bound to accept Muir's advice. The time had inevitably come when his body could no longer bear the double strain of literary and industrial work. For fifteen years at least his life had been one long strain. Those concentrated hours of night study with their consequent lack of sleep had cut their furrows in him. Until he was fourteen years old he had been engaged upon farm work of a most strenuous nature. Then had come the factory period with its years of ceaseless labour, with the journeys into Swindon, early and late, day after day, year in, year out, sun or rain. Williams had not lived one man's life; it was only his certainty of aim and joyous zeal for scholarship and literature which had given him the strength of three. But if he walked out of the railway works for ever he knew he could not exist alone upon his literary earnings. And there was Mary to think of, too. How would they manage? What would he do? Would friends help him? It was not an easy decision for any man to make and especially for one of his calibre.

He felt his position desperately and acutely. To Dowsing he wrote on 2nd April: "I am sorry to feel that neither of us has been able to make anything out of our books. One or two of my poems books sold out but *I* did not get anything. Not likely! . . . Well, never mind! I, like you, have not written much verse lately, and I doubt whether I shall trouble to write much more at all, unless things alter.

People do not really want it; and there is an end to the matter. Newspaper reviews do not sell your books, unless you can be like Masefield, and put out something sensational. At present I am on prose work more. People will look at that, but they won't have poetry !"

Reuben George was so concerned about Williams at this time that, after discussing the matter with him, he wrote on behalf of the Swindon W.E.A. to Alfred Zimmern and Fitzmaurice in order to try to convince them that Williams should receive a Civil List Pension. Zimmern, as ever, was most sympathetic, and discussed the question in the first place with John Bailey. The latter thought that the best and most immediate way in which to help Williams and his wife was to give them a holiday. Accordingly, he sent them a cheque for £20 and made all the arrangements for them to go away together to the seaside for a complete change. So, a fortnight was spent at Ilfracombe, a week at Aberystwyth and a week at Pwllheli. What must have been their feelings, these country lovers, when they realised that they would be spending the whole month of May together, far from the stifling heat of the Swindon factory and the petty gossip of South Marston ! They had not been to the seaside since their honeymoon at Torquay—thirteen years before. But Williams was not entirely idle, for while away he finished the first draft of the Upper Thames book.

Zimmern then approached Gilbert Murray and Fitzmaurice; Lord Crewe also promised to support the project. When the preliminary ground had been covered, overtures were then made to the Prime Minister for the inclusion of Alfred Williams' name in the Civil List. Mr. Asquith was given the fullest particulars of his career, work, and needs.

When Williams heard in the April of what was being proposed for him, he wrote to Fitzmaurice: "I earnestly hope that there will be no confusion arising from Mr. Zimmern's desire to help with the proposal. . . . Personally, I would rather have been kept in ignorance of the matter." He told Fitzmaurice of his recent ill-health and of how he had lost more than a thousand hours from his work during the previous two years. What was more, he had at last definitely decided to leave the factory during the coming autumn and if unsuccessful at making a living in England, to emigrate.

The application to Mr. Asquith was unsuccessful, being rejected on the grounds that Williams was only thirty seven years of age. It was considered that to recommend him for a Pension would be to establish a precedent that would open the door to others not so deserving. But Mr. Asquith was so interested in what he had heard about Williams and so moved by the story of his courage and high ideals that he suggested to Zimmern and his friends that a subscription list should be begun to form the basis of an annual pension for Williams.

He himself was willing to head it with £150. When Williams heard of the subscription list idea he was angry and embarrassed and in his usual independent and forthright manner told Fitzmaurice, very bluntly, that he objected to the whole scheme. But Fitzmaurice begged him not to oppose the idea, since his wife would be involved. Williams carefully considered the matter for a week and then consented for the project to continue, but on the express condition that there should be no begging in order to swell the fund. Since he desired only the barest necessities of life, he did not wish that the money collected should reach any large amount. He thought that an annual pension of £30 or £35 would be ample, and, "I should feel then that I had not been guilty of covetousness." This latter to Zimmern who had been to see Reuben George in Swindon. Williams also told Zimmern how disappointed he was with himself and how he had been hoping, by staying away from the factory, to recuperate solidly. He had been unable to publish his book about the Railway Factory and still had by him his factory poems. And he had not been able to make the final revision of the Upper Thames book.

The seaside holiday ended. The couple came back to Dryden Cottage refreshed and strengthened. Williams reported to Muir and said he would like to return to the factory in order to put his health to the test. Again he was warned as to the consequences of such action; Muir would give him no guarantee as to the future. Williams, however, began work again in the steam hammer shop, but before June was out there was a severe recurrence of the dyspepsia and indications of heart trouble. Muir then warned him that if he did not leave the works at once he would be dead in six months. So there followed another bitter period with Williams trying his hardest to win back his health. While at home he wrote very little but, with Mary as his companion, took long walks about South Marston, climbing Liddington and wandering by the Cole. The summer of 1914 was such a sunny one that by July, Williams felt so much stronger that he decided to make one last effort to continue as a hammerman. If he failed, he would nevermore set foot in the works but would try to make a living by writing, or, alternatively would become a farm labourer again. Muir told him he was mad to think of returning to the factory and said that the state of his heart made farm labouring much too strenuous. Some quiet and gentle gardening was another matter.

Williams worked in Swindon for just six weeks longer and found himself at the end of this period in a state of utter exhaustion. The end had really come this time. On 3rd September, 1914, Alfred Williams laid aside his hammer for ever and left the service of the Great Western Railway, a young man broken in health, and embittered in spirit. The latter mood was not to last, however. He was too much of an idealist for that.

Before he bade farewell to the shop he wrote in chalk on the iron plate over his furnace the single Latin word VICI. As he did so he must have recalled those struggles of his earlier days when he had scrawled the characters above his forge and he must have heard again the mocking jeers of the sneering foreman. But what a gesture! VICI. I have conquered. I have conquered my enemies. My books, my study, my labour are all living witnesses of my triumph.

The future lay uncertain before him. The subscription list had not yet been closed, so he had no idea as to what he might expect in the way of a pension. He had very little money saved, but, as he told Byett, "so long as I can get pure air and a crust of bread that is all I want."

He decided to take Muir's advice and do a little quiet gardening, but very soon he began seriously to consider the possibility of market gardening of an intensive nature and looked about for new land to develop. He had always cultivated the garden at Dryden Cottage, but now he turned to that piece of the Hook which had been promised to him by his mother. He began to dig it over within three weeks of leaving the factory and not satisfied with this, he rented the old garden which lay at the back of what had once been Mark Titcombe's cottage, and began to till this, too.

CHAPTER TEN

LIFE IN A RAILWAY FACTORY

THE Great War came to Williams in 1914 with as great a shock as to most people. He, like the majority, was caught up immediately in the intensity of its atmosphere and sprang to arms in verse. From the beginning, his new poems were full of deep hatred for warfare and for Germany. His very first war poem was a sonnet called "Right Inviolate" and this, published in the *Swindon Advertiser* on 24th August 1914, had for its theme the triumph of freedom and truth over might—

> ". . . right inviolate
> Unshaken sits on her Heaven-guarded throne,
> And Truth peals louder than the battle guns."

Further poems of the same *genre* followed. In September, after the loss of the cruisers *Aboukir*, *Hogue*, and *Cressy*, he wrote "The British Naval Disaster", which was also published in the local press. In

October, his "Battle Song", designed for recruiting purposes, attracted much attention in Swindon and the county. In December, "Albert, King of the Belgians" paid a tribute to the indomitable soldier and ruler who had captured the imagination of the world by reason of his heroic defiance of the enemy. The poem was sung at a moving re-union of Belgian refugees in Swindon that month.

Williams was deeply affected by the mounting losses and suffering occasioned by the war, but he was no pacifist. He was convinced that the only sure way out of what he called "a most cursed and damnable and hellish situation" was for all men to fight the common enemy. He did not think very much however of the standard of his war poems, and, writing to Dowsing that Christmas Eve, he said: "Have you done any poems on the war . . . I have done a few pieces for the local papers —well, not *poems* but verses, you know ? A few pieces might be passable, but still, they are *not up to a lot.*"

Ever hopeful, ever constructive, Williams, in December, embarked upon a fresh and inspiring venture savouring more of the days of peace. With *A Wiltshire Village* and *Villages of the White Horse* safely published and the new Thames book ready for the public, he decided that he would collect the folk songs of the Upper Thames district with a view to making an anthology of them. Before the year was out and while snow still lay on the roads, he began cycling methodically to various nearby villages in search of the old people and their songs.

When he left the Works that autumn he was rather at a loose end for some time in spite of his gardening operations, but he told Dowsing that he was "just scraping a little bit of bread and butter together". Quite apart from the horrors occasioned by the war, Williams' depression and lowness in spirit were on the increase. His future loomed uncertain before him. Yet he was cheered when he heard that in October, Melba had sung Roger Quilter's setting of his "Cuckoo Song" before an enthusiastic audience in London. Then, the *Wilts and Gloster Standard* had accepted his book on the Upper Thames for serialisation. Loveliest of all he had found himself one day, about Christmas time, in Wroughton and had kissed Mary Hunt, aged 95, under the mistletoe ! This after she had sung him an old song. There was, however, still no news of the proposed annual pension, but he had heard from Lord Crewe that an application had been made on his behalf for a grant from the Royal Literary Fund. And he was flattered by a striking article which had recently appeared in *Great Thoughts* and which, entitled "A Wiltshire Poet", gave a Miss Priscilla Moulder the opportunity of surveying his life and quoting two of his best lyrics.

But to Dowsing in January he poured out his heart, and bitterly wrote, "It is disappointing that people will not buy poetry, but it is the same down here. You can give your books away but you cannot sell them. I do not sell one in two months, sometimes I'm not asked for one for five months. I do not care 'a tinker's curse' as we say in these parts. When I am dead I shall be remembered as a little poet, and you will at least be no worse off. That must be our meed. The others—those who will not recognise us—will be DEAD. It is not a great reward, but—the others have *no reward*. Remember this—and don't get downhearted." Yet he himself had cause to feel downhearted.

By April, 1915, he said that he was feeling better in health than he had been for five years previously, eating and enjoying food, which, in his factory days he could not have stomached. He had got down to his gardening now with renewed enthusiasm and hope but the work often overtired him. As he had not yet reaped a crop from the new allotment, he was uncertain as to whether he would become a market gardener after all. Mary Williams, gentle and encouraging as ever, worked with him on the garden when ever possible and did as much of the heavy labour as Alfred. But their joint struggle for existence was always uphill and always a gamble.

Early May saw a final revision of *Life in a Railway Factory* which Williams had hopes of publishing that autumn. The Thames book, which was being called *Round About the Upper Thames*, was now being serialised in the *Wilts and Gloster Standard*; by the middle of the month he had collected some three hundred folk songs in North Wiltshire and the Vale of the White Horse. "This terrible war has shattered many of our dearly cherished theories and set back the hand of civilisation's clock many centuries," he wrote to Fitzmaurice. "I have faith, however, that in the end our glorious Britain will prove triumphant, both in overthrowing the German master and in showing the world how it is possible, by honourable politics and right dealing, to advance the real civilisation and the lasting welfare of humanity generally."

The folk songs expeditions continued, day outings full of joy and promise. Eager to complete his picture of the life of the locality, he had by the end of August convinced the editor of the *Wilts and Gloster Standard* of the worthwhileness of printing a selection of the songs and ballads which he had gathered. Williams was most anxious that the revived pieces should be brought to the notice of the general public. It was eventually planned that twenty-five instalments of the songs, with an introduction, should appear in the paper. They were to be printed in sheet form so that readers could cut them out and keep them. Thus did Williams ensure the survival of many of the Wessex songs, though he did not wish in any way to pose as an expert in philology or folk literature.

Gardening, writing, song collecting, cycling, and a gradual return of strength, swung in the autumn. And in October, 1915, Duckworth published *Life in a Railway Factory*. Williams' main object in launching this book at that particular time was that he believed the moment was then ripe for master and man to set aside old industrial prejudices in favour of a well-founded judgment which would be the first step towards a happier agreement between Capital and Labour after the war. Yet he well knew what reception his outspokenness would have. The Great Western Railway Company, or its employees, would dispute the greater part of what he had written, especially where he had dealt with administrative problems and condemned the evil conditions in the factory itself. In November he wrote to Fitzmaurice- "My views of the labour position are quite unorthodox: I mean, the Trade Unions would not accept them. I do not care too much for Trade Unionism, for the reason that it is materialistic: nevertheless, we all acknowledge the sterling work it has done."

Life in a Railway Factory was fittingly dedicated to Alfred Zimmern who was then occupying a chair at Aberystwyth University College. At one time Williams had thought of inscribing the book to Reuben George, but finally decided against this because Reuben was a staunch Socialist. "It may give rise to misconception and damn the book; my object in writing the book, for instance, might be considered due to socialistic views, with which I have only little sympathy." This to Henry Byett.

The eighteen chapters and three hundred and fifteen pages of *Life in a Railway Factory* represented the most daring and comprehensive condemnation of factory life that had appeared in Europe for thirty years. In his usual logical preface Williams tells the reader that his aim is to describe simply the actual life of the railway factory with a survey of the several causes of labour unrest and a few suggestions as to its remedy. He intended to draw upon his own experiences and observations since he did not want his book to be merely a treatise on economics. Yet that is just what it is. Williams furnished the most concrete evidence of cause and effect.

Life in a Railway Factory is a massive masterlink in that chain of books which began with *A Wiltshire Village* and which several years later was to reach full circle in *Folk Songs of the Upper Thames*. The general plan of the book is that of *Villages of the White Horse* and *A Wiltshire Village*. This time it is the factory which is the well defined area. In the earlier books he had delighted in the peoples and things of the countryside, comparing their richness and innocence with the monotony and materialism of the town. Now in *Life in a Railway Factory* we find a reverse process. Williams turns to the town for his information so that in a subtle manner he is able to make an even more telling contrast between country and town, and to throw into sharp relief that kind of life which he himself so greatly admired. Such a dual method ensured a most comprehensive survey of Williams' own development, both as a lover of the countryside and a workman in the town.

Naturally he has a great deal to say about the many and diverse characters who made up the personnel of the factory. There are again the usual full descriptions of incidents, customs, and processes, and the same simple and honest writing. His mind fastens upon the details of almost every section of the factory, each, as it were, corresponding to a village, as was his method in *Villages of the White Horse*. The various characters of the factory form an integral part of the general pattern in much the same way as the country folk do in the earlier books. We become spectators of the life of the factory throughout its entire year and nothing is kept from us.

·Williams is more than a detached bystander. His personal observations and forcible arguments against the wretchedness of the factory system are skilfully marshalled, and strengthened by his understatement of them. The whole book is, for this main reason, an authoritative and revealing social study—a historical document of permanent value. It was bound to be a bitter book, though its onslaught was chiefly directed against officials and officialdom. His sympathies were entirely with the underdog and oppressed. During his stamping shop days he met many coarse types and witnessed rough and brutal conduct, but on no occasion in this book does he speak contemptuously of his workmates or show any patronage or signs of superiority. He was too much of an Elizabethan for that. Not that Williams could not use biting invective and strong language when necessary, but it was always to, and about those, in whom he found injustice, snobbery, or hypocrisy. In *Villages of the White Horse* he had once written: "It is not unusual for the farmer and his men to disagree, and I have known them even to indulge in a hand-to-hand fight, and go on working as if nothing had happened; but there is never the dreadful hatred and long pent-up smouldering passion about the farms as there is in the factory sheds; it is altogether unnatural and dehumanising there."

Life in a Railway Factory furnishes many proofs of how often and how determinedly he had kicked against these irksome conditions and how deeply he loathed the many crudities he regularly encountered. Though in his early factory days he welcomed the rigours and realities of heavy manual labour, as the years went on, he withdrew into his spirit more and more, finding himself, as far as the factory was concerned, finally marooned and frustrated. Since he possessed in some measure that quality which the French know as *panache*, and needed a life of essential rightness, colour and freedom, he could find no abiding place in the instability and confusion of the factory system.

Dante's imaginative representation of hell is no more horrible than

Williams' descriptions of the Swindon railway factory. We can feel within us, deep down in our insides, the whole awful place shaking and trembling, echoing and re-echoing with the ceaseless noise and beat of stamping, rolling, coaling, shunting, forging, shingling, and smithing. Noise upon noise, continual thunder, crash and reverberation shatter our senses and stifle our protestations. We meet an endless train of coalies and shunters, smiths and fitters, forgemen and boiler makers. Here come the carriage finishers and painters, the washers-down and cushion beaters, the ash wheelers and waggon builders—a procession of gesticulating automatons. Clerks, draughtsmen, stampers, checkers, storekeepers, and overseers pass like zombies on leaden feet continuously backwards and forwards, in and out, here and there, round about and across the floors of these steaming factory sheds. Such interminable travail, such waste of human effort, such degradation of man, the lord of the universe, make one marvel how Williams and many another were ever able to continue and retain sanity. He especially would have gone mad if he had not been able to see some signs of nature's quiet sensitivity even amid the tumult and broil of the banging and the shouting of this terrestrial colony of Hades.

But Williams was a poet, ever on guard for, and in quest of, beauty; among the shadows he was able to discern some lights. And how he needed balm ! There were the hares and rabbits that used to frequent the factory yard before the premises were extended and the grass and bushes cleared away. And within a stone's throw of the workshops he found it possible "to revel unseen in a profusion of flowers that would be sought for in vain in many parts of the countryside." Near the factory fence he discovered in one single year, rosebay, toad flax, ragwort, mignonette, melilot, ox-eye daisies, mayweed, willow-herb, meadowsweet, ladies' bedstraw, pansy, yarrow, and cinquefoil. "The wild rose blooms to perfection and the bank is richly draped with a vigorous growth of dewberry, laden with blossoms and fruit. Beside the streamlet in the corner is a patch of cats' tails, as high as to the knees, and a magnificent mass of butter-bur. The deliciously scented flowers of this are long since gone by, but the leaves have grown to an extraordinary size. . . . Here also are to be found the greater willow herb with its large sweet pink blossoms and highly-scented leaves, the pale yellow colt's foot, medick, purple woody night-shade, hedge stathys, spear plume thistles, hog weed and garlic mustard, with many other plants, flowering and otherwise, that have been imported with the ballast and have now taken possession of the space between the lines and the fence. The shade of the trees and beauty of the flowers and plants are delightful in the summer when the sun looks down from a clear, cloudless sky upon the steel rails and dry ashes of the yard, which attract and contain the heat in a remarkable degree, making it

painful even to walk there in the hottest part of the day. Then the
cool shade of the trees is thrice welcome, especially after the stifling
heat of the workshop, the overpowering fumes of the oil furnaces, and
the blazing metal just left behind."

He looked for, and welcomed, his beloved birds. Rooks and
sparrows were regular visitors, the former inured to the smoke and
noise, busily happy as scavengers. But he missed the starlings, robins,
martins, and swallows; the factory was no home for them.

Most precious of all, not far from one of the sheds, he could lift up
his eyes to the hills, and there "on a fine day, from between two
towering walls, in the little distance, blue almost as the sky, and yet
distinct and well-defined, may be seen a great part of Liddington Hill
crowned with the *Castellum*, the scene of many a lively contest in
prehistoric days, and the holy of holies of Richard Jefferies, who spent
days and nights there, trying to fathom the supreme mystery which
has baffled so many great and ardent souls." On a very clear day, the
details of the hill could be seen with its hedges and white chalk pits
and "you might imagine yourself to be standing within the mound and
looking out over the magnificent valley—north, east, and west;
towards Bristol, over Cirencester, and beyond Witney and Oxford."

What of the factory characters ? We are introduced to such men as
Herbert the bricklayer's labourer, Charlie the moulder, Harry and
Sammy, hammermen, Paul, Baltimore the drop stamper, "Double
Stoppage" Charlie, and Jim Cole. Of "Tubby", whom Williams considered to be the best furnaceman in the factory, he writes: "He hails
from Wales, 'the true old county where the men comes from', according
to him. Tubby is short, fat, and round, about the size of a thirty-six
barrel, and he is extremely short-legged. His head is quite bald and
shines well. His features are regular and well-formed. He has an
aristocratic nose, thick neck and shoulders, shapeless with fat. At the
fire he strips off his outer shirt and only retains his flannel vest. The
sleeves of this are cut short to the shoulders and it is fastened at the
neck by means of strings threaded with a bodkin. He drinks an
enormous quantity of cold water, and it is singular that he never uses
a cup but swallows it from the large two-gallon pot. To this habit
he attributes his uncommonly good health and fine proportions. He
is a genius at the fire. Whether the furnace be in good or bad condition
he will soon have it as radiant as a star, and he is marvellously cool at it.
His speech has a strong Welsh accent and he talks with great rapidity,
especially when he happens to become excited. At such times it is
difficult to understand him; he pours out his words and sentences like
a cataract." "Tubby" is thus recorded for all time, his greatness
achieved rather than thrust upon him.

 Then there was Jimmy Eustace, or "Jimmy Useless" as they called him, who, though something of a rake, was a skilled workman when the spirit moved him. "His long grey hair hung down as straight as candles and his grey beard had the true lunar curve. He chewed half an ounce of tobacco at a time, and spat great mouthfuls of the juice about everywhere."

And "Budget" with "only half a shirt to his back and hair six or seven inches long and as straight as gun barrels; whose face, long before breakfast time, is as black as a sweep's; who slaves like a Cyclops at the forge and is frequently quoting some portions of the speeches of Antonio and Shylock in "The Merchant of Venice" which he learnt at school and has not yet forgotten."

In the stamping shed Williams worked with such men as "Baltimore", "Sambo", "Strawberry", and "Gustavus". "Baltimore" was the joke of the forge, but he kept his good nature and was never upset by the frequent sarcastic remarks which were levelled at him by his fellow workmen. Though not a very skilled artisan, he was heart and soul in his work, never wasting a moment. He would spend the greater part of the night thinking over some problem connected with a difficult piece of forging. He was dressed in an "old-time Militia uniform— scarlet tunic much too big, with regulation white belt, baggy trousers too long in the legs, heavy bluchers on the feet and, instead of the swagger head-dress worn in the Service to-day, the old Scotch cap with long streamers behind and a little swishing cane in the hand or under the arm."

"Sambo", whose mother had been a West Indian, had a gift for pantomime, and amused everyone by reason of his funny expressions and ability to contort his face grotesquely. He was the bait of the bullies of the factory and suffered many indignities.

"Strawberry" had been cobbler, flautist, photographer, cyclist, and antiquarian in turn. He was always ready to try some new hobby, but, says Williams "he will suffer the furnace-man's fate in the end and perish of the smoke and heat of the fires."

Life in a Railway Factory is a treasure chest of similar portraits of men real and living. Day by day Williams worked with them, and their deeds, histories, and sayings are the life-blood of his book.

But its main purpose was to show the general public how degrading life in a railway factory was at this stage of industrial history. It is hard to believe that such conditions could possibly operate in a civilised land; it was these which shocked every critic and reader, and which amaze at the present time. There is hardly a chapter which is entirely free from criticism of them. It is true that it would be difficult to avoid many of the conditions in a large factory of this type, no matter how scientifically and humanely managed. And Williams did not always realise this. In a railway factory, with its complicated system, and widely varying types of workmen, it is to be expected that many of the conditions will be irksome and unnerving. There is bound to be misunderstanding. The whole tradition of the factory makes for it. But Williams had his picture to paint and his tale to tell and deliberately chose to be supercritical.

He speaks in the strongest terms of the lack of recognition of the rights of the individual by those in authority, and points out that the workmen and their protective organisation were systematically and deliberately ignored. The general principle seemed to be to regard the average labourer as less than a man. There is one dreadful and searing example of this mentioned in the book. On one occasion an ex-furnaceman, who had been severely scalded, began work again after recuperating, as an ash wheeler. "One morning, while they (i.e., the managers) were present, the ex-furnaceman came to wheel away the debris. Then a manager turned to me and said, 'Who's that ? What's he doing here ?' I explained who the man was and what he was doing. 'Pooh ! what's the good of *that thing* ? He ought to be shifted outside' replied he. In a short while afterwards the furnaceman was discharged." This, in brief, represented one attitude towards a crippled employee.

More than once Williams had to stand up for himself with his fists, and even when his literary achievements began to be known and admired outside the factory, there was, in general, no pride in him, or appreciation of his dogged efforts within the factory. There were, of course, exceptions, and Williams always paid tribute to those who acknowledged him and sympathised with his ideals. The pomposity of the officials is a continual target for Williams throughout the book. He knew from first-hand knowledge that the autocratic treatment and severity of many of the foremen were largely responsible for much of the prevailing unhappiness and dissatisfaction among the workmen. Jealousy was rampant. Only a few of the foremen were generous and humane; the behaviour of the great majority almost forced the workmen into open rebellion.

Williams knew, too, that the installation of new and modern machinery in the sheds, with the general speeding up of the processes, had had a bad result on the workers. He condemned the lack of initiative on the part of the factory staff and dismissed the piecework system as a thing of evil. There was an enormous waste of iron and steel, with no attempt made to use scrap material on the premises. The hours were much too long. The men had little freedom and were not even allowed to express their political views openly without incurring the disfavour of officials. If a workman thought of some improvement in processes, he was not encouraged to pass on, or make use of, his discovery. There were generally insufficient tools. There were many petty thefts. The long standing at machines and un-natural combat for the necessities of life, in a tedious and confined atmosphere, frequently led to a complete breakdown in mental and bodily health. The story of Gustavus, one of the saddest in the whole book, instantly springs to mind. His wife contracted milk fever after a confinement and became a hopeless lunatic. "Gus" had five small children, one a mere baby, to care for, and this he did with only a little assistance from a friend. The eldest child, a boy, helped whenever possible; "Gus" did as much as he could when he came home from the factory. He washed all the clothes on Sundays. Sickness haunted them and in the end he himself had to stay at home, completely ruined in health. Wicked tongues in the stamping shed suggested that he was only shamming, and when he began work again, an overseer did his best to have him dismissed, following a medical examination. "For several weeks he dragged himself to work, in a last desperate effort to keep a home for his babes and supply them with food, though anyone might have seen that he was in positive torture all the while. At last he could bear up no longer. He came to work the forepart of the week, then stopped at home; in three days he was dead. His little boys and girls went to the workhouse or to charities."

Williams waxed vehement at the unhappy position of the boys and young men employed in the factory. "You can always tell these young men of the steam hammer or rolling mills, whenever you meet them. They are usually lank and thin and their faces are ghastly white. Their nostrils are distended; black and blue rings encircle their eyes. Their gait is careless and shuffling, and their dress, on a holiday, is a curious mixture of the rural and urban styles."

And again, "A great alteration, physically and morally, usually takes place in the man or the boy newly arrived from the country into the workshop. His fresh complexion and generally healthy appearance soon disappear; his bearing, style of dress and all, undergo a complete change. In a few weeks' time, especially if his work is at the fires, he becomes thin and pale, or blue and hollow-eyed. His appetite fails; he is always tired and weary."

Over and above all these there was the smoke from the oil furnaces, the noise of the boilers and steam hammers, the curse of the night shift, the frequent accidents, the extremes of cold and heat.

Such then, was the Swindon railway factory in all its appalling nakedness and crudity. But Williams was no mere destructive critic and the first and last chapters of *Life in a Railway Factory* contain carefully considered suggestions for the amelioration of the majority of the troubles. There is an impassioned plea for the recognition of the individual. There is his wish for an end of the piece-work system, for a 48-hour week, and higher wages in the lower grades. The wage table, given in an appendix, shows, among other things, that whereas a foreman was paid 70 shillings a week and his assistant 50 shillings, a boiler maker received 34 shillings and a stamper 28 shillings. Men in such skilled occupations as waggon building were paid 68 shillings weekly; carpenters the same. Unskilled labourers received no more than 20 shillings weekly, this representing 54 hours work at less than 4½d. per hour. Williams himself never earned more than 35 shillings weekly.

If he had been living in 1939, he would have been more satisfied with conditions in the Swindon factory. The 54-hour week had given place to one of 47 hours. All the factory workers were able to have a week's holiday with pay each year. Closer attention was given to prevention of accidents and fire, while new processes and improved machinery had greatly simplified labour. The piece-work system was, however, firmly established and much hard and dirty work still continued.

It would be unwise to claim for Williams that he was directly responsible for these improvements. But he certainly had a hand in influencing public and official opinion, and the grim story which burst upon England in 1915 was no flight of fancy. Williams had toiled and suffered agonies of frustration within these walls for twenty years. He knew the facts, since he had seen them with his own eyes, and he wrote truthfully of them. And they who know security and peace of mind and spirit will for ever rise up in righteous anger when they read his description of the stamping shop. "And what a terrific din is maintained! You hear the loud explosion of the oil and water applied for removing the scale and excrescence from the iron, the ring of the metal under the blows of the stampers or of the anvil under the sledges of the smiths, the simultaneous priming of the boilers, the horrible prolonged screeching of the steam-saw slowly cutting its way through the half-heated rail, the roaring blast, the bellowing furnace, the bumping Ajax, the clanking cog wheels, the groaning shears, and a hundred other sounds and noises intermingled. There is the striker's hammer whirling round, this one pulling and heaving, the forgeman running out with his staff, the stamper twisting his bar over, the furnaceman charging in his fuel, the white slag running out in streams sparkling, spluttering, and crackling, the steam blown down from the roof through the open door, the thick dust, the almost visible heat, the black gloom of the roof and the clouds of smoke drifting slowly about, or hanging quite stationary like a pall, completely blotting out the other half of the shed, all of which form a scene never to be forgotten by those who shall happen to have once viewed it."

CHAPTER ELEVEN

INTO BATTLE

L IFE *in a Railway Factory* created a minor sensation. Opinions outside the factory were divided regarding the accuracy of some of its more outspoken comments, though every critic but one paid tribute to its courage and honesty. In November, 1915, John Bailey wrote to Williams, "I shall not enjoy reading your book, I expect, but I equally expect it will interest me and do me good. We who live sheltered lives, and leisured lives, ought to face the ugly facts of the toil and weariness and discomfort which fills such a large part of so many other lives. And there is no doubt, that conditions, though I suppose much improved, are far from what they ought to be, and will be." *Life in a Railway Factory* came as a great shock to Bailey, for he was perplexed and disappointed at the tone of many of its pages, seeing in them much that he thought foreign to the spirit of Williams' poetry. Yet, though not in agreement with the general atmosphere of the writing, he was bound to admit that Williams had more than sufficient cause for bitterness, especially against the senseless and brutal bullying in the factory. It is interesting to learn that Bailey believed that the only ultimate solution of the factory problem would be some form of partnership between masters and men.

Alfred Zimmern, on the other hand, much better informed and much more of an expert on industrial matters, considered that *Life in a Railway Factory* was monumental, and was proud to have his name associated with it. "Its strength" he wrote to Williams, "is in its fineness of detail and in its self-control. It is real description without a trace of rhetoric. I envy you your simple directness of style. No one can help believing what you say. Cabinet ministers might take a lesson from you. There is much in the book I should like to talk over with you. It makes me feel the very great difficulty of trying to improve things from the outside. How can I ever feel and understand the life and needs and outlook of the workers? I can realise the oppression intellectually, but I cannot live myself into the mental atmosphere which the oppression creates. Many of the workers seem to be just like the Balkan Christians after generations of Turkish misrule: they have the aspirations of free men without the qualities which freedom alone can give." And Zimmern, knowing how difficult Williams was finding things in those early war days, asked him to regard it as a pledge of honour not to keep his financial anxieties from him.

The reviews of *Life in a Railway Factory* ranged from *The Globe,*

which considered that it deserved to stand alongside Prince Kropot-
kin's sociological works, to *The Times*, which looked upon it in the
light of pure literature as well as a social study. "A book of revelation"
said *The Daily Chronicle*, while *The Yorkshire Post* observed that it was
literature "in the Carlylean sense being an actual transcription of life
as lived by the writer."

Yet the appreciation which most pleased Williams came from
Felix Potter, the General Manager of the Great Western Railway.
In praising the book, he said that the Swindon conditions were well
known to exist by the Paddington staff, and could well be improved
were it not for the attitude of certain high officials. He begged Williams
to call on him if he was ever in London. Williams, not forgetting
that he had once been a hammerman, considered this invitation a
most unusual honour.

But in spite of the excellence of the notices, copies sold very slowly.
In the spring of 1916, Williams was complaining to Dowsing about
the paucity of the sales, perhaps forgetting that peoples' thoughts and
interests lay in other directions in 1916. "If I were doing fiction
I should sell by the *thousand*; as it is, I cannot go beyond a few
hundred."

A damning and soured review appeared in the *G.W.R. Magazine*.
This began cautiously, with praise for the book because of its high
literary value. It then went on to suggest that, in spite of this, the
author had been entirely out of his element in the factory, since his
thoughts were more often far away in the countryside or with the
books in his library. He detested the factory simply because it was
a factory; what the reviewer called his "oblique mentality" was due
largely to the uncongenial environment of the works. "What man
in a normal state of mind would bemoan that the workshops were
not situated in a flower garden?" And again, "The man is a nature
lover, and no blame to himself." Williams had been unnecessarily
severe upon the workmen; he seemed to have a down upon everyone
and everything. "The author's bitter spirit against the management"
the notice continued, "gave him an ungovernable disposition to credit
the most uncharitable rumours or idle tittle-tattle about them." Many
of his statements were challenged. It was considered that he had a
biased view of life in the factory which was not shared by the other
workers. The review concluded: "If one of the objects of the book
is to gibe at labour because it is labour, we can only say that, after all,
labour is honest and manly—since man was born to it; and it is to be
hoped that until we reach the millennium there will be plenty of it.
In the past, the lack of it has given great trouble. But Mr. Williams
is a good writer and we recommend his book to impartial perusal."

Williams was distressed at these criticisms and was determined that

they should not pass unanswered. Accordingly, he asked the editor
of the *G.W.R. Magazine* to allow him the courtesy of a reply. But this
was refused on the grounds of shortage of space in wartime. Williams
then turned for advice to "Lou Robins" who had himself once worked
in the factory; he suggested that the editor should be quite firmly
told that if he persisted in refusing Williams a hearing, an account of
the whole business would be published in all the leading magazines.
Consent was eventually forthcoming. Williams' reply to the reviewer
ran into two and three-quarter columns; the review of his book had
occupied five and a half columns.

He did not attempt to apologise for himself. He stood by everything
he had written, for his remarks had been based on obvious and actual
facts. He denied that he was abnormally sensitive, or possessed of
an "oblique mentality" and said that it seemed as if the reviewer had
been embarrassed by Williams' outlook and unconventionality of
behaviour. Descriptions of factory life had been mistaken for con-
demnations of them. "As a matter of fact, many of my most happy
days were spent there. There I learnt the lessons of life. There I
became linked with humanity. There, also, I consolidated my studies,
and, while working at my steam hammer, peered through the world,
and out into the universe beyond. I consider the best gifts I possess
I owe to my connection with the factory, always excepting that in-
estimable one—the original spirit within me, and determination never
to be beaten, to master my conditions, and not to let them master me."

The review was not a fair one since it had unfaithfully represented
the tone of the book in general. But *Life in a Railway Factory* had
already passed into history.

Williams now decided to publish a selection of his war poems which
Erskine Macdonald was anxious to have, since there was some demand
for this type of writing. The usual co-operative arrangement held
good. On the last day of 1915 advance copies of *War Sonnets and Songs*
lay on his study table at Dryden Cottage. Most of the songs and
sonnets had already appeared in the local papers; all of them were
directly inspired and influenced by the stirring events of the first few
months of the war. Yet, had it not been for the insistent persuasion
of some of his friends and acquaintances, it is doubtful whether
Williams would have thought of publishing what he himself considered
to be rather second-rate material. But he did think that the spirit and
tone of the verses would attract the admiration of the public, especially in the Swindon district, and swell the sales of the collection.
Because of his desperate straits at this time, it seems obvious that he
was looking for a quick return, for the poems, in spite of their vigour,
add little to his literary reputation. How Alfred and Mary Williams
existed at all at this time is past comprehension; it is fairly certain that

both of them were denied the essentials of living. His total earnings for the latter part of 1915 rarely averaged more than five shillings weekly. What Mary meant to him during these days of hardship and privation cannot easily be reckoned. There is no evidence that he turned to friends for charity, though it is certain that had any of them known the circumstances, he would not have lacked whole-hearted assistance. Very few at this period, even amongst his intimates, knew the actual position at Dryden Cottage. His letters to William Dowsing reveal the true state of affairs. His attempts to push the factory book with local booksellers were generally unsuccessful; during the whole month of November he had so many attacks of dypsepsia that he was quite unable to contact booksellers or to do any gardening or writing. The couple's first wartime Christmas can well be pictured.

Yet *War Sonnets and Songs* sold well, though Kyle said there was some loss on the edition. Williams had successfully gauged the public mind. He, of whom *The Times* has once written that his poems were those of a man whose life was lived in a world where the prizes were things not measurable by the scales used in the camps of capital and labour, was only too gratified by the returns which the book brought him in. For a wartime publication it was well produced and sold at half-a-crown. More copies were sold in the Swindon district alone during the first three months of 1916 than of the factory book during the whole year. But Williams published no more poetry of this type, though the demand for it grew as the war continued. He dubbed the book "little war scribbles" and of it wrote to Dowsing, "at the beginning of hostilities the public wished to read *war* verse; in time, however, they became sick of it, and the bards perceived this and stopped. My publisher urged me to print a few of my poems, on purpose to keep me in view. . . . They are really but little good and I know it." He told Fitzmaurice that *War Sonnets and Songs* had few merits, and to Dowsing again he confided, "They are of no value— merely a local collection. I am rather sorry I 'messed about' with them."

War Sonnets and Songs reveals the change which was taking place in Williams' outlook. The war had a lowering effect upon him in that it helped to increase his growing bitterness of spirit and accelerated his determination to look to the present rather than to the future. The really sad thing about the book is that he knew how poor in quality many of the poems were. *Life in a Railway Factory* was full of the noise of machinery; *War Sonnets and Songs* is full of the noise of battle. Both concern themselves with hatred of systems and people. There is no gentle hand here. The poems deal with such incidents as the attack on Belgium, the Battle of the Marne, the *Emden*; Lord Roberts, the *Lusitania*, the British Cabinet. They are intensely patriotic and often imaginative. But as a serious contribution to poetry they detract if anything from his stature as an artist.

He was still collecting folk songs whenever he had the chance, and felt well enough. He sought out the old singers and wrote to any source where he thought there might be copies of ancient ditties. He devoted the early months of 1916 to this task. He scoured the ground most thoroughly, not only visiting the villages near at hand but night after night cycling into the Cotswolds and to places as far away as Bampton and Burford in Oxfordshire. He had heard of the work of Cecil Sharp, and admired it, but he was not influenced in any way by what he and others had done. No project gave Williams greater joy than this one, for it brought him into contact with people. He always stressed that he was no expert at folk song collecting. He interviewed humble men and women of all types, many of them over ninety years of age; he was inspired when invited to enter into the dimnesses of the old cottages and to chat with the aged folk dreaming in the inglenooks, forgetful of everything but the fragrant memories which they recalled when "that tidy young stranger" questioned them. Williams was certain that the valley of the Upper Thames would produce material as valuable as any in England. By February, 1916, he had noted over five hundred pieces and realised, with some consternation, that it would take him from eighteen months to two years to complete what promised to be an interesting and comprehensive collection. "The ground I am working on is extensive: it is the whole of the Thames Valley this side of Oxford. The outside line runs through Cirencester to Tetbury, to Malmesbury, to Marlborough, to Ramsbury, Lamborne, Wantage, Steventon, to Abingdon, to Oxford, to Witney, and thence, by Burford to Cirencester again." This to Fitzmaurice that spring.

By March he had cycled nearly seven thousand miles in pursuit of the songs; in addition, he had discovered a wealth of fascinating and forgotten information about the countryside. He was simply amazed at the thousands of songs still in circulation. He kept a record of the places he visited and the people he met, in a small black notebook which he carried everywhere. Then he diligently went through all the songs, classified them, added explanatory notes, and published the results each week, as had been planned, in the *Wilts and Glos. Standard*. He now thought of offering the collection to Duckworth when he had completed it.

His doctor warned him that he was doing too much cycling, but Williams ignored the advice and went on with his task all that summer. He was literally folk-song mazed. He talked to the Swindon W.E.A. on *Folk Songs of the Upper Thames*, and *Highway*, the monthly journal of the W.E.A., published a folk song article by him which gave an exquisite picture of the "dreamy villages, and the placid and seemingly imperturbable folks of the countryside". It told of country songs that were rooted in the hearts of the people, of the old-time Morris dances, mummers and wassailers, wrestlers, boxers, back-sword players, and dancers. It had much to say about the worthies. "One, the eldest, who died last year, was ninety-nine, and sang to me but a few hours before his death. Another, aged ninety-four, toiled in the fields as a young man with those who fought at Trafalgar and Waterloo, and relates stories of these battles".

Williams corresponded with people, many of them experts, all over England, about the songs, for they were attracting unusual attention as they appeared week by week in the *Standard*. His old friend, Jonathan Denwood, then living in Whitechapel and pining for a smell of the Downs and the mists of his own northern fells, sent him information about Cumbrian folk songs. And Frank Kidson, a real authority, advised him that many of the so-called "folk" songs of the Upper Thames valley were no more than Victorian drawing room lyrics which could all be found on contemporary sheet music of which he had original copies. But this did not daunt Williams, and by autumn, two-thirds of the work was done and the field of exploration had been extended west to Chippenham and east to Wallingford.

Yet all the time Williams was worried that he was not a combatant. He had felt all along that he ought to volunteer for military service so that he could be a defender of liberty and avoid the criticisms of those who might think that he was a slacker. He was affected by the general war situation like most people and especially by the letters which he used to receive from boyhood friends who were now serving in the forces. He would have liked particularly to join one of these who was in Greece. He imagined himself in the country whose ancient culture he so fervently admired and whose language he had studied and read since his early factory days. Further, he knew he would be better off financially. It was a pretty soul-destroying existence he and Mary were living then, in spite of all their activities; service in the army would at least mean regular food for him and a service allowance for Mary. But he was afraid they would not take him because of his health. He did not think he could stand up to anything really vigorous again. He was still a martyr to dyspepsia and as he had once told Henry Byett, "One day I feel rather fit and for the next few days following I am rather shaky. I have no stability." The factory had, in short, ruined him in more ways than one. And he did not help matters himself by his exertions. But what else could that active brain do? It could never be idle.

Early in September, 1916, they were in such straits financially that he had to ask Fitzmaurice to back an application he proposed making to the Royal Literary Fund for a monetary grant. He was then firmly of the opinion that his medical record for the past three years would bar him from all military service. Yet, a few days after his letter to Fitzmaurice, Williams received a notice to appear before a medical board at Devizes. He attended and was put through severe tests; to his complete surprise he was passed by the doctors as fit for home garrison duty. Consequently, there was now no need to submit an application to the Royal Literary Fund, and he was hopeful that after the war he would be able to return to his writing as a reliable means of livelihood. Had the artist not been called up, Williams would have been able to publish his Upper Thames book that autumn, but the sketches were not finished; the book would now have to wait, with the folk songs and the factory poems. There was always the further possibility that the Prime Minister's offer made in 1914 would still hold good. Williams had heard nothing further of the proposed subscription list and annual pension, so that it now seemed clear that the whole project had been shelved because of the war.

As soon as Zimmern heard that there was a distinct possibility of Williams joining the forces, he arranged a meeting with Reuben George, "Lou" Robins, and the Williamses at South Marston, the aim of which was to discuss the latters' future. Zimmern saw at a glance that help would be needed. After the meeting, and while returning to Swindon, he told Reuben and "Lou" that he was going to set aside £500 upon which Alfred and Mary Williams could draw when necessary. They were not to know of the existence of this. Zimmern appointed Reuben and "Lou" as trustees of this sum and said they were to make use of it whenever they thought a real need had arisen.

On the night of 2nd November, 1916, Williams left home for Devizes. He had volunteered and been accepted as a gunner recruit in the R.F.A., the unit being a territorial one. The officer in charge at Devizes advised him to return to forging where he would be more use to the war effort, but Williams had had enough of the hammer and the shop; he preferred the guns to munitions. He was proud of the fact that he was a volunteer and thought that his duty lay in soldiering. He was certain he had made a wise choice though he knew Mary would be vexed at his decision.

Two days later he had left Wiltshire for High Wycombe feeling pleased with himself and his new experiences, though missing the privacy of a separate bedroom in his billets. He wanted to get on with what he called his "bit of scribbling". At the end of his first week in the army, he proudly sent his "Mim" (his nickname for Mary Williams) the whole of his first week's pay—five shillings. He told her he was living like a lord as an orderly in a sergeant's mess and that the only excitement he had had was a little wood chopping! There were several Wiltshire men in the unit, though none from his immediate neighbourhood; several of them had read his books. Most of the men in this camp were in the C1 grade, as was Williams himself. By the end of the month he had received his complete uniform, and had written to Mary: "I've walked out to the town and swanked (in the dark)." But the early thrills of army life were wearing off and he was beginning to regard a great many things as a waste of time, money, and energy. He had soon discovered that his pay did not go very far.

As soon as opportunities presented themselves, Williams got down to the serious business of writing again. He was particularly disappointed about his folk-song book, for he had been so keen on getting this piece of work finished. But there it was and it couldn't be helped. Instead, he began a book about army life and by the beginning of December was well ahead with this. He had been hearing regularly from his home and from his friends. Robert Bridges and Mrs. Bridges had written to tell him how interested they were in his folk-song articles. Besides, as shareholders in railways, they had been distressed to learn of the miserable conditions in the Swindon factory. Bailey had sent him a copy of Horace, a Greek Testament, and a leather case for his special papers. The world looked good in spite of the war. His spirits were rising. "I can see beyond to-day. I know my position in letters and my value. If I should be killed in action it would be glorious for me, and if I go into action and come home safe, it will be accounted to my honour." This to Mary in November, 1916.

The unit moved on. Three days were spent in a camp at Great Baddow, near Chelmsford—"a very middling place", Williams called it, where nearly all his companions were Scotsmen, and, "like a lot of madmen". Williams was working and finding pleasure with horses here; his country knowledge had come in useful. On 3rd December he was in billets at Sible Headingham and one of the keenest members of the 328th Brigade R.F.A. There was much he still found attractive about army life in spite of the obvious drawbacks, and he told Henry Byett that he much preferred it to life in the factory, especially in peace time. "I would much prefer the colours if it were not that I feel the call for literature in civil surroundings. Nevertheless, I shall make copy out of this. At Wycombe I struck off four chapters. Since leaving there I have not penned a line."

What of Mary Williams during these early days of separation? She was completely lost without Alfred, for the whole of her life had been devoted to him and to his interests. She was lonely and often depressed. She had unpleasant neighbours who irritated her and made her unhappy while her shy and retiring nature did not permit the making of new friends. She might often have visited the members of her husband's family who lived near at hand, but she preferred to withdraw into herself to making the contact. For a long period after Alfred's enlistment she received no separation allowance, and at one time was actually short of food, though no one knew that this was so. He guessed from the hints dropped in her letters that all was not well for in December he wrote: "How do you live and pay the rent? Have you enough to eat?" He never knew how miserable she really was. It fell to "Lou" Robins and his wife to discover what was happening at Marston and they immediately invited Mary to spend Christmas in their home, which she did, and gladly, for they were true and sympathetic friends. And they sent her Alfred a parcel of food, too. She stayed on for three months.

On the very last day of the year, Williams' thoughts went winging to his little cottage and he was reminding Mary to put the early potatoes on the floor for sprouting and to look to the little apple trees which he had planted before leaving Marston. His heart was often in the villages and with the old singers and he pined for congenial companionship. He was thrilled beyond measure when he met a clergyman near Headingham who knew something about folk lore and dialect. Every day he read from his Greek Testament. He was keen on his work and proud of the way he could polish a gun.

But the Battery did not stay long in Essex, nor indeed in England, for on the night of January 12th, 1917 it left for Ireland. Williams' first journey outside England and on the sea was a nightmare. He sailed from Liverpool and wore a life belt all the way. The ship was on her side half the time and two horses were lost in the heavy Irish seas. "I was sick, sick, sick, all night—not half," he told Mary. On the following day the 328th Battery of the R.F.A. took up its quarters at Newbridge Barracks, County Kildare. And Alfred Williams was a far cry from Dryden Cottage, and Liddington, and the Cole.

CHAPTER TWELVE

IRELAND, SCOTLAND, ENGLAND

THE Irish winter was a bitter one and Williams felt the cold intensely. Newbridge Barracks were draughty and uncomfortable, there was no attempt at privacy, and the food was generally uneatable. He had insufficient money with which to buy extra food so that he had to regularly write home for both. In mid January he hailed with delight the unexpected arrival of half a pound of cheese, a cake, and some Wiltshire apples. Books he had in plenty and these he freely

loaned to officers as well as men. He was grateful that he had a bed
to sleep in, but he spent most of the night balancing himself on it
for it was always in danger of complete collapse. He had become
friendly with the chaplain who had prevailed upon him to address
a meeting of the men; this was apparently so successful that it had
to be repeated. Many of them now knew he was a writer and several
were reading his books which he got specially for those interested,
from his publishers. Williams got on well with most of his fellow
soldiers and was certainly no prude, but he was genuinely shocked
by the swearing and loose talk. He liked most of the officers, especially
one, Lieut. Mackenzie, who had been a tutor in Greek at Edinburgh
University; Williams had many interesting discussions with him.
The officers as a body respected Williams' scholarship, which led him
to write to Mary: "What a contrast to the treatment I received at the
Swindon Works. But these fellows are intelligent and have knowledge
of life and human nature which the *Upstarts* in the factory never had."
Some of the N.C.O.s he greatly disliked, for he found them so ignorant
that he mentally compared them with some of the foremen in the
factory.

He was constantly worried about Mary's plight, for he well knew
how scanty her separation allowance was; it is therefore surprising
that he should have bothered her so frequently for money. She was then
receiving an allowance of 12/6 weekly which barely kept her from
starvation. "I am going to write to the War Office and ask for further
assistance for you." This on the last day of January, 1917. And he
was adding very little to his book on army life, though he was giving
considerable thought to politics and the general course of the war.
He led several informal debates at Newbridge, on several occasions
voicing the opinion that the Government was underestimating the
strength of Germany and her allies. To Fitzmaurice he wrote in
this strain: "If we succeed in smashing Prussianism, and in breaking
up the armies of the Kaiser, there is still the German people. They
are a strong, stubborn race, intelligent, proud, and I for one do not
think it within the range of possibility that we shall succeed in imposing
or dictating a future policy indefinitely to them. That seems to me
to be too much to require, and I feel that we ought to at least take the
pains to examine ourselves, and to ask what we should do under
similar circumstances, and to try and approach the final settlement
in a spirit of 'give and take', for assuredly all the 'take' cannot be on
our side. The thought has struck me that our continental policy
has not been as happy in its issues as it might have been. . . . Life is
changed. All history depicts change. Nothing endures for ever, and
our position on the planet is not permanent. I seem to see, in the
present struggle, the beginning of a vast expansive movement by

Germany which we shall be powerless finally to arrest, unless it be by showing a conciliatory spirit, and acknowledging the greatness and genius of her people and institutions, which, at the present time we are most of us very loth to do. It is not a pleasant truth to face—if it be a truth—but I cannot help pondering these things, and wishing that we might find means of co-operating with our enemy in the future."

But besides being a prophet, Alfred Williams was also a very good soldier. He had made such progress with his training in three months that he was asked to take a course of gun fitting at Woolwich Arsenal. He was very willing to do this, for he realised that he might afterwards receive promotion, and Mary an automatic increase in her allowance. In order to qualify for the Woolwich Course, it was necessary for him to pass a difficult practical test of exactly the same standard as that given in peace time to journeymen fitters seeking employment. He had a first hand knowledge, of course, of forging and smithing, but had had no previous experience of fitting. So there followed a week's preliminary training at Newbridge which included some complicated bench work; then he presented himself for the entry test. This he passed with high marks, a really creditable achievement for an erst-while hammerman. He now awaited admission to Woolwich, after which he had high hopes of becoming Battery Fitter, with the rank of Sergeant Major, with more pay, greater leisure and the joy of doing really skilled work. All this took up much of his time, and, "As for writing (literature) it is out of the question" he wrote to J. B. Jones in February, "but I am living the life and getting plenty of experiences and impressions which I hope to record some day."

While he was waiting to become a fully qualified fitter, the 328th Battery moved on to Fermoy Barracks in Co. Cork, and on 14th February he was writing to Mary about the little Irish town, "It is not very large, but it is very pretty. It lies in a hollow beneath a towering mountain. The River Blackwater runs through the middle of the place. It is a lovely stream and there are two very large weirs alongside the bridge."

There he had an accident. He was in charge of the limber gunners for his section, and one day towards the end of February he injured his back while lifting the trailer of a gun, the total weight of which was just over a ton. Examination showed that a few strands of the spinal cord had been damaged so he was admitted to Fermoy Military Hospital for a prolonged rest cure. Here, the pains in his back and stomach were, at times, so severe that he could scarcely breathe. This unhappy misfortune spoiled his chances of going to Woolwich for the gun fitting course; during his first week in hospital he heard that he was expected there on 27th March. This was really a very great disappointment to him, for it was unlikely that another opportunity would arise.

From the beginning of his stay in hospital he was fortunate enough to be tended by an Irish nurse who was not only an expert at her job but also was keen on reading, and interested in Williams' literary career. She was a keen Nationalist and a member of the Poetry Society. Williams soon struck up a firm friendship with her and they passed much time together discussing Irish literature, particularly the work of Yeats, A. E. and MacGill. From Ida Levinge, Williams learned a great deal about the Irish, and first heard from her lips another side of the history of her unhappy country. He listened to her for hours on end while she told him the legends and stories of ancient Ireland; together they read much Irish poetry at a time when the weather was so often wet and dull (Fermoy was barely thirty miles from the open Atlantic) that Williams was low in spirits and tired of being inactive. He told Fitzmaurice that during his short stay in Ireland he had found the people to be "kind and warmhearted but under-educated, dreamful and unpractical . . . their enthusiasm is greater than their wisdom and intellectual capacity." Fitzmaurice's ancestors had been Irish so he was pleased to send Williams a *History of Ireland* which was read with sorrow and shame; he found the whole story a terrible tragedy in the development of which the English had played a rather ignoble part. Williams early realised that the problem of the Irish was a complex and difficult one and thought that their inveterate lack of unity in the prosecution of common ideals was their greatest weakness.

Alfred Williams, from the first, told his wife about his friendship with Ida Levinge. Mary Williams, harassed and fretting in her loneliness in England, and full of worry for her husband, was peeved and hurt that he should find it necessary to turn, if only in spirit, to another woman. He reassured her with loving messages, "You're a foolish old thing, but I understand your heart . . . you are my all, Mim." He told her that his nurse, who was engaged to an Irish doctor, was a kindred spirit because she was such an enthusiast for poetry; in fact, he was going to write a poem for her as a souvenir. Alfred Williams wrote two poems about Ida Levinge, "Love's Memory" and "To Niam on Duty".

While in Fermoy Hospital he heard of the sudden death of Jonathan Denwood with whom he had been in regular correspondence since the early days of his literary career. Then he received the news that Elijah Iles of Inglesham had died at the age of 95. It was the latter, known more familiarly and affectionately as "Gramp", who had sung many old songs and told many stories to Williams when he was collecting folk songs. Of Elijah, Williams wrote in an appreciation in the *Wilts and Gloster Standard*: "In my perambulations of the Thames Valley I have met with many fine old characters, but none of them were quite as distinct, original, and rich in memories as 'Gramp'.

The songs he sang were all very old. Several of them he learnt from his grandfather, while only a lad: they must have been in the family for generations. One of his oldest pieces was 'Pretty Susan, the Pride of Kildare' . . . When the Battery was stationed at Kildare recently, I had the pleasure of sending him some Kildare plug tobacco, which gave him peculiar delight: I may say that about the first thing I thought of, on reaching Kildare, was Elijah's song."

And Robert Bridges, who had sent Williams one of his recent books, had had his house burned down at Boar's Hill and his son badly wounded at the Front. Saddest of all, Elizabeth Williams, who had been an invalid for a number of years, lay on her deathbed in Rose Cottage. Mary had now got an extra four shillings allowance weekly, but she was sick with eczema; Williams himself was feeling that the war was seriously checking his creative faculty.

All these disturbing tidings, together with the sense that, as an artist, he was being frustrated (he did actually write four poems in hospital) had the cumulative effect of making him introspective to an advanced degree. Fermoy was bleak and cold and there were severe snowstorms in April. He had been vaccinated and it had taken badly. Even the warmth and sparkle of gay Ida Levinge could not shake off his restlessness. Only the rich Irish scenery brought his spirit any permanent balm. From his bed he could see the hills, and thinking of Liddington and Barbury, he wrote to Mim in the first days of spring: "In the morning, clouds rest upon the highest peaks. They gradually disappear and melt into the blue. . . . There is a range of lowish hills which always remind me of the Cotswolds".

His back slowly yielded to treatment and it was not until the end of March that he was able to hobble as far as the Barracks and back again. The doctor, however, was satisfied with his recovery and said he had the vigour and appearance of a man of twenty-five. On Easter Monday the weather was fine enough for Williams to walk into a wood near the hospital where he read the Crucifixion from his Greek Testament, a habit of his for several years, while he sat for several hours feeding on the beauties about him. "It was very sweet", he told Mim, "I know of nothing like it. Picked a large handful of anemones, violets, wild strawberry blooms, celandines and gorse, not like ours, quite, but nearly thornless, with very graceful spikes of bloom. I also found some exquisite ferns. I carried the bundle back through the town to the hospital and attracted the attention of most I met; I expect they thought it very singular to see a soldier laden with flowers. The children ran after me in admiration and the older people looked at them covetously."

Elizabeth Williams was growing worse and was not expected to live much longer, so Alfred applied for leave on compassionate grounds.

He was also worried about his wife and wanted to see how things actually were at Dryden Cottage. Leave was at first not granted as the doctor said he was not fit enough to travel; there were still days when his temperature was up to 100°. But at last, on St. George's Day, he was discharged from Fermoy Hospital and recommended for a fortnight's sick leave. He left for England on the following day—so penniless that he was unable to break his journey at Dublin where he had wanted to see some Irish art. On 25th April he was home in South Marston.

While at home he attended a W.E.A. ramble at Shrivenham, where he met Richard Garnett again. On 5th May he was back at Fermoy, having said a last farewell to his mother still lingering on with dropsy and heart trouble. He found, when he rejoined his Battery, that a new major was in charge, who was hated by everyone because he was a positive slave-driver, "as cold-blooded as a snake" said Williams, who was convinced that he was a madman.

Eventually, the conditions so exasperated Williams that he applied for a transfer to the R.G.A. and at the same time asked if he might have a day's leave to visit Cashel, the seat of the ancient Irish kings. Leave was granted, but only after he had told the officer concerned that he was an author and lecturer and had been asked by the War Office to prepare a series of papers on Irish archaeology! He was disappointed with Cashel—and his fare had cost him ten shillings.

On 9th May, 1917, the Battery left Fermoy for the Curragh, 110 miles by road. Alfred Williams had seen the last of Ida Levinge, but he would never forget her companionship. On the last evening they met, in the soft and gentle Irish twilight, he gave her her souvenir poem:

LOVE'S MEMORY.

The cloud remembers the hill,
 The moon remembers the sea,
The dew forgets not the flowers,
 And I will remember thee.

The blue tide foams on the shore
 With its passionate kisses wet,
The winds know their trysting-place;
 Then how could my soul forget?

Soft as the rose-leaf falls,
 By spirit-fingers prest,
So sweet thy memory lies
 Full-perfumed in my breast.

The long route-march was undertaken as a demonstration against disaffected Ireland, but though Williams had actually met several

Sinn Feiners he had heard no very irrational opinions expressed. On the road to Dublin the people gave the soldiers milk by the bucketful and emptied their houses of food without charging a penny. From Borris-in-Ossory, County Kerry, he wrote to Mary to tell her how tiring he was finding the march (they were doing nearly twenty miles daily) and how, in spite of the continual rain, he had slept with his two mates under their gun.

The Battery was on the Curragh by the 1st June and the long march was over. The wet weather continued, yet they were immediately put under canvas and found conditions more than trying. Williams was suffering from severe chaps on his hands, was, as usual, short of money, and was being exasperated by "a perfect swine of a sergeant". He occasionally visited Dublin, thereby escaping his immediate surroundings, and liked the city in spite of its squalor. One day he visited Tara, first going by the slowest train in Ireland thirty-two miles away to Kilmessan and then walking to Tara where he saw the still visible ruins of the famous banqueting hall and the mounds of Irish heroes. He was enthusiastic about this adventure, and when he sat on the base of St. Patrick's statue and gazed on the view about him he thought he had never been so cheered while in the army; so he sent Mim two large moon daisies which he had picked on the sacred hill itself.

It was confidently expected that the Battery's next move would be to France, but on 2nd July, Williams, with eighty other artillerymen, had left Ireland altogether and was in Scotland, at Radford Barracks, Edinburgh, and waiting to be sent overseas. Though he was sorry to leave Ireland and the friends he had made there, Williams was immediately attracted to Scotland. He was more than satisfied with the Barracks, built specially for the Scots Greys, the "mad" major had been replaced, and he was enjoying himself working in the stables for the time being, no longer a limber gunner. And at the first opportunity Williams went to see the Forth Bridge and sent Mim a picture of it. But, as usual, his initial enthusiasm soon wore off. The Battery was put through the drudgery of initial artillery training again, being grouped with five hundred new recruits for this purpose; there was also daily physical jerks which Williams found "excruciating". The food, never very eatable, went from bad to worse and he jumped at the opportunity of attending a short service at an Edinburgh church because of the free feed that followed!

Williams remained in Scotland for about a month when he received his transfer to the R.G.A. A few days before the end of July he was sent to Avington Park Camp, near Winchester—Gunner Alfred Williams, No. 661546, R.G.A., a busy member of the gun laying class and dealing in the main with five-inch 60-pounder guns. Conditions

were easier than at any time since he had been in the army, though the
damp and heavy air of the Winchester district rather tried him. "We
lead a gentleman's life", he wrote to Henry Byett. He had a comfortable bed and sufficient leisure to permit him to continue with his army
book and he often used to retire to a little wood near the camp to do
his writing. By the 18th August he had completed twelve chapters
in pencil; by 29th August—confident now that he would be on the
next draft for France—he had added another six, though John Bailey
warned him that he was writing too quickly. He had now decided on
calling the book *Boys of the Battery* and was so anxious to finish it that,
though he was quite handy to Wiltshire, he did not ask for leave, for
he knew he would have no chance of writing while at home. He
needed about a fortnight in which to finish the book. Mary was still
far from well, still upset by friction with her neighbours, still spending
long and weary hours in the garden at Dryden Cottage. She did most
of the heavy digging herself and was proud to tell her husband that
she had picked thirty pounds of blackcurrants that summer.

Early in September, Williams won his badge as a gun layer and shot
the highest in his class with the rifle while doing the musketry course.
Then the Battery was informed that it was to be drafted to India and
almost immediately. He had just six more chapters to write to finish
his book and wondered whether he might get them finished before
leaving England. Nevertheless, he decided to go home for a few
days' embarkation leave, where he found Mary very disturbed that he
was going so far away from her. But he reassured her by telling her
that in India at least he would be safer and have less work to do.
And there in Rose Cottage he saw his mother for the last time. He
then returned to Winchester with Mary's farewell present—a watch—
in his pocket and immediately continued with his writing. He spent
every spare minute copying out the chapters in ink, for he had now
finished the first draft of the book and was overhauling it in readiness
for publication. He even went so far as to buy himself a fountain pen
in order to do the work more speedily—and he detested fountain pens.
On 24th September the Battery left Winchester for Devonport where
Williams boarded the *Balmoral Castle*; he had only seven chapters
copied out. While waiting to sail he wrote to Mary: "If anything
should happen, you must see to my literary interests to the best of your
ability. Zimmern, Bailey, and Lord Fitzmaurice would doubtless
take action. . . . I will try to write to the Laureate."

On 28th September the troopship steamed out into the Sound and
Alfred Williams had begun the greatest adventure of his life. As the
summer darkness fell across Penlee Point, he wrote to his mother:
"You've been a good mother to us all, and taught us to be upright
and honest, and if we have turned out rough and bad it is not your

fault. I shall never forget you, and I shall always love you as long as I have breath in me. So be brave, dear mother, and think of the time when we shall meet again, and know each other in a happier world than this."

CHAPTER THIRTEEN

TO INDIA

IN the Channel, the *Balmoral Castle* was attacked by submarines, but she successfully shook off and evaded her pursuers. Alfred Williams was under fire for the first time in his life. Then for several days, the troops, crowded from stem to stern, were in great danger owing to heavy weather, often standing by patiently in their lifebelts prepared to make a jump for it. The ship rolled considerably and Williams, with most of the others, was frequently sea sick. Doggedly she made her way past Gibraltar and down the west coast of Africa; after nearly a fortnight at sea they were still north of the line.

Conditions on board were appalling. The food was of the poorest quality and the men were half-starved; Williams pined for the sweet, clean food of Fermoy and the Curragh. What couldn't he have done to half a pound of Wiltshire cheese and a fruit cake ! Every day he continued with the copying out of his precious chapters though he was so unwell during the third week at sea that he could hardly walk the length of the deck. He suffered badly from diarrhœa and could not stomach the unwholesome food.

They lay for four days off Sierra Leone, not daring to move on because of the fearful lightning and awe-inspiring tropical storms. The heat was deadly and every man was half eaten by lice. Then slowly they sailed to Capetown, a few days out from which Williams completed his copying and revision of *Boys of the Battery*. He carried the soiled manuscript under his lifebelt all this time, not daring to let it go out of his sight.

They spent three days at Capetown and here the troops, about a thousand artillerymen, were sent ashore on arrival absolutely penniless, to wander through the streets of that rich city, without the wherewithal to buy even a picture postcard, or yet an orange. Williams had been unable to provide himself with much money on embarkation and the men were only paid one week's pay. But in spite of his misery, he was greatly impressed with Capetown and its harbour, and he climbed to the top of Table Mountain to pick a silver leaf there to send back home to Mary. On the afternoon of the last day there, all the men were invited to tea at the Troops' Institute, where the South Africans were sympathetic and generous to them.

On 28th October, 1917, the *Balmoral Castle* sailed from Capetown, with Williams praying hard for a good English rainstorm. A few days later she was at Port Elizabeth where she remained for two days unloading cargo; she then made for East London where there was more unloading for a day and a night. Here Williams felt nostalgic as he observed half a train load of Wiltshire milk being delivered into the port. It was planned for the troops to go ashore here, but there was a heavy ground swell on and any disembarkation would have been troublesome and dangerous. From East London the next move was to Durban where they all hoped they might stay for a while, as they were tired of the sea and anxious for a change of food before sailing on to Bombay. To his mother and sisters he wrote: "We're sick of bad bread and stinking butter that you have to put on your bread with a spoon by tea time. I washed my shirt and pants yesterday and dried them. You have to walk about with them in your hands, for if you put them down a few minutes and turn your back, somebody steals them. . . . We all have the *itch*, enough to drive one crazy by night, and we are all, or nearly all, *lousy*, which is a disgraceful thing on board a first-class Mail Boat. But nobody has ever cared about us since we came on board, to see whether the men kept themselves clean or not. The result is that many of them have been wearing the same clothes these six weeks and stink as they walk about." And again, to Fitzmaurice: "The boat, a Union Castle Mail Liner, is like a floating palace, half-empty, alas, except for Tommies, sixteen hundred of whom are carried in her bowels." The normal complement for third-class passengers was one hundred. The trip should have been a pleasant one and a unique means of real education, but Williams cursed the whole wretched system which made for such disgraces.

After ploughing her way through some unusually rough seas off East Africa, the *Balmoral Castle* arrived at Durban early on the morning of 2nd November, 1917. The men had been six weeks at sea, had no money, and were owed a fortnight's pay. "Upon disembarking from our ship, we stood on the quay in full marching order, in a broiling sun, for nearly three hours, and then marched two and a half miles to a "rest" camp. When we had been installed in our tents and assembled for tea we received one pint of tea and one slice of bread. There was plenty of food of several kinds, but no requisition for food had been made to the quarter-master, and we went hungry". This to Fitzmaurice upon arrival.

The troops remained in Durban for nearly a week. The citizens were again very kind, otherwise the men would have been in difficulties, as they had still received no pay. As at Capetown, the soldiers wandered up and down the streets, as poor as beggars, sick at heart, hungry and angry. They were, however, permitted to ride on the trams free, and eventually the Wesleyan community entertained them daily to tea and supper in their chapel, thus satisfying a real need. One day there was a serious flood and the troops were called out to deal with it. On another, Williams went to a spiritualist meeting where the medium told him that he was surrounded by a very fair guardian spirit in the form of a lifebuoy with ivy wreathed round it. She told him that he would return to England safely though he would meet with an accident. Williams was impressed by the medium, whom he found to be clever, quiet, and unassuming, and would have attended another service had he remained longer in Durban. He was always attracted to the mysterious and occult. On the last day in the city, he posted the manuscript of *Boys of the Battery* to Duckworth.

Late on the evening of 6th November, Alfred Williams left Durban on the *Caronia*, a Cunarder taken over by the government; the *Balmoral Castle* remained behind in Durban, the troops being glad to see the back of her. But there was overcrowding again on the new vessel with 4,500 soldiers on board, though 400 of these were landed at Kilwa, in German East Africa, the last draft of artillerymen to arrive in this colony before it was conquered. Military operations were proceeding in the south, so the men were disembarked as near to the actual fighting as possible, and, as the *Caronia* lay at anchor off Kilwa in sweltering heat, Williams could see thick clouds of smoke sweeping across the horizon from the battlefield. He was never to be so near to a battle again.

Then they began to sail across the Indian Ocean. The men wore neither boots nor stockings and Williams foolishly bathed his feet under a large tap in the fo'c'sle with the inevitable result that he was severely scalded and burned by the sun. For the rest of the voyage he suffered acutely from swollen legs and wondered whether this was the accident prophesied at Durban. He used to sit under one of the lifeboats, amusing himself by reading Pat MacGill's *The Big Push* which he thought had admirable subject matter, but a wretched literary style. There were also the porpoises and the flying fish to watch.

At length on 12th November, 1917, the *Caronia* steamed into Bombay and Alfred Williams had set foot in India. There followed a 1,500 mile journey by rail for three nights and two days and his first impressions were disappointing, for he thought India a vast and wild place, sun-baked and uncharitable. Though there were huge plantations of unending tea, cotton, and maize, for hundreds of miles the train passed through nothing but rock or dried mud left from the monsoons. Over lofty mountains and across mighty rushing rivers it carried the fascinated and wondering Wiltshire villager to deposit him eventually with several hundred other overheated and exhausted artillery men at Roorkee. And there 75 miles away on the distant horizon were the

Himalayas towering 30,000 feet into the mists and sky. Williams, the lover of hills, was awed and inspired by the sight, but he still pined for the quiet and privacy of his little home, and wished he was with Mary and walking with her on a Sunday through the fields around Marston. He was particularly anxious for news of his mother. Half humorously he comforted himself and Mary with the laconic observation: "I am quite alright among the snakes, elephants, buffaloes, camels, and monkeys. The sun shines all day and every day and we are not overworked."

The Battery, the 68th R.G.A., went under canvas on arrival. Williams found Roorkee to be a place of noise and evil smells, and they were all disappointed with the food, which was badly cooked and short in supply; they had expected better of India. Life was dull for some time and Williams often wished he could converse with the natives, but unfortunately for him, their religion hedged them round with insurmountable barriers, and, at that period, he did not think it worth while to learn Hindustani, which was rather surprising considering that he usually found such delight in language.

What of Mary during these latter months of 1917? Shortly after her husband sailed from Devonport, she went to stay with some friends at Highworth where she waited anxiously for news of his arrival in India. The English winter set in early that year, with dark, windy, and bitter days, and on her return to Marston she found life more lonely than ever in Dryden Cottage, often going a whole day without seeing or speaking to a single soul. And that winter she was thirty eight. Nearly every day she made an effort to see her mother-in-law at Rose Cottage, whose life hung now on the slenderest thread, but often she turned back to the solitude of her own home, with her enquiries about the dying woman's health frozen on her lips. That December, while Alfred was writing an article on "Winter in India" for the *Wilts and Gloster Standard*, there were heavy and continuous snowstorms in the Swindon district. Mary became really concerned when the snow drifted in through the roof on to his books. She was so worried that she walked into Swindon to ask "Lou" Robins to do something about this; the blind man walked through the snow-drifts over to Dryden Cottage by himself to make arrangements for the necessary repairs (for which he paid) on the same day, thus relieving her anxiety. It was then that "Lou" learned that Mary had not received any separation allowance for several weeks, this being the second occasion on which this had happened since her husband had volunteered. "Lou" went to see Reuben George to tell him of the circumstances and suggested that Zimmern's trust fund should be drawn upon. Reuben was not convinced that there was yet a real need, but said that he would look into the matter. Nothing was ever done, however, and the fund remained intact. In consequence, "Lou" Robins and his wife invited Mary to stay with them and their children for it transpired that she actually had no money with which to buy food, though she could easily have obtained food if she had turned to relations and friends. She gladly accepted the Robins's offer and, though her allowance began again and all was well, she remained with them in Swindon for three months, and assisted them in their shop and with the newspaper round which "Lou" was developing.

That winter Elizabeth Williams died. Her passing, at the age of sixty-seven was a deep and heavy sorrow to all her family, and especially to Alfred who was so far away from home. The war had preyed very much on her mind and she was grieved that he was in the army. Of her, he wrote to his sister Bess: "She loved us all with a deep and wise love, and we can never forget the great debt that we owe to her who laboured always for us, when we did not know it, and set us such an example of modesty, virtue, and honesty. Generally she was right, and now, more than ever, I acknowledge how much I owe to her teaching and example to us all."

As soon as he had settled down at Roorkee, Williams began to write another book, which was to deal in some detail with Indian life and scenery. He just couldn't help himself; he was a born commentator. He took every opportunity of acquainting himself with the customs and habits of the people. On Boxing Day, after a quiet Christmas, he went to see a Mohammedan festival. This was taking place at the village of Mela, some six miles away, a holy place, and site of an important mosque. Williams walked over from the camp, being accompanied for part of his journey by a young native boy who could speak a little English and who carried a scared cock underneath his arm for sacrifice. The lad told Williams that he was going over to Mela to pray for his mother who had once visited the mosque there, and he gave him much information about the ceremonies which they were going to witness. This was Williams' first experience of an eastern religious meeting, and of the twenty thousand people who were present, Williams was the only white man. He was so carried away that he came again for the second day of the festival, bringing two companions with him.

India slowly began to cast its ancient spell upon him and he was more than disturbed when he heard a rumour that the Battery was going to be drafted to Mesopotamia for he had not yet obtained enough authentic material for his book. To Mary he wrote, in the last days of 1917: "I more and more feel compelled towards gazing to the hereafter. If I may say it and be believed, it is the soul and spirit of us that has my attention, rather than any matter touching our worldly and material interests. At the same time, there is Life's battle to fight. I am in the Army. We are at war. I am a writer of books, a painter of life—a realist. Yet that is not all. These things are superficialities to me. Down, deeper down than this, is the real man, and if I get back home safely, I intend trying to cultivate the philosophic mind, and, before I die, to write something serious and intense."

And here spoke both the hammerman and the poet of *The Testament*.

CHAPTER FOURTEEN

FROM ROORKEE TO RANIKHET

ALFRED WILLIAMS was soon gripped by India and was glad that he had not been drafted to France. He was getting used, as well, to the poor feeding at Roorkee, was looking forward to more visits to places of religious and historical interest, and whenever opportunities presented themselves he attended lectures on Hinduism and Mohammedanism. His sympathy with, and consideration for, the various aspects of the religious life of India began to be asserted. In January, 1918, for instance, he went out of his way to make a journey to see the cremation of an Indian soldier after which he wrote a lengthy account of the gruesome ceremony to Mary, who was horrified by the realism of his description. He was particularly anxious to get to Darjeeling to catch a glimpse of Everest, but was prevented from doing so for some time owing to further trouble with the leg which had been scalded on the voyage from England and which made him slightly lame for several weeks. He also had to take great care with his back which still caused him occasional pain; he dreaded the oncoming of the monsoons because of malaria to which he felt he might easily fall a victim.

At Roorkee, however, he had a fair amount of leisure which enabled him to continue with his writing. Slowly, he was accumulating a vast store of information about Indian life and scenery (in high glee he told Mary that he had seen kidney beans growing near the camp, 23 inches in length!) and was making copious notes of all his observations; now he turned his attention to a new book which was to describe in detail the voyage from England. He found at this period that he was able to write, in the rough, about a chapter a week. He was still patiently waiting to hear the fate of *Boys of the Battery*.

Mary wrote to him regularly for she knew that he always keenly appreciated local news. She told him that his mother had willed him his promised part of the "Hook" field, upon which information he commented: "Of course when I return, I can see what I want to do, though I am not coming home to make a slave of myself in the Hook or to turn agricultural labourer". He advised her to get the new land dug over, cleaned, and turned into a garden, and gave her suggestions as to what seeds should be sown.

Since the death of her mother, his sister Bessie had been living alone in Rose Cottage, and Williams, who was very attached to this sister, was anxious that she should have company. Accordingly, he was relieved to hear that Ada and her family had moved into the old home and that Bessie would now have someone with her who would understand her gentle nature.

In January, 1918, Alfred Williams spent one long day exploring the village of Sohalpur when he walked in the fields of sugar cane and saw the natives refining sugar by primitive methods. He was fascinated. He might have been back home on the farm lands of Wiltshire, where the same kinds of things were happening. That night, completely tired out and with his head a whirl of excitement, he returned to Roorkee by oxcart, lying on his back the whole way on top of his piled up kit and rations, with the oxen patiently plodding homewards along the moonlit banks of the Ganges. After the Sohalpur adventure, he wrote to a former comrade, Cackett, who had been with him at Fermoy and who was still stationed in Ireland, concerning the mysteries and the splendours of India, "If I were to attempt to tell you of them, I should not go on parade for a week."

Military duties continued to be of a light character and there was now no physical training for the artillery men; parade did not begin until 9 a.m. and the day's work was finished by 3 p.m. It was only when there were guard duties or journeys into the jungle with the guns, that the days were longer. Thus Williams had unusual opportunities for the fullest observation of the Roorkee countryside. His health, for the time being, caused him no great concern and daily he practised a few of the Müller exercises. Roorkee, set on the fringe of the hills, cool and invigorating, was a most satisfactory winter training station.

The animals were his favourite study and his training as a naturalist stood him in good stead. He saw them in their natural haunts, recorded his impressions of them, and wrote a great deal about them to his friends in England. How often, too, must he have thought of those others running wild and beautiful in their Wiltshire meadows and lanes. On a freezing night in February he stood on guard in the hills just outside the camp. "The hyenas" he wrote later to Mary, "were making a terrible noise about a mile away. They make a noise something like this 'Yur! Yur! Yur!' and prowl around on the lookout for poultry, a young kid or fawn." He told her, too, of the porcupines he had seen, "considered quite good meat"—and of the shy hares, and of how "a lovely fawn, startled by the drums of the native regiment quartered near us, came springing down the hill past the hospital and came close up to me and would not leave me all the afternoon but followed me up and down . . . licking my hands and nibbling the grass round my feet." To Cackett he wrote, full of wonder and astonishment, and in almost childlike fashion, "The trees are full of monkeys and parrots and other brilliant-looking birds, and camels and elephants are as common as horses. And jackals and hyenas prowl round the tents at night, and the earth is full of snakes and mongooses. And tigers and panthers visit the neighbourhood nightly." On one occasion when they had a break of three hours, being mess orderly at the time, he went into a nearby wood to do some quiet writing, only to find himself the object of attention of a crowd of monkeys, who solemnly sat round him at a little distance, peering at him as country children do when a stranger sets up an easel and sketches in their village. One night he woke up startled to see a wolf sitting in the moonlight and looking at him from the bottom of his bed. But with one fierce glare the animal bounded out through the window. Then Williams was excited to hear that a man-eating tiger, which had devoured several natives, and for which a reward of two hundred rupees was offered, was at large near Roorkee—he half hoped he might see the curiosity. He was horror-struck, however, when he learned that some Ghurkas from the adjacent native camp had been shooting peacocks in the woods and taking them back to their quarters and roasting them.

There were the birds, too. The robin, the tiny fly-catcher, more minute than the English bird, the huge kingfisher and the stone grey blackbird were new marvels. "But" he wrote, "I like the birds best that more nearly resemble our own at home."

By Easter, 1918, he had gone further afield. He had visited the holy city of Hardwar, witnessed religious bathing in the Ganges, besides writing ten chapters of the new book; he had done nothing further to his Indian nature book. He believed that *Round the Cape to India*, which was to be the title of the voyage book, would create a real stir when published and would undoubtedly offend many in high places, as *Life in a Railway Factory* had done before. His main idea was to point out the difference between the old officers who were gentlemen and men of experience, and the new officer class which so often consisted of mere upstarts who were coarse, ignorant, selfish, and untrained. "A feature of the book will be a little romance on board, between Lieut. John Catchmie, posing as the Honourable Reg. Augustus Le Vert (the Green), and Polly Smith, pretending to be Miss Sibyl Gwendoline Goldsworthy, and Lieut. Simon Sharpe, and Miss Kate Kissquick. Polly Smith is going out to get a situation in South Africa. She had been a bar-maid, but posed as the daughter of a big politician at the Cape, John Catchmie's father was a whitewasher and paperhanger, Simon Sharpe's father a pork-butcher, a maker of prize sausages and black puddings, and Miss Kissquick was a sort of female professional, a very immodest and amorous young woman, the cause of much scandal and a little fighting among the officers on board. I've made it all very, very ridiculous. . . . There is a duel at the end, and afterwards the General made them fight it out with gloves. It is all founded on facts."

He worked steadily at the new book in the sure belief that his future as an author was brightening and that when he returned to England he would have much success with his writing and never again be short of money. "We have great friends" he wrote to Mary, "They are all pleased with and proud of us. And this should strengthen us to keep up the fight" He had heard that Zimmern was making serious inquiries into the conditions on the *Balmoral Castle* on its recent voyage to India.

But much as Alfred Williams was enthralled and excited by Indian sights and sounds, he still yearned for Wiltshire and South Marston. "Oh, dear me ! it seems ages ago . . . I hope you will get a nice apple year. I expect our little trees will grow nicely . . . and the currant trees will bear lovely by the time I get back."

Early in March he visited Hardwar again in order to strengthen his impression of the city; he had also learned a number of Hindustani words. He travelled the eighty miles to Hardwar by ox wagon, the fare costing him eightpence. While there he witnessed several interesting ceremonies and bought a curious hand-engraved brass lamp in the bazaar. This was just large enough to hold a small candle and was really no more than an ornament, but Williams could not resist the exquisite quality of its workmanship. The lamp cost him three rupees —nearly the whole of one week's pay.

On 13th March he had written the last chapter of *Round the Cape to India.* On 19th, the Battery, after many rumours, had been transferred to Cawnpore, three hundred miles further south, where Williams was immediately bowled over by the heat, and was suffering from acute diarrhœha. "Roorkee", he wrote to Mary, "is cold beside this place, and it is only spring. There has been a little air to-day, and as I was coming from the parade ground, as the wind blew, it reminded me of the hot blast and flame that used to come from the oil furnaces in the stamping shop." The Battery remained at Cawnpore for about a month and Williams was ill more or less all the time with fever and dysentery. The punkas were going from early morning till late afternoon, with the prospect of even hotter weather to face in May and June when the usual temperatures were 120 degrees in the shade. The whole routine of the Battery was changed, too. There was a parade from 7 till 9 a.m., after breakfast had finished at 10 there were odd jobs until 11 (Williams more often than not cleaned out stables), and from 11.30 until midday there was musketry practice when the day's work was over but for guards.

Williams began to explore Cawnpore from the first. The city streets, the trams, the electric light, and the large public gardens with their orange trees, mangoes and limes, and the Europeans who hardly noticed the soldiers, all these were very different from the primitive hill station at Roorkee. His first major discovery was an industrial exhibition of native products which he visited, as it was free, on several occasions. Here he fell in love with a four-folding screen of carved wood, a beautiful piece of handmade workmanship, "one of the things a man might in a sense worship because of its inspiring and elevating influence." It was priced at £13 and he badly wanted to buy it, but he could not afford to do so, for, though there was a certain amount of back pay due to him, he was losing 1/4 weekly because he could not prove that he had attested earlier. He did not find the mile-wide Ganges, "more like a sea than a river", so fascinating at Cawnpore as at Hardwar, in spite of the fact that he had a morbid interest in the corpses which floated down the holy waters and in the skeletons of natives which could be seen when the river was half empty. He also visited the famous well and Massacre Ghat where Nana Sahib had sat and watched the slaughter of two hundred women and children in boats on the Ganges.

Unfortunately, Williams' health did not improve. One day he simply poured with perspiration and could just bear to lie on his back in the shade. On another, his temperature soared to over 100 degrees and for three days in April he ate nothing at all. The heat affected his liver so that most days he felt uncomfortable. The earth was like concrete, and while out on the range doing his musketry course, his elbows got badly skinned and then sunburnt. He loathed the sight of the parade ground with its blinding light and merciless sun. "I'd just like to be by the claypits and to see a white mist of rain sweeping over Liddington Hill down upon the valley." But instead of this prospect, he had to endure the swarms of flies, ants as big as bees, hornets, mosquitoes, and elephantine wasps. On the other hand, he liked to see the little lizards running up and down the walls and was still disappointed that he had not seen a big snake. With memories of Wiltshire and home, he watched the Indian harvest being reaped, with the corn being cut, and being brought straight in to be threshed. Happily he gazed on the sitting reapers and on the oxen patiently treading out the corn and he let the warm iron grains of barley and wheat run through his hands. He must often have thought of his mother and how she had gleaned in the Four Docks Field in the days of his childhood.

Early in April the English mail arrived, with letters from Mary, Zimmern, and Mansbridge. A question had been asked in the house about the *Balmoral Castle* and its voyage. From Mary he learned that Mark Titcombe's cottage, which for many years had stood upon the ground rented by Williams as an allotment, had at last tumbled down. A link with the past had gone. Mary used what wood there was as firewood. The bricks, and other rubble, remained where they were: but their history was by no means over. And did both Mary and Alfred give a thought to Nellie Kempster, and to Mark, who had once his soul to the devil? He also heard that Duckworth, to his great sold disappointment, had declined to publish *Boys of the Battery*. As ever, he accepted the situation philosophically and went on with the revision of *Round the Cape to India*, though he doubted if he would be permitted to publish this during wartime. *Boys of the Battery* had now gone to Zimmern, who was trying his best to find a publisher for it.

By mid April it was clear that Williams would be dead if he remained any longer in the tropical heat of Cawnpore, so he accepted with alacrity an offer to be transferred to the hills. On April 12th, he and nineteen other artillery men left Cawnpore at midday by rail for Ranikhet, some 350 miles to the north, where they expected to remain for two months. The men arrived at Lucknow that afternoon where they learned that they would not be proceeding further until 9 p.m. Naturally Williams began to explore the city and was interested in the chief mosque, with its ancient tombs; in the native market, he bought a brass stag for Mary. About midnight, they boarded the train for Katgodam, the terminus of the line, into which station they steamed, entirely exhausted and very irritable, at 1.30 the next afternoon. Here they were joined by eighty other artillery men from the fort at Allahabad, all more or less on their last legs, and the whole company was then told that it was to escort a mule train carrying ammunition to Ranikhet, fifty miles away, through the lower Himalayas. After dinner, a hundred tired artillery men left Katgodam to march fourteen miles to their first camping ground, each man carrying a rifle, haversack, mess tin, water bottle, and bandolier with twenty rounds of ammunition. They marched until midnight and in so doing climbed four thousand feet. "I never had such a day in my life", he wrote to Mary, "but the scenery was splendid. Of course it was dark by eight. There was afterwards a moon and brilliant stars. We saw hordes of monkeys of several kinds, including great grey apes."

The company rose at dawn the next day, which was a Sunday, and marched another eight miles in seven hours, climbing a further two thousand feet and then dropping two thousand feet. On the Monday they plodded on and wearily climbed to six thousand feet, on Tuesday they dropped four thousand feet, and on Wednesday they were at

Ranikhet where they arrived after five days on the road, completely worn out. "It made one giddy to turn one's eyes from the road. You have seen pictures of companies of men with mules twining round the mountain side. It was what we were doing for those five days. Snowdon is only 3,000 feet. And we were up 6,000 feet! The road was chiefly blasted out of the rocks, and we followed a tremendous ravine for at least thirty miles out of the fifty."

The Himalayas were a revelation; they staggered and humbled him, took his breath away, and made his heart sing for joy. Seventy miles away he could see seven ranges of hills, with twenty-four snow-covered peaks, all above 20,000 feet in height. One, Nanda Devi, was over 25,000 feet. There were glaciers, too, and beyond the ranges, two tremendous and awful peaks a hundred and twenty miles away. "The hills open out into a great theatre. We are on a high hill, or a series of hills, and the theatre is in front of us. . . . I should never dream of such a sight. It is simply amazing. They are covered with snow and look like a soft silver in the distance." To Henry Byett he confided: "Oh, it's a jolly, jolly spot, and I just love it. The Himalayas are divine. It is great to see. What material I shall have for books—if I live. . . . I would not have missed India for five years of life."

Ranikhet camp was surrounded by fragrant pine forests, and there were also deep copses of oak and walnut trees. The mountains, on arrival, were covered with massive plantations of rhododendron trees in full bloom, and with jasmine, and white and pink wild roses. Each morning for a month Williams heard the cuckoo, and within a week of leaving the plains, he had gathered violets, willow herb, and cranesbill, making notes upon them and recording their differences in form and colour from the English varieties. Maidenhair fern grew freely by the roadside.

Of course his health immediately improved, though Ranikhet had extremes of temperature and was not as bracing as he thought it was going to be. But he was quite content, for every day he saw something of interest. One day it was a wild elephant, another day two striped panthers, and by the middle of May he was boasting to Mary that he had seen tigers, leopards, black bears, antelopes, gazelles, wild boars, mountain sheep and goats, and golden eagles.

But he just could not get the Himalayas out of his mind. They inspired him most of all, and daily he looked into the distance to the peaks of Nanda Devi, Kamet, Nampa, and Bartakhanta, all over 23,000 feet high and linking earth and heaven. "To look upon them is like a glimpse of eternity" he wrote to Mary. "If you were only out here with me I'd not worry to come to England for many years, for here in the hills, it is simply divine."

Poetry welled within him again and he wrote something nearly every day. By June he had a book containing fifty new poems. On 12th May, 1918, he sent the following poem to Mary:—

AT RANIKHET

Where Dawn puts forth her flame-white hand,
    And suns and moon successive rise,
Lo ! Trisul, Nandadevi stand,
    And prop the empire of the skies.

Westward the velvet glooms abide,
    Till dawn and dusk have kissed and met,
And, stealing o'er the mountain side,
    Part on the hills of Ranikhet.

Now south the circle runs; o'erhead
    The archèd azure slow declines,
Whose gauzy veil is lightly spread
    Above her myriad oaks and pines;

Where burns the tiger, fiercely vext,
    The panther, crouching in his den,
And rugged lion, leaping next
    To rend the ruby hearts of men.

And there the snowy roof ascends
    Eternal, silvering in the sun,
And with the azure sweetly blends
    Till heaven and earth are mingled one.

There were drawbacks, nevertheless, even at Ranikhet. Williams was not enamoured of several of his fellow artillerymen and on more than one occasion he spoke to them in no uncertain terms about their coarse and filthy language. "When I consider all things in connection with the life of the masses, the crowd, or whatever one likes to call them, I become more and more convinced of my opinion so long held—namely, that I'll never be a *democrat* and that Democracy as a ruling power would be fatal to England, for when you give one of them an opportunity of showing what his rule would be, he is the most terrible tyrant and hog you could imagine. I am especially thinking of the manner in which they treat the poor natives here." This to Mary; and when he was acknowledging Dowsing's *War Cartoon Sonnets* which had been forwarded to him from England, he told him how refreshing it was to come in contact with so cultured a brain again, for "in the army you can find no chums and I'm really a lonely sort of fellow.'"

As the spring wore on, the weather began to get hotter and hotter and there was thunder and storm. In spite of their altitude everyone was looking forward to the monsoons, which had already begun in Ceylon and the South. Williams went down with fever at this time and was in hospital for four days during which time he wrote several new poems. He had also received orders from the Battery Office at Cawnpore to write a detailed account of the voyage from Devonport of the *Balmoral Castle*, for the government had decided to institute an inquiry into the many complaints which had been made. He was both gratified and flattered by the request, and finished the report in two days, which was then forwarded direct to England; the evidence he gave was serious as touching both the Steamship Company and the officers who had been in charge of the troops.

On the day Williams left hospital, the monsoons began in earnest, and describing this newest of his experiences, he wrote home, "We have had thunder showers, much vivid lightning. These storms usually come in the evening. The lightning is wonderful and shows up the mountains magnificently." The men now moved into bungalows for they had been under canvas since their arrival. Immediately in front of the bungalow which Williams shared was a huge pine tree around which the local Hindus had built a platform from which religious services were conducted and to which they had tied two red and white flags with which no one interfered. Beyond the pine tree on the hill side was an oak tree beneath which Williams used to retire in order to do his writing. For several evenings running while he was sitting there, a large wolf sprang down from the roadside on the hill and jumped over his head without seeing him as it made for the dried river bed lower down the hill.

The changeable weather did not improve his health and he suffered from several attacks of malaria. "There is some difference in my appearance now from what it was when I came home to see you from the Curragh twelve months ago. I've got the old factory appearance now." Williams dreaded the prospect of having to return to the plains because of the vapour and damp heat there. But the days sped on and now the snows on the Himalayas could only be seen about twice weekly; the early mornings were as foggy as any in a Scottish autumn and the clouds were set among the hills and valleys before Ranikhet.

Williams walked freely about the district learning all he could about the people and their habits. He met a native wedding one day with its child bride and noisy band of horns, flutes, and drums and the sight both fascinated and horrified him. There were hours of rambling by the river, with its rushing icy torrent, dashing and foaming between the bleak rocks, so different from the broad, flowing Ganges at Cawnpore. There were myriads of new and strange butterflies to study, delicate ferns, and oxlips whose cousins bloomed in the water meadows of Wiltshire. Nightly he heard the frogs croaking from the river bed, and one night he killed a scorpion which was climbing up the wall by his bed.

He was growing to be a part of India, so that in June, 1918, he wrote to Mary: "What is there in England, *except you*, for me to come back to? Well, you and my tried friends. There will be all the old bitterness, I daresay, the little slanders and jealousies, and the quibbling. I think I have learned a lesson by travelling. A man's own home, his wife, and himself on a small scale, otherwise, the world and mankind as a whole are what he should think of."

So he lay dreaming of the past and the future in the snowy fastnesses of Ranikhet.

CHAPTER FIFTEEN

IN THE PLAINS

AT South Marston, Mary Williams had been working for the local branch of the Red Cross Association. She continued to make herself responsible for the main of the gardening, including the cleaning and preparing of the new piece of the Hook which Alfred's mother had left him. He was not quite clear how the remaining portion of the Hook was to be shared, so he asked Mary to measure off what had been willed to him on the side upon which his garden lay, next to where his fruit trees were growing.

At Ranikhet, Alfred Williams had sent some poems to the *Englishman*, a paper published at Calcutta and having the second largest circulation in India. The editor of this, not only printed the poems, but also inserted a paragraph in one edition about Williams' career as an author; he also asked him to write a special poem in the recruiting interests. "To India" resulted, which was read with enthusiasm by his fellow artillerymen. Further poems were accepted by this editor for which Williams was paid, though the *Englishman* did not as a rule buy verse. "So, after all, I am not dead yet, either as a poet or a prose writer. . . . I have an improved power in verse, I think, for I have got rid of a certain formality of expression which I used to show in my more common pieces." This in answer to a letter from Mary telling him that his sister Laura had had some of *her* poems printed in the *Western Gazette*. Artillerymen stationed at Allahabad wrote to Williams asking him to write more poems for the *Englishman*.

But he was having no success with *Boys of the Battery* and on 15th

June, 1918, he heard that Chatto and Windus, to whom Zimmern had submitted the manuscript, had declined to publish the work, so he decided to split it up into separate articles and submit them to various newspapers. He was not now so disappointed about the failure of the book to find a publisher, for he believed this was largely due to the critical war situation and to the disinclination of the general public to be interested in anything relating to the army but not specifically identified with action. "If it had been war, the battlefield, I should have had no difficulty. But never mind! I don't care a bit. By and by I'll improve it and it will do some day." On 20th June, he sent the now completed *Round the Cape to India* to Zimmern. He was anxious that the work should be submitted to Duckworth, for he preferred to keep in touch with this publisher for he knew his method of business. He had received very little from royalties since he had been in the army, although *Villages of the White Horse* had now been issued in a cheap edition at 3/6 in Duckworth's Readers' Library.

With some of the money which he received from the *Englishman*, Williams bought three silver fox skins and two wolf skins and sent them home to Mary. The fox skins were to be made up into a stole and muff for her, "as a souvenir of Ranikhet", while the wolf skins were to be used as bedroom mats so that she might have something soft to put her feet on when she got out of bed each morning. With the furs he enclosed for the garden at Dryden Cottage some oxlip seed, which he gathered on the banks of a nearby river, and which he believed might grow in England in a sheltered place.

The Battery was daily riding and manœuvring in the Ranikhet district when the weather permitted, in order to exercise the horses. The men were also receiving instruction in bayonet fighting as all artillerymen had to learn something of this, and musketry. Williams soon gained the reputation of being the best bayonet fighter in his section. "My mates say I'm a proper old Guardsman. Well, I try to do my best everywhere", he wrote to Bess in the July.

As Alfred Williams learned more about Hinduism and Mohammedanism, he found himself faced with the fact that the English Church, and western religions in general, were not the only ones with divine sanction. He was greatly affected by the high moral characters of the majority of the natives and was struck by their prayerful attitude. Since his earliest days he had always given considerable thought to the meaning of the Universe and man's place in it, and now the poet who had written "Natural Thoughts and Surmises" and "The Testament", was exploring other philosophies. Shortly after he had sent *Round the Cape to India*, he wrote to Mary about the book as follows: "In the eleventh chapter we were having a discussion on the War and Christianity and Pat asked me if I believed in Jesus Christ and the Bible and I said 'I believe in it *all*, Pat'. I must get that *all* cut out, because I don't profess to believe in *everything*, being advanced on many points, and my assertion that I believed in it *ALL* would imply that I was no further intelligent than the *superstition mongers* (of the burning hell order) and I don't want readers of me to think I'm one of those. So I want you when you hear that the book is likely to be published (if it so happens) to write and ask that that *ALL* in this chapter shall be cut out."

He wrote again to her in the same strain at a later date: "The Hindus, and especially the Buddhists, have a very lofty spiritual conception of God, even though the masses are poor, and, (to us) dirty and superstitious. But the more intelligent Hindus are very fine people and would scorn to do the dirty things which we western people practise. . . . We English folk (especially the religious bigots) are an extraordinarily narrow-minded race: when we get abroad and see the many hundreds of millions of other people on God's earth that we count *damned*—well ! ! ! we think no small beer of ourselves. I must confess that I am something of a universal being. So are we all really; for we are all of one brotherhood. And I'll never believe that all these splendid people out East are God's outcasts. He cares for them as much as he does for the Westerners".

Williams had now been three months at Ranikhet and there were many rumours that the artillerymen would be moved, some to France and others to Mesopotamia. Eventually they learned that they were to return to Cawnpore, but the move was delayed owing to landslips on the way to Katgodam and a serious outbreak of cholera in Cawnpore itself. India had had its hottest summer since 1896 and the monsoons had not arrived on the plains. Consequently, Williams was thankful to be still stationed in the hills, where work finished at 11 a.m. for the day, where there was a holiday every other day and only one church parade on a Sunday. Ranikhet was as gracious and lovely as an English spring, all soft and green and luscious, now that the rains had come and gone. "The hillsides are covered with orchids now, like English greenhouse plants, and wild dahlias and begonias, and brilliant red flowers like anemones. I spend many hours down the khindside (hillside) by myself among the foxes, hares, and jackals. It's very jolly".

On 9th August a new party arrived from the plains with grim tales of heat, fever, and sunstroke. Every man in it looked like a ghost and nearly all had been ill; others were waiting to be sent home to England because of heart trouble caused through the excessive heat. Others of this party had died in Cawnpore.

On 11th August, when the new party had taken over, Williams very reluctantly said farewell to his beautiful and unforgettable Ranikhet,

whose name would for ever be written across his heart. With him he
carried the book of poems which he had written while in the hills and
which he thought might find an Indian publisher before he left the
country altogether. One of the poems, "India", was in blank verse
and ran into thirty foolscap pages. "It tells about the burning heat of
the cities, Indian birds, the Ganges, a Hindu funeral, the juggler, the
snake-charmer, the fakir, and the farmer. The second part describes
the journey up to Ranikhet through the hills, the wild beasts, the Himalayas, Ranikhet, and all its curious life." He wrote this to Mary on the
evening of his last day, in sight of Nanda Devi and the other peaks.

They trotted out of Ranikhet on mountain ponies on the fifty mile
journey to the railway terminus at Katgodam. On the first day,
a Sunday, they were thirteen hours in the saddle and rode twenty-nine
miles to the village of Bhowali. Williams found this mode of travel
very tiring but vastly preferred it to marching. On the second day
they ambled another twenty miles, which completed their journey,
taking a new route to Katgodam by bridlepath. "The scenery was just
wonderful: the richest I've seen at all, I think, but the heat in the
pockets between the hills is tremendous. Fancy us strung up in belts,
bandoliers, haversacks crammed full of kit, water bottles, ammunition,
and rifles slung at our backs, overcoats, and our week's washing that
was too late to go with the advance baggage from Ranikhet. My
clothes, tunic, breeches, and everything were saturated with perspiration. The hills and forests were full of wonderful flowers, including
delphiniums, wonderful begonias, balsams and autumn anemones
(such as we have white) red and salmon-coloured. . . . The monkeys
sat on the hillsides in thousands . . . and cracked nuts and ate berries
as we went past." So they arrived at Katgodam where they slept
the night under canvas and where it rained from dusk until dawn.
The following morning they left by rail for Cawnpore and slept that
night in the train. At midday on 16th August, 1918, the artillerymen
joined their main battery again, which, since their sojourn in the hills,
they learned had been commanded by a new major of the slave-driving
variety. Alfred Williams remembered with a chuckle another member
of that species who had once thundered at Fermoy.

Williams found Cawnpore much cooler than he expected, cooler
than in fact it was at Katgodam in the hills. Nevertheless, many of
the soldiers who had remained in the city were suffering from prickly
heat rash, but he hoped, as the season was wearing on, that he would
avoid this. Within a few days of settling in, he had finished in the
rough a long poem called "The Monsoon" which he had begun at
Ranikhet, and had sent it to the *Empress* as Calcutta, the leading literary
review published in English in the east. And he heard that his poem
"On Seeing the Body of a Hindu Floating down the Ganges" had

appeared in the *Englishman*, the editor of which now sent him 22 rupees for poems which he had used earlier in the year.

The Ganges, swollen with melted snows, was two miles wide and like a great sea: the monsoons were creeping slowly on Cawnpore. There were frequent steady showers or frightening downpours and yet every day Williams was soaked through with perspiration. It was a miracle that he escaped malaria, for many of his comrades had already succumbed; daily he drank a quart each of beer, tea, and milk. Night after night there was tropical thunder and lightning and the frogs croaking from the river banks kept him awake. Then, early in September he saw his first real snake and was at last satisfied—"it stretched all across the road, about 14 feet".

Patiently they waited for the weather to change. Williams went on writing poetry. "At Cawnpore" appeared in the *Indian Daily Telegraph*, a paper widely read by the white fraternity in the city, another was printed in the *Cawnpore Civil Reciter*, but neither publication paid him anything for his work. He was steadily adding to his store of knowledge about India and was looking forward to the cooler weather so that he could continue with his prose work about its life and scenery. He was also anxious to amass such information as would be sufficient for him "to be able to write and speak a little about India when I come home".

On 12th September he was reminding Mary that it was a year since they had last met and, in order to cheer her up a little and to show her that he had not forgotten the occasion, he sent her a parcel containing four coconuts, two maize cobs, a brass ball, a brass butter dish, eight little clay figures of Indian servants, and a very fine beetle in a box ! She was undoubtedly amazed, and certainly cheered on receiving this collection. An early visit to the Industries' Exhibition, which was still open in Cawnpore, revealed that the screen he had set his heart on buying was still unsold. This time he succumbed and, as he had received a further seven and a half rupees from the *Englishman*, he bought the screen, and got Cook's branch office to store it for him for sixpence a month and arrange for its despatch to England as soon as restrictions were removed.

For the first time since he had been in India, Williams was earning enough money from his writings to provide him with adequate pocket money. Mary had regularly sent him money with which to buy extra food, but when on 14th September he received a guinea from her, the proceeds of an article of his which she had sold, he told her not to send him any more. It is strange that he did not send her any of his earnings to give her some pocket money for he knew how short she was. Mary was doing her best to sell the serial rights of *Boys of the Battery* to the *Wilts and Gloster Standard* for £25, though Alfred did not think the book was entirely suitable for serialization, as he said the chapters were too realistic.

He had always set his mind on visiting Agra to see the Taj Mahal, and when on 19th September, 1918, he applied for, and was granted, a few days' leave, he made for Agra immediately, where he arrived by mail train shortly after midnight. The only bed available for him was a charpoy in the open at the Soldiers' Home. Early next morning he set out in a tonga with a guide to explore the city, paying some rupees in advance for such luxury. He first drove to Akbar's Tomb, five and a half miles out, where he admired the famous Entrance Gate. Then he went back to Agra, over the Jumna River, to the tomb of Itimad-ad-Daula, who had been Akbar's prime minister, where he got into conversation with a party of Brahmins who had come from Madras to visit the shrine and with whom he discussed the merits of Indian architecture, Indian customs, and literature. Then he went back over the Jumna to the Taj Mahal itself where he stayed, spell-bound, for two hours, completely carried away by the matchless beauty of this world wonder. "I mounted to the top of one of the minarets, 160 feet— a magnificent view! The Taj is of white marble, the finest, and it is inlaid, within and without, with 29 kinds of precious stones. All the floral work . . . is of precious stones; beryl, onyx, agate, jasper, emeralds, carbuncle, malachite, turquoise, lapis lazuli, etc., etc. This is inlaid. I can't tell you how exquisite it is. There are millions of pounds worth of precious stones in the Taj. The building is like a beautiful lily, as pure, lovely, perfect, elegant, and just as simple as she. . . . St. Paul's and Westminster are mere ugly piles of dirty stone beside the Taj. They really are." For the remainder of the day he walked about in a dream. The artistry of India had spirited him away.

In the afternoon he visited Agra Fort which contained the royal palaces of former Mogul emperors and the finest mosque in India, with its gleaming marble and many inlaid gems. After a rest and his first meal since breakfast, he returned to see the Taj in full moonlight. Everything now had an added mystery and beauty and he did not go to his charpoy until the early hours of the following morning. This was a Sunday and before leaving for Cawnpore at midday, he stayed a further two hours admiring the Taj.

India was all wonder and loveliness to him. All was promising. Life was full of promise. Then the blow fell. On 5th October, a fatal letter arrived from Mary. The Marston Estate was to be put into the market. Dryden Cottage would be sold. They might have to seek another home. "Thank goodness we haven't any great possessions". So he comforted himself and the sorrowful, fearful Mary. "It is you and I who are rich and other people are poor, because they have no intellectual possessions, no real life about them. And we have many good friends everywhere."

Williams had always thought that the war would be a lengthy affair and never considered that the Germans would be defeated easily. In fact, he believed that when the enemy launched their spring offensive in France in 1918, they would gain much ground and eventually beat us in the land war. He considered that the British people were disillusioned and he had certainly lost his first fine enthusiasm for the war. He no longer wrote poems about it; India, nature, people, were now his themes. "It is all very well to talk about giving your life for your country" he wrote. "Newspapers feed us up with all kinds of tasty dishes, but they cannot deceive the soul's appetite, which is for something better than blood and death." Then he had heard from Robert Bridges in the summer, of the failure of the German offensive and of the large number of prisoners and quantity of equipment which the Allies had captured. Yet even the Laureate believed that the war would last for another eighteen months at least, if Germany was to be thoroughly defeated.

In spite of his comparative safety in India, the easy life, the opportunities for writing and observation, Williams was indeed weary of the war. Like many another, he wanted to get back home, to his wife and garden, to Wiltshire and the Downs, to stability and the future. "I must try hard to produce good literature and not allow myself to be stifled by the material things of life, not to *kick the bucket* spiritually, I mean", he wrote to Mary.

In October he heard that Bulgaria had surrendered and that Turkey had been defeated in Palestine, but he still believed that Germany would hold out on the western front for some time with stubbornness and determination. He told Fitzmaurice in a letter at this time that it was obvious that the war had been a very great blow to civilisation and had changed men's thoughts. "I feel that we shall gradually lapse back into the old ruts, not of carelessness and quarrelling but that we shall recognise that the ways of beauty, peace and naturalness are preferable to all that we have witnessed and lived through during the past four years."

As the autumn wore on there were further rumours that the Battery would be sent to Mesopotamia, and though Williams did not want to leave India until he had had a fill of her, he said he would very much like to see a new country. He was looking forward to wintering in the hills again at Roorkee, so that he could complete his Indian book, but while at Cawnpore he continued steadily with his writing — mainly poetry. Influenced somewhat by the work of Bridges, he had now written several new love poems, all imaginary in substance and artificial in feeling, which he thought would very well fit in with his love pieces in *Cor Cordium*, "in fact, I suppose they really belong to them. All love lyrics are a little artificial, however one might wish to delude oneself in the contrary belief". He had also been reading some of Tagore's poetry, whose work to him didn't seem so wonderful, read in India, because one could perceive the springs of his fancy and origins, which were the Hindu religion and philosophy. He had also finished reading a book of Indian history for which he had sent specially to Calcutta, as there was no such book in the Battery library. And in the first week of November he had finished five long chapters, packed with a wealth of material, of his Indian survey. He had also written another article called "Jerks", which was published in the *Indian Daily Telegraph*.

Since September, an influenza epidemic had been ravaging Cawnpore, and though Williams had had a slight attack, he had shaken it off by using plenty of quinine. The city was plagued with mosquitoes and sandflies and in October had a record high temperature of 102 degrees in the shade; 500 to 1,000 natives were dying daily in Cawnpore. "Every morning for a week before breakfast I have been down to the Ganges watching the arrival of corpses to go to the river. They bring them down in ox-waggons—scores of them—say a few prayers, pour ablutions over them, and float them out."

On 11th November news came of the Armistice, and a letter also from Zimmern which said that Duckworth had decided not to publish *Round the Cape to India*. Williams was excited by the former news and not very disappointed at the latter. He has described the scene at Cawnpore on Armistice Day. "We were all abed and I was asleep last Monday night, 11.30, when the officers came to the bungalows and routed us out. The bells were ringing in Cawnpore and we could hear the people cheering. There was a lively scene with the Battery I can tell you. We ran to the sheds and got out the guns at midnight and fired 31 rounds, sang and cheered and sang till we were hoarse. A little whisky was afterwards to be had and I secured several drops of rum, but there was very little drunkenness."

At South Marston on that day, Mary was ill with chest trouble and hardly went outside the house. She was still gardening every day, still doing work that was much too heavy for her, and trying to make ends meet on a separation allowance of 12/6 weekly. And at Manchester, the Poetical Society, on the eve of the Armistice, had been listening to a learned lecture by Dean Swayne, on "Alfred Williams and his Poetry".

From Cawnpore, Williams wrote to Mary, "If I were young I should never come back to settle in Marston, or perhaps in England at all, for its a poor narrow-minded place." And to Dowsing he wrote, "India, mysterious, the vast, the wonderful, and the (almost) incomprehensible, has imbued me with a different spirit. Its peculiar atmosphere suits me. Here is indeed poetry. Every tenth man you meet is a poet, and a darned great one, too. He writes nothing. But he is a poet. For poetry here is religion and religion is all poetry."

On the 1st December the Battery had left Cawnpore, and Williams was back at Roorkee and finding the nights so bitter that he needed four blankets and a greatcoat on his bed in order to keep warm. But he was glad to be back in the Hills.

CHAPTER SIXTEEN

FROM CAWNPORE TO BOMBAY

FOR some time he was so busy with soldiering at Roorkee that he was unable to do any writing. This distressed him, for he was of the belief that he would have finished the Indian book had he remained at Cawnpore; now that the war was over it was uncertain when it would get done. He was still wondering about what was going to happen to the Marston Estate and whether they would have to quit Dryden Cottage. "It will be a pity, in a sense, if we have to clear out after my planting all those nice trees. But that is always a speculative matter, and one's loss is another's gain, and if there were no sowers there would be no reapers." He had no idea what he was going to do on his return to England, but he thought they might manage to scrape along for a little while while he earned a few shillings with some of the material he already had on hand. Indeed, he looked into the future with some trepidation; it is certain that had he been younger, Williams would have remained in India and sent home for Mary to join him. There were many excellent jobs available for Europeans. Supervisors were needed in factories, and the Indian Forestry Department had lucrative vacancies for outdoor officers. "But my age is getting advanced, and, of course, I am booked for other activities: I mean that I have devoted myself to literature. But even out here, if I were staying, I should continue my literary work, as there is a fine field and a market for your productions." The *Empress* had already published the first part of *India*, and the *Englishman* had sent him more money and was asking for further poems. Williams' work was getting known in India and he had received several congratulatory letters from Europeans. In England, however, *Boys of the Battery* and *Round the Cape to India* were still going the rounds. Whatever happened to both, Williams wanted them correctly and well produced, with no "nasty paper and binding or too crowded print" so that people would get a wrong impression of him.

Two things brought him real comfort at this period. One was that there had been several references in the English press to *Life in a Railway Factory* which led him to declare: "I believed myself that it must have a good effect, since it's the only good book on factory life that we have in England written by a working man. And just fancy how cool and cruel Swindon people themselves were about it!" The other was that he had received a letter from the Poet Laureate containing this sentence: "I think I ought to address a poem to you—the subject matter will be characteristic". Robert Bridges greatly admired Williams' philosophy of life.

In January, 1919, Williams learned that Dryden Cottage had been bought by a South Marston farmer named Banwell, who had decided to live in it. Williams thought that the new owner might well make provision for him and Mary by offering them another house, especially as he was in the Services and away from home. His first intention was to look for a modest cottage in the neighbourhood, and then to get some light work somewhere, while he looked round for more permanent employment. Finally he decided that he would be beholden to no one but would build a house himself on the "Hook". He knew he might look forward to an army gratuity of about £15 and that this, with another £15 saved from journalism in India, would enable them to exist, at least, until the future had been decided. It is natural that he should at this time feel embittered and disillusioned. He wrote to Mary about war profiteers in this strain: "It's the usual thing again, for the fellows who have gone out to shoulder the rifle and bear hardships, and protect the homes of others, to have none of their own to come to in the end. I feel a bit mad, because these damn farmers have been fattening their bank accounts at our expense, and have been looking around to fix themselves up in comfort." Of the General Election which was then proceeding in England he wrote: "I cannot vote for the Labour Party myself though I admit the necessity for them, and the great good they do. But their policy of social salvation by pure little-mindedness in managing the big matters of state has no chance of being successful". Yet he heard with pleasure that Reuben George had been nominated as Labour candidate for Chippenham, and would have liked to see him returned as Member for his own, rather than his party's sake.

Although Williams was mostly unhappy and unsettled, he had now got on with his writing, and seventeen long chapters of *Indian Life and Scenery* had been composed by the middle of January. The whole book—nineteen chapters in all—was finished by the first week in February. The second part of the poem "India" had now appeared in the *Empress*. He thus had three books in manuscript, and regarding the publishing of them, he told Fitzmaurice that he believed his work was not being accepted because "I suffer from the lack of the ability to stir people, I am sure: it is my sluggishness or my undramaticness." John Bailey had already told Mary that though her husband's writings

*Alfred Williams at his
steam drop-hammer*

*Alfred Williams (in helmet) at his gun in India during the
World War 1914-18*

Alfred Williams and his wife

about India and Indian subjects were suitable for certain popular educational magazines, they would not be easy to place because their matter had, in one form or another, been reproduced before in other books. Williams did not perhaps realise that though the matter was new and original to him, it would not necessarily be so to readers of his writings.

During that worrying winter, the Battery did much arduous training, with constant firing practice in the jungle and in sight of the Himalayas. On one lengthy exercise there were two batteries using 30-pounders, a field battery, over a thousand men, a detachment from the R.H.A., and aeroplanes. Williams was thrilled with all this and has told of how they used to proceed by night to new positions, dig themselves in, camouflage the surrounding countryside, fire all the following day and then move to new sites. As there had been only two days' rain while Williams had been at Roorkee (the first rain in eighteen months) the sand where they manoeuvred was nearly a foot deep, and when the Battery was on the move, the horses couldn't be seen for dust.

Then the unexpected happened. All men aged 41 and over were notified that they were to stand by in readiness to leave for Bombay for embarkation to England. Rumour had it that they would be out of India within a week. Williams, highly delighted, passed on the joyful news to Mary, telling her to look out for another house, but not to leave Dryden Cottage before he had received the notice to quit. "If I am not satisfied with things at home, I shall shift clean out, as I'm not going to suffer the semi-starvation we put up with before the war. But I must come home and try and get rid of some of the writing I have, and the Folk Songs. I should not think of at once building a cottage . . . we must first see what we are going to get in the shape of wages. We'll let them see that there's life in the old *Gunner* yet." Had he been home, it is certain that he would have made an attempt to buy Dryden Cottage himself.

But hopes of leaving India were dashed. All previous orders were suddenly and inexplicably cancelled, and men of the 41 age group were now informed that they had been placed sixth on the list for demobilisation. Someone had also discovered that if an idiotic mistake had not been made in the Battery office, all the older men in the 68th Battery would have been embarked for England at the end of 1918.

By the end of March, Williams had left Roorkee and was back in the swelter of Cawnpore, where time hung heavily on his hands for some months; he was not in the mood for writing and the Battery had very little to do. One afternoon he was so bored that he hired a bicycle for eightpence and rode ten miles to see the Agricultural College and Museum on the other side of the city. Naturally he did a great deal of reading, being particularly interested in Mohammedan literature in translation, and eventually arriving at the opinion that it was Mohammed who had been responsible for giving to the world the works of Aristotle, Plato, Sallust, and other classical authors. Williams also re-read during these months the whole of the Old Testament, afterwards making the comment to Mary: "It's wonderful what a new point of view you get out here among Eastern peoples. Biblical times and things were nothing like we always thought them to have been, sitting in England."

He brooded a great deal, worrying about the future, angry and hurt in spirit that "I should have done my whack in the Army while others were earning great wages in safety." But all the same he was "pretty proud about it and I scorn the beggars who got fat while we've remained thin". He was anxious about Mary's health; she was suffering agonies again from rheumatism and found it very difficult to exist on her army allowance. He believed, too, that his reading public in England had forgotten him, and to Dowsing he confided: "In my town nobody reads me, and only a few read me in other places. In spite of very good reviews, very few people know either you or me, and I should be quite unknown if I stayed in India many more years." *Boys of the Battery* was still unpublished either in book form or as separate articles, and as for *Round the Cape to India*, Williams thought the only hope for it would be to entrust it to an established literary agent. "I am sure of my own literary qualities" he wrote to Mary, "and am not going to cry small on any account. Only, my writings are not sensational, and on this account don't appeal to novel readers."

But his work was still finding favour with editors in India. That March an article called "An Indian Idyll" appeared in the *Englishman*; another on "The Development of the Forge Hammer" was published in *Railways*. The latter article had an interesting sequel. An engineering firm in Calcutta, Saxby and Farmer, Ltd., wrote to the editor of *Railways* to ask him to approach Williams for detailed information regarding the American Hammer which had been brought to the Swindon factory by "Yankee" Watson many years before. Williams, flattered, sent the firm half a dozen sheets of descriptive matter and several rough sketches of the hammer, and later learned from the firm, when they gratefully acknowledged his assistance, that he would be able to find plenty of highly-paid work on the Indian and Mesopotamian railways.

In May, trouble broke out in Afghanistan and all demobilisation was suspended. The Battery was given instructions to stand by in readiness to proceed to Peshawar, and every day new drafts came in from the various depôts to fill up the strength. This was another disappointment to Williams, who had lately been informed that he would be leaving for embarkation on 6th May, but "we are soldiers and have to obey orders without demur". Knowing how the disheartening news would affect Mary, he sent her home a crocodile skin and a leopard skin "in order to cheer you up a bit", having been able to buy these because he had recently received payment for another article, "A Cawnpore Cameo" in the *Englishman*. As a matter of fact, that month, Williams developed a mania for buying skins for his friends and relatives, and expended on them nearly £12, the whole of this amount coming from his journalism.

But Alfred Williams did not leave with his Battery for the Afghan front, for in mid-May with the temperature 117 degrees in the shade, he fell ill with malaria and went into Cawnpore Hospital. He had barely recovered from this and was looking forward to a return to the hills, when an ulcer developed on the pupil of his left eye. For six weeks he was in agony and was nearly blind; the doctor pointed out that he had been straining his eyes for years—information which did not surprise Williams very much. He lay fretting in hospital, still worrying, still thinking of the future. He thought of the many letters written to him, which he could not possibly answer. He had nightmares about Mary, he grieved for his brother Henry who had died that spring, and ever he went over the same ground as to what he was going to do when he got back to England.

With treatment, the eye slowly improved, though it was thought that a permanent scar would be left on the pupil. In the third week in June he was transferred from Cawnpore to Kailana Hospital at Chakrata in the Himalayas, where the eye responded to specialist treatment, reduction of light, and the cooler atmosphere; and at Chakrata he was in the mountains again and could see once more their mists and snows. As soon as he had recovered, he was sent back to Roorkee again, where he found many strange faces. The heat was excessive, 120 degrees in the shade; "a damp, steamy heat", and most nights he slept outside his bungalow with nothing on but a thin khaki shirt. In the early mornings, thunder storms were frequent, so he had to pick up his bed and make a dash for it to his quarters when the rain came suddenly upon him. Then he had an attack of prickly heat and found it maddening. "The heat doesn't come out, and you can't see much on the skin, but the flesh seems to be burning clean off your bones: I walk about in agony with it for about two hours a day, especially in the morning. About 10.30 I go to the washhouse and sit under the cold water for about 20 minutes. This cools the temperature, and I am some hours before I get as warm again, as I keep out of the sun. But you have to be rubbing and scratching yourself all the time."

The eye worsened. Poor miserable Williams was unable to do any reading or writing and the camp doctor expressly forbade him to do anything else but eat his food. But he soon disobeyed orders and wrote several letters to Mary, using his right eye only. Arrangements were quickly made for him to go back into the Hills.

And on 15th July he was at Chakrata for the second time, where he was told he would have to remain for at least a month. It was while he was here that the signing of the Peace Treaty was celebrated. Every patient in Kailana Hospital was given a bottle of stout, a cake, and some apples; in the evening, Williams, in company with three other Wiltshiremen, watched a football match.

The eye was carefully covered up and padded with cotton wool, but was slower this time to improve. Though he could not see them, Williams was told that pink roses were growing in wild profusion on the slopes behind the hospital; the cuckoo and thrush sang daily, and he pined more desperately than ever for home. By the beginning of August, the eye was just strong enough for him to do a little reading and writing. It had once been suggested to him by the editor of *The Globe*, in 1916, that he should write a novel with a railway background, making it largely autobiographical. At the time, Williams had had no opportunity and very little interest to deal with this matter, but now at Chakrata, as the eye improved, he thought about the idea again and made a rough sketch of a probable plot. That was as far, however, as the novel went. He was later to return to it. Another article appeared in *Railways*, this time on "Stamping", and for this he received 25 rupees, with which he bought some ten pounds of Lipton's very special Orange Pekoe tea and had it sent home to Mary. He had again heard from Bailey, who, having read the poem "India", expressed the view that much of it was reminiscent of Milton and Cowper.

Williams was discharged from hospital in the first week of August and ordered to report at the railway junction at Saharanpur. Here he remained for three days only, but during this time he discovered that there was a small railway factory near the station, managed by an Englishman; Williams obtained permission to tour the works. He showed the manager his articles on stamping and the latter was so impressed with them and with Williams' all-round knowledge of railway work that he told him he was mad not to offer his services to some of the railway concerns in India, many of whom would be willing to pay him a thousand rupees a month. Williams thought seriously again about remaining in India, but finally decided against doing so. He wrote to Mary in this wise: "I've got to choose between two things, and I think, upon consideration, that it will be best to try and 'carry on' at home in a congenial climate, and not try to be grabbing, and in so doing, to lose my literary values, and, perhaps, shorten my days. If it wasn't for my books, I'd stay in India and have you out with me;

but I mustn't betray myself now and disappoint all my supporters. And India might not suit you, at least, Calcutta would not." It is interesting to conjecture what would have been the fate of Alfred and Mary Williams had they settled in India.

After Saharanpur, a day or two at Muttra, and then, on 25th August, Williams was back in Cawnpore. In spite of the increasing heat, he was feeling much fitter and more settled in his mind. The food was excellent—the best since his Irish days—and duties were light. For three hours each evening he strolled about the Cawnpore streets as a garrison policeman, being free during the whole of the day time. Eagerly he renewed his acquaintance with the Ganges and the crocodiles.

His stay at Cawnpore was a short one, for, early in September, after another rumour that he was to be drafted to Mesopotamia, he left for Roorkee. On the way up into the hills he spent one morning in Delhi, where he ascended one of the minarets of the great Jumna mosque, being duly impressed with the view of the surrounding countryside from it; and on arriving at Roorkee he was greeted with the glad news that he was to be discharged in about six weeks' time. As his demobilisation now seemed a certainty, he wrote to Mary to tell her to get in a stock of faggots and to kill the "fatted pig" on his return. There was also a letter from England from Kyle asking him to make a selection of his Indian poems for publication when he got back.

When on 12th September Williams was informed that he was definitely going to Calcutta in preparation for embarkation from Bombay, he applied for, and was granted, three weeks' leave with free railway travel anywhere in India. He was in his element. There now began a succession of breathless sightseeing tours. He crowded all he possibly could into his last weeks on eastern soil. From Roorkee he travelled to Lucknow where he spent a day, then through the whole of one night to Benares, where he had another long day. By the 19th he had got as far as Calcutta and was in residence at the Y.M.C.A. The whirlwind tourist did not rest. A demon drove him out to explore the lordly streets and squares of Calcutta, the parks and the gardens. He went for a sail on the Hooghly, "like the Mersey at Liverpool", stood in admiration under the largest tree in the world in the Botanical Gardens, spent a lazy evening at the Zoo, and visited the Kalighat to see the sacrifice of goats. The greatest pleasure of all, however, was when, in Calcutta, "I went to an Indian Theatre: didn't tell anybody I was going. Four miles from where I was staying. We went in at 8 p.m. and came out at 4.10 a.m. the following morning. This is how the Indians do it. There were three plays altogether, Bengalee plays. It was a special night, a Benefit night, and two famous Bengalee retired actors were giving their services. I got in at half price in the Dress Circle (2 rupees)—I was the only European there. But the people

were very civil and courteous. And, by criky, the plays were famous.
The scenery was excellent, the acting quite great, and the singing and
dancing by the chorus of Bengalee girls charming in the extreme . . .
I should never have stayed there for eight hours wet through with
sweat if I had not been pleased with the plays." He was challenged
by a military policeman while entering the theatre and advised to turn
back because he would be in danger of his life. Nevertheless, during
the performance, Williams talked with the Hindus around him who
gladly and willingly told him all about the plays and the general proceedings. After leaving the theatre he managed to find a Chinaman
with a rickshaw who ran him back to the Y.M.C.A. which he reached
at five o'clock. It had indeed been a night out. When he opened the
newspapers the next day, it was to read that a man had been murdered
just outside the theatre during the performance. But it had all been
a most unforgettable experience and Williams was as impressed as he
had been at Agra.

From Calcutta he made a twelve-hour journey by the Madras Mail
to Puri, rushing all the while through myriads of lotus blooms, forest
and jungle, through leagues of rice and wheat fields. At Puri he bathed
in the sea, climbed the largest minaret in the city at sunset, visited the
Juggernaut, the Lord of the Earth, and then returned to Roorkee,
via Calcutta, to be demobilised. From Calcutta he sent Mary four
pounds of China tea, with the words: "I've had about all I want of
India and now I hope to come home to you and sleep without fans,
punkas, or mosquitoes." He said goodbye to Roorkee on 2nd October,
stayed one more day in Delhi, and then after a journey of four days and
nights through magnificent Bengal scenery, he arrived, one of 2,500
men, at Deolali Camp, near Bombay. From the camp he could see
hills—the Western Ghats. And he thought of the Downs, to
whose bosom he knew he was returning, at least with faith, to scratch
out a meagre livelihood again. He thought of the Himalayas, too.
He sailed from Bombay in *The Huntsgreen* on 10th October, 1919; and
his very last act before so doing was to send Mary a pound of tea.

CHAPTER SEVENTEEN

HOME AGAIN

*T*HE *HUNTSGREEN*, a small boat, was badly overcrowded,
having 2,500 troops on board. Rations were poor and short;
there was never any sugar. Williams, with several others, had a touch
of malaria in the Red Sea, and all were suffering from lack of sleep.
On 31st October they were in the Gulf of the Lion after a rough passage

through the Mediterranean. All were shivering and shaking with cold. They landed at Marseilles where Williams lost all his kit but his haversack; luckily he had posted his MSS. and his gratuity money, about £21, home. There followed a three-day journey across France to Boulogne; Williams wanted to visit Paris, but was not allowed to break his journey. He reached Plymouth on Armistice Day, where he was demobilised, and on the following day he was with Mary in Dryden Cottage. They had under £40 to their name. When he had enlisted, he had been placed in Category C (home service only), but on demobilisation the doctor said that he was fit enough for Category A (active service abroad). It is probable that the military authorities thought that Williams might make a claim for a disability pension and had placed him in a higher category than may have actually been justified, but it is clear that all things considered, he had gained in health and his general physique improved.

He took some time to acclimatise, and the cold, dull weather towards the end of 1919 depressed him and made him sigh for the light and life of India. He could not settle down to anything very positive or definite. He naturally found many changes in South Marston and in England. He had little sympathy with the spirit of the purely political world to which he had returned; every man seemed to be out for his own ends and to do as little work as possible. To him just then, England appeared to be the home of selfish people, full of sham and silly conventions and taboos; he confessed to Dowsing in December that he had been happier among the Hindus and Mohammedans than he was now with people who were so complacent and self-sufficient "I long to *see*, and still to *see*, and to feel new influences. Money I don't care a scrap for; the ocean, strange countries, and men appeal to me. Well! this will soon appear to be a Jeremiad, but I'm not whining at all. Thank the Lord! I've a decent appetite, a strong pair of boots, and a new suit presented me by the War Office! What more should I need? Let's carry on with patience, and bad luck to any who would presume to walk upon our prostrate bodies". Alfred Williams was indeed in the dog days.

In February, 1920, after reading a book on spiritualism he wrote to Henry Byett, "If we are going to believe all the horrid nonsense going about at the present time, then Hinduism is true, demons are true things: Animism (demon worship and spirit worship) is true, witchcraft is true, and all the devils and hells ever imagined are probable. I felt this while I was in India. But there! It's the public temper at present. It's strange, I confess. But Mohammed was strange, and Gautama, and thousands of them. But we can't believe them all, no matter how we'd like to." Later in the month he talked to Byett about Christianity, and said he did not consider the claim of Christ to be God as well as man, a strong one—like Buddha he claimed too much—though he certainly looked upon Christ as a model for all men. In short, Williams considered Jesus the Christ from the unitarian viewpoint. Such then was Alfred Williams' mind; he had changed a great deal in his outlook.

In the midst of his worries he heard from Kyle, who said he was still anxious to publish a selection of his poems—a book of about 160 pages —and to include some of the new ones which he had written while on active service. Williams was keen for this project to go forward, for he had far too much unpublished work by him, including the folk songs which he wanted to dispose of as soon as possible, but "I haven't a pound to deposit on the scheme: I should have to do it chiefly by subscriptions".

He also realised with a pang that since he had been in the army he had more or less been forgotten as a writer in England; a new book would re-establish his claim as a poet worth reading. So, early in the new year, he began to think of some general pattern for the proposed *Selected Poems*. He planned that the book should have seven definite sections and should contain the best of his early poems, sonnets and translations, with selections from his love, nature, and Indian poems. Bailey approved of the form of the book and the choice of poems and promised to write an Introduction; Bridges said he would be honoured to accept the dedication. Kyle was willing to publish without a deposit, but Williams guaranteed to sell 250 copies at five shillings per copy. The selection was duly made and soon in Kyle's hands. Williams was excited about the whole business and told Fitzmaurice that "it may be the most important book of verse I have done, since upon it will rest my claim to be a poet in the least degree. I am not disheartened at the prospective result; even if reviewers should snuff me out like a candle, I would not on that account shed tears, or behave indecently."

In January, Williams gave a lecture on "India" in Swindon. The Mayor, who was Chairman, gave him an official welcome home, and told the audience how proud the townsfolk were to have so great an author and poet among them. After the lecture, Williams walked home with Byett and told him that less than a dozen copies of *Life in a Railway Factory* had been sold in Swindon though the book had now been on sale for six years.

His small capital was dwindling. Nothing was coming in from the garden yet awhile. Williams wrote several descriptive articles on India and one very outspoken one called "Why I am not a Labourite" in which he made a declaration of personal policy. Henry Byett typed these articles for him and they were submitted to the *Daily Mail*, but none were accepted. Williams just could not write sensationally. So journalism brought him in nothing. He revised *Indian Life and Scenery*; renamed it *'Mid Palm and Pine*, included some excellent photographs and sent it to Duckworth who had to refuse to publish because, owing to the high cost of production, no book would be profitable to market unless it could immediately sell 2,000 copies.

Slowly, embitterment and disillusionment ate into him. Was he to have *no* rewards ? He was often unwell and frequently catching cold. Mary suffered all that winter from rheumatism. They were living on about ten shillings a week, blessing the stores of tea which they had. And over them there hung like a pall the shadow of their impending departure from the cottage that had been their home for nearly 20 years.

In March, 1920, their financial position was becoming so desperate that Alfred was forced to ask Fitzmaurice and Bailey to support an application for a grant from the Royal Literary Fund. In his letter to Fitzmaurice he said that, though he was grateful for all that had been done for him by his friends in the past and though he tried to accept all that happened to him with calm and philosophy, "Yet I am driven to confess that one requires to exercise self-control this Easter-time: and it is difficult to induce oneself to believe that one is comfortable and happy beneath these sullen skies, and amid this chilling atmosphere at present embracing our island. Still, the countryside is becoming very fresh and green and the fields and hills are sweet and the sun is pleased to look down upon us out of the cloudy heights."

Fitzmaurice was much moved by this letter and backed the application strongly, which was all to the good, as the Fund had many pressing calls on it at the end of the war. Williams was granted £20, which he thought would see them through the summer, when he would have garden produce to sell. He had got down to gardening in earnest and was digging and seeding three large pieces of land, Mary giving him the usual very practical assistance. But it was hard graft and once again he toyed with the idea of emigrating. It was another parting of the ways—finally he decided to remain in England and go on with his writing. He was helped in this decision by the Laureate whom he met at Oxford and with whom he discussed Asiatic poets, and his own writings. Bridges was interested and encouraging and said he would do all he possibly could for Williams.

Then at the height of the planting season, the left eye began to trouble him again and he had to go for treatment as an out-patient at the Bath Military Hospital. By now his health had begun to deteriorate seriously; he was not half the man he had been when he had sailed from Bombay six months before. The eye trouble was a most unfortunate and ill-timed set-back for he had recently been offered by a small Bristol publisher some proof reading which reluctantly he had to refuse. For weeks he travelled up and down to Bath, during which period he could do neither reading, writing, nor gardening, for he suffered continually from neuralgia in both eyes. The specialist told him that the left eye would not be better for a year, and blamed its general condition to India and Williams' low bodily health. Williams himself at one time thought that his eye had a touch of some tropical disease which he might have caught while in Cawnpore Hospital. He had two pairs of glasses but neither were entirely satisfactory for he could not work with them for any length of time. Henry Byett advised him to apply for a disability pension, which he did in June, but it was not granted, though there was a possibility he might later be granted eight shillings weekly for a limited period. All that summer, neuralgia continued, and he was never without a cold, either in his ears, eyes or teeth. He found it difficult to get about in bright weather. He just could not endure arduous physical labour, but he tried his best to do some gardening, with Mary helping him valiantly. On 23rd June he managed to scrawl to Fitzmaurice: "I am a rather successful gardener, but one of the worst of *sellers*; commercialism is what in my heart I absolutely detest, yet one must suffer the taint if one is to live in the present time. I am frequently told that literature also is commercial, but . . . there is a vast difference between receiving a few pounds in royalties for intellectual work, and bickering and grasping over an additional halfpenny a pound for potatoes and peas; it's quite demoralising."

One Sunday in June, Henry Byett came to see him in order to discover how he was faring. In the evening they went together to the Parish Church. After the service, Williams told Byett that he felt it was hypocritical for him to attend because he could not say the creed sincerely. His idea of true religion embraced the world as a family, goodness of life, and purity of purpose. He continued, "I really have a sincere regard for religion, and I consider that the church is, and must be, a permanent institution, if it is not something more than this. I make no narrow definition here, however, since I would allow equal liberty to those professing other faiths all over the world. That there is a wide difference of belief and doctrine is immaterial, for there is no substantial distinction as to the object in view or goal to be reached."

Williams now learned that Banwell had decided to convert Dryden Cottage and its neighbour into one large dwelling place. He was thankful that the Rents' Restriction Act protected him from being evicted until he had other suitable accommodation, for there was an acute shortage of houses in the district. He had now decided that when the time was ripe he would build his own house and with his own hands —on the "Hook".

That summer, every day was a struggle for existence. There was little money coming in either from royalties or garden. Henry Byett, who had visited the couple on several occasions and had observed their sad condition, was so worried that, feeling it to be his responsibility' unbeknown to Williams who would have been furious, he wrote to Zimmern and frankly told him the position, and of the book Williams had in MS. Byett knew how independent Williams was and how difficult it was to help him better than any man living. He suggested that the fund which was to have been raised before the war to purchase an annuity for Williams might be re-opened, or another effort made to obtain a Civil List Pension. Byett's letter was prophetic with its sentence: "Of course he will die in want, like others of his kind before. He asks for nothing else, but it's a lasting shame if want is allowed to hasten that end, displaying lack of gratitude from his fellows for all his work, and robbing posterity of the benefit of what more he might have written."

Zimmern, who was in Paris, was much moved by this appeal. When he replied to Henry Byett he said, "I am not hopeful that anything can be effected through publishers. Paper is appallingly dear just now, and publishers consequently timider than ever. The Civil List is also not hopeful. I got a promise from Mr. Asquith in 1914 that £150 would be given if enough was raised privately to make a decent annuity; but for the two lives this would have to be a large amount. I'm going down to Wales in a day or two to spend the summer studying. I hope to be able to invite Mr. and Mrs. Williams for a short stay if I can get him to accept the railway fare. . . . I'm quite determined to save him for English literature."

Then in July, Williams heard from John Bailey who had been informed by Fitzmaurice of the eye trouble, that he regretted the smallness of the Royal Literary Fund Grant. Accordingly, he had approached a few of his friends and told them about his difficulties. Bailey enclosed £15 with a promise of a further £10 to come. "I have had no difficulty whatever in raising the money, which is a great proof of how much people respect you. Those who have subscribed at present to my little appeal for you are Professor W. P. Kerr, Professor of Poetry at Oxford, Dr. Bridges, Mr. Andrew Bradley, former Professor of Poetry, Mr. Edmund Gosse, Mr. Bruce Richmond and the Editor of *The Times Litt. Supp.*" Bailey constructively suggested that Williams ought to go in for gardening on a large enough scale to earn money and yet leave himself sufficient time for reading and writing. He also therein added the hint that Williams might write a series of imaginary letters to working men, of his experiences in India, his views on the Indian, Irish and Labour problems, and the general political outlook. The money came as a godsend. Immediate embarrassments were avoided. Since June, too, Williams had been Clerk and Assistant Overseer to the South Marston Parish Council at a salary of £30 a year. His main duty was to collect some £6,000 in local rates, and there was considerable clerical work attached to the posts.

His duties for the Parish Council, the gardening, and the hours when he was unable to do anything because of further damaging his eyesight, left him with no time for writing either prose or poetry, or for much private reading and study. What was worse, the inspiration for these did not come so often or so easily. "I *felt* more strongly when I was at the factory, and wrote my best things then" he confided in Dowsing. "The work was obnoxious, but the daily release gave me opportunity. It was the contrast and I always *felt intensely* at the weekend. And you have the wherewithal to live and keep your family. Now I have practically nothing. That book of mine (*Railway Factory*) helped to get the shorter hours for factories. My old shed runs four days a week, and the men get double and treble the pay; but if I would go back they would not take me. *I'm too old* ! ! And I have nothing now, and am forced to plant potatoes, dig and sell them. You'd find that a much meaner business than working in a factory. I've had a good trial now, and I often wish I was back at the forge, as usual. If I were to voice my real sentiments I should say, 'damn the land ! !' It's good enough for . . . those without a *spirit*, but to me it's little less than agony. . . . I am struggling through this summer somehow, but I hope I may get a little chance next year. . . . I haven't written a poem since 1918, and I don't think I shall do anything more yet. . . . There's no advantage in shutting one's eyes to the fact that people don't care anything for small poets now". Dowsing had suggested that he and Williams might publish a joint book of poems, but the latter was not keen to do this for he doubted whether such a work would succeed unless it were well financed beforehand.

Zimmern kept his promise and invited Alfred and Mary Williams to holiday with him in Wales. Both were glad to accept the offer, which came as a pleasant surprise, though neither knew that their old friend, Henry Byett, had been responsible for its having been made. On the day before the couple started, Williams got ready five cwt. of potatoes for a customer in Swindon and worked well into the early hours of the morning on business connected with his Overseership. The holiday was spent in August at Maentrog near Penrhyndeudraeth, with Zimmern and other guests. One day they motored to Caernarvon, around Snowdon, climbed Moelwyn, and then continued by way of Barmouth and Dolgelly, to Machynlleth, and Williams was in the hills again and thinking of Ranikhet. Zimmern discussed Williams' affairs in detail and made several suggestions as to finance. Williams told him among other things that he had decided to build his own house.

The couple returned to Wiltshire, refreshed in body and spirit, but still beset by the same problems of how to exact a livelihood and where to live. Back home in Dryden Cottage, Williams' eyesight began to fail again. In desperation he turned for advice and help to Fitzmaurice, and as of old, Fitzmaurice was there and ready with assistance; he offered to place Williams under the care of his own oculist, Dr. Burden Cooper. The offer was gladly accepted and Williams immediately consulted the specialist who, to his surprise, favourably reported on the eye and said that with the right lenses there would be no permanent disability. He thought that Williams had been treated badly in the matter of a service pension. In September the new spectacles had arrived and Williams' sight began to make rapid improvement. He was able, in thanking Fitzmaurice, to tell him that he was feeling happier and more settled within himself and was continuing his study of Hinduism.

That autumn was an eventful one. By October, Alfred Williams had decided to make a start with the building of his new house on that portion of the "Hook" meadow which he had inherited from his mother. He had by him some £30—the whole of his capital. An intimate friend offered to loan him a further £100, free of interest, and for as long as he needed it. On October 10th he was well on with his preparations and wrote to Fitzmaurice: "I have 60 perch of land, a well of water, and about £30 worth of fruit trees upon it, and it seemed to me that with a little courage I might build myself a small cottage upon the holding and be secure. I bought an old stone cottage and have taken it down; there are about 50 tons of good stone. It only cost me £12. I am buying very good timber from Chiseldon Camp and I have a very good man acting for me as carpenter and joiner, and have also secured the services of a local stonemason. I shall do the labouring myself. We shall qualify for the Government subsidy, we hope (£240) with the necessary 780 feet of floor space, and I imagine that at the end of operations I shall owe no more than £200, perhaps less. I shall not begin my walls until the spring." Williams had also bought timber from the aerodrome at Minchinhampton which was being dismantled. He believed that once his cottage was built he would be able to wrest a living from the land.

The "old stone cottage" which he had bought for its stone was none other than the ruins of Mark Titcombe's cottage situated on a piece of land fronting the road "at the point where the field path from Stratton Church merges on to the road". All that autumn and then on into the winter, Alfred and Mary Williams spent some time every day, whatever the weather, pulling down the ruins of the old gentleman's cottage by hand. They then hauled away in handcarts much of the stone and mortar to the "Hook", slaving like navvies until nothing remained of the ruins. Once on the "Hook", every stone was graded and piled in readiness for the building in the spring. The price of new building material, both brick and timber, at this time was quite prohibitive.

On 15th December, Williams lectured on "The Religions of India" at the Swindon Mechanics' Institute, thus making his début on the popular lecture platform. Henry Byett, by whose efforts Williams had received the engagement, has described the occasion.

"The evening of the lecture duly arrived. The lecturer was in fine form, voice and diction but that marked the limit of the commendatory features. The subject was not interesting to the majority of the audience, and, although that was not the lecturer's fault, the misfortune was his (and the audience's). . . . The lecturer stood upright away from the reader's desk, perfectly erect as though on a parade ground, except that his hands were plunged into the pockets of his tightly-buttoned jacket, looking the picture of discomfort—a feeling which infected his audience. To crown it all, he committed the unpardonable offence of continuing his lecture for over an hour. The audience were bored; they fidgeted, coughed, shuffled their feet, perused their programmes. Many left the hall, but still he went on. At length he thought the audience had had sufficient, and ceased. . . . I imagine I was the most uncomfortable person in the room. I felt much as a fond mother listening to her son performing the feat which has to determine his whole future. . . . It was 'Good-bye' to any future chance of six guineas (the fee they paid) while he so badly needed it. The relief was great when the lecture ended. The audience applauded, partly in thankfulness for its conclusion, and partly from sympathy with the lecturer. Many had attended because he was a local man, because of the fame which had come to him, and out of curiosity to see such a wonderful genius. I was greatly disappointed. That which I hoped would increase his popularity, and add to his admirers, had failed, and worse."

Williams too was disappointed at his failure and knew he would never be asked to lecture in Swindon again. But he was not downcast, for he had hope for the future burning within him at last. He was building again; not this time in words, nor in speeches, but in his eyes was growing the picture of his own Taj Mahal, his poem in stone, a new testament of faith flowering in beauty in the lap of Liddington and Barbury.

CHAPTER EIGHTEEN

BUILDING

NEAR the village stood some derelict locks of the disused Wilt-shire and Berkshire canal whose weed-thick and sluggish waters had first fascinated Alfred Williams as a boy, when he had left school to work at Longleaze Farm. He had not thought in *those* far-off days that a time would come when he would eye the bricks of the locks with very practical design. He enquired of the owners of the canal as to whether they were willing to dispose of the entire lock walls as they stood. They agreed and he bought them there and then. As soon as Mark's Cottage had been finally demolished, Alfred and Mary began work in similar manner on the canal locks. This venture entailed, to begin with, a daily journey of about two miles from Dryden Cottage up to the main road. Then they spent long and weary hours pulling down the lock walls. The bricks were loaded on to a handcart and painfully pushed back along the bye-road to the "Hook". On good days they were able to make about four return journeys, but they eventually had to make use of a local haulier.

So this undaunted couple continued, oblivious to the world, intent on their aim. While dismantling the cottage they had, on moonlit nights, worked until nearly midnight. They followed the same plan of campaign at the locks. There now followed a succession of un-comfortable and exhausting days when, back on the building site, they chipped the old mortar from the bricks, sorted and stacked them, and pounded and screened the mortar to make rubble. Night after night they retired to bed so physically weary, so bruised and so stiff that they were unable to sleep. Their hands and wrists were cut and galled, their nails broken and bleeding, their feet swollen and tender. The fine dust from the mortar hung in their clothing and set up irritation in Alfred's weak eye. For a whole month Mary worked with a festered forefinger.

By the end of the year they had carted to the "Hook" 120 tons of stone, 20 loads of sand, and 3,000 bricks. A few weeks later, when the journeys to the canal had been completed, they had piled up a further 12,000 bricks and a dozen cartloads of broken mortar. Alfred estimated that, in this manner, they had saved themselves about £170.

They were now given notice to quit Dryden Cottage by Christmas Day, but it was impossible for them to make the move. They stayed, but the landlord's gesture greatly angered and hurt them.

All through the biting months of that downland winter they went on steadily with their preparations. The villagers eyed the venture with mixed feelings, and not without some amusement, but the children used to help them with their mortar-chipping and brick stacking. Williams then thought of raising a mortgage on his portion of the "Hook", but this happily proved unnecessary for Fitzmaurice offered to give him £200 towards the building expenses. They were overwhelmed by such munificence, and on the 4th January, 1921, having heard from Lloyd's Bank in Swindon that this sum had already been placed to his credit, Williams wrote, "It may be that in years to come I shall sit secure in my cottage and think with gratitude of the pleasant time and your lordship's favour. I shall feel more happy and free when I have my own house, though I take no delight in the mere possession of anything. . . . I am sometimes led to wonder why I should take the trouble to build me a house, but I suppose that my more practical or 'conditioned' self prevails over the unpractical or 'unconditioned'. One may doubt the truth of this but there is an unparalleled pleasure in the quest of Reality. And clearly to have conceived that 'majestic tranquillity of the soul' of the authors of the Upanishads is in a great degree to have attained it." In reply to these sentiments, Fitzmaurice suggested that he should come over to South Marston to see the beginnings of the cottage, but Williams, wishing to save the aged man such a journey, went over to Bradford-on-Avon to see and thank him personally for his benevolence.

On the 16th January Williams informed Henry Byett, "We were brick hauling all last week; tomorrow we must begin the cleaning of the last 5,000. Laus Deo! It is a tiresome and tedious business; the mud has been terrible. But we keep steadily on."

In February, on days when the weather was propitious, Williams began digging the foundations; sometime in March these were finished. The "Hook" was scarred and water-logged. Because he knew that many houses in the Marston district were in danger of collapse and had had to be supported by massive buttresses, Williams shovelled in nearly 20 tons of concrete into the foundations. He might have been building a church. It was while doing these excavations that he laid in a barrel of strong beer, a daily drink of which seemed to keep him going.

On the March quarter day Williams resigned his office of Assistant Overseer to the Parish Council. Nine months' experience as a collector of rates had been quite sufficient to convince him that such work was not for him; on many occasions he had had to make repeated calls on people who had not paid their dues and whom he knew were quite unable to do so. He loathed dunning the poor; the whole business was repugnant to him. In addition, though the work took up far too much of his now very valuable and limited time, the pay, about twelve shillings weekly, was hardly worth considering.

Ranikhet: in embryo, 1920

Ranikhet, South Marston

Derelict lock

The village school, South Marston

He knew, too, that if he continued in office it would be necessary for him to employ another man to do the labouring on the house.

Freed of his overseership, Williams now tackled his house problems, one by one, with redoubled energy of body and spirit. The Ministry of Health had informed him that it would be willing to pay him the £240 subsidy, but suggested that he might have moved into a Council house. Williams pointed out to the Ministry that, since he was in receipt of no regular income, it would have been impossible for him to pay rent and rates. On the 3rd April, 1921, the walls were started. The local stonemason whom Williams had had in mind appeared on the scene, being engaged to do all the expert masoning. This man was the 72 year old Jesse Head, formerly employed in the Swindon railway works. He was an able craftsman but very obstinate, and there was friction between him and Williams from the beginning of their contract. The old man praised the foundations, but insisted on being allowed to do the remainder of the work in his own way, threatening on several occasions to resign if anyone interfered. Not wishing to lose him, Williams gave him a free hand and consented to act as a labourer under his direction, but when the opportunity arose, and the mason was absent, Williams altered parts of the building to suit himself. Whether Head observed what had been done is not known; anyway he made no comment.

During the whole period, Jesse Head was paid at the full Trade Union rate of 1/2 per hour, with a bonus of 1d. per hour when the work was completed. Over and over again he insisted that he was a mason and only a mason, even requiring Williams to climb up on the scaffolding to empty a bucket of mortar which had been carried up before, and was actually standing by his side. As had been his intention, Williams did the whole of the labouring and serving, built up the inner courses, and with Mary's help mixed every bit of mortar by hand.

The walls were eighteen inches thick from the floor to the wall plates, except at the rear of the house where the thickness, in order to reduce the number of bricks required, was reduced to fourteen inches. But Jesse Head said he would down tools there and then unless all the walls were eighteen inches thick. There was a scene, and some hard words were said on either side, but in the end the mason gained his point. In consequence, Alfred and Mary had to make for the disused canal lock again, where they dismantled a further section of the walls, and, during May, carted back a further 2,000 bricks to be cleaned and graded.

During building operations the pair had many visitors, most of whom were not welcome. One day two exquisitely dressed ladies drove up to the "Hook" in a magnificent limousine, and enquired of a bystander where they might find Alfred Williams the poet. The bystander happened to be "Lou" Robins who, with his wife, had tricycled out from Swindon to give the couple what help they could. Alfred and Mary were actually standing quite near, though hidden by the stonework of one of the walls, then about seven feet high; they were laboriously mixing mortar. Overhearing the enquiry, both quietly ceased shovelling and hid in another part of the building. No wonder, for Alfred was collarless and was wearing a mortar-plastered coat and trousers, worn and torn at elbows and knees, and mortar-splashed boots out at the toes. Mary was equally disreputable. Both were dog tired. "Lou", knowing that they were in no mood for such fine company, directed the two ladies to Dryden Cottage, a few yards away. The chauffeur backed the car. Several minutes later the ladies returned to say that they had knocked, but in vain. So away they drove, saying how sorry they were that they had not been able to meet Mr. Alfred Williams "the poet". It was only then that Mr. and Mrs. Alfred Williams, "the mortar mixers", emerged from their hiding place, and with thanks to "Lou", went on with their work.

Clothes, in fact, became a pressing problem, and it seemed at one time that they would have to wear their best clothes to work in. But by means of a typical ruse, Henry Byett got Alfred to accept a second-hand suit. Knowing how independent he was, he told him that having been recently discharged from the army as unfit for further military service, he had been fitted out with a suit of civilian clothing. As he already had his pre-war clothing, the army suit was therefore spare, and as it was also too large for him, but would certainly fit Alfred Williams, it would be admirable for the rough kind of work he was then doing. Further, he would be doing him a kindness by accepting it, as he did not wish to store it and, as the suit had cost him nothing, he could accept no payment for it. The ruse succeeded. Williams accepted the suit with the words, "If you do not care for the suit, I will indeed gladly discover my respect for you, accept, acknowledge, be pleased with, and triumphantly wear the garments. It may be in a more honourable capacity than as a mixer of common sand, mortar, cement, or contemptible earth and ashes; for I am getting in need of a second suit, and that would be quite nice for me for many occasions."

By 5th June, the house was joist high. Nearly 50 tons of mortar had already been used, much of which contained road scrapings which Alfred had collected in his wheelbarrow from the surrounding lanes. Whole days, thirteen hours at a stretch, were spent in stone-cutting. The higher the walls got the more strenuous were his exertions, but he told Fitzmaurice that he was undaunted when he reflected on his good fortune in the possession of such true and honourable friends. That summer a heat wave lay over the district and on the 10th July

Williams wrote to Henry Byett, "My, this is some hot weather! The heat is nothing to me, for it's only warm, really, but the drought! Oh dear, I don't know whatever to do for water, and we are all the same. By the end of July, if my mate lasts out—he's rather fagged of late—I ought to finish the walls. Thank God! It has been real slavery, and no mistake; but I'm cheerful at the end—or not the end yet, but hope to be soon. Well, the 'jobbing' after the walls, won't be so bad. . . . We are very tired, for we work early and late."

Hour after hour, day after day, the couple slogged on, hardly stopping for meals, in a determined and combined effort to get the outside work finished before the coming on of the winter. Many a morning they started at daybreak, long before Jesse had arrived, worked all day and then continued into the moonlight, so that on the following day the mason should not be kept waiting for bricks or mortar. Henry Byett speaks of leaving them at 9.30 p.m., quite worn out, but still desperately and madly mixing mortar for the next morning. They hated the smell, sight and touch of mortar, but dared not leave it alone. On, on, they strove. Blinded with tears and grit, noses running, ears singing, bodies soaking with sweat, their whole world was a sea of brick and mortar. During the whole of the building period they existed on about £1 weekly, and it is certain they were deprived of necessary food. But by the end of July the four walls were complete, and there was a house waiting impatiently for a roof.

The two chimney stacks followed. Every time they got to a chimney pot, Jesse Head struck work and went on the drink. He said that at his age he could never climb a chimney stack until he had steadied his nerves by a visit to the local inn. When he returned, muttering and trembling, Williams had to tie him to the scaffold pole to ensure his safety, for he was a stout and stocky man. From this vantage point Jessie Head would hurl down curses and mortar. But by mid August the chimneys were finished and the carpenters had arrived. Soon the roof principals were in position.

The roof was on and the floors laid in October. They were now waiting for the plasterers. The roof was of first class asbestos which, with the grey horizontal tiles that covered it, cost Williams close on £50. He had been eager to have Welsh slates on his roof because of their durability and appearance, but these would have involved an extra £40. He had already calculated that by the time the whole house was finished he would owe nothing.

In the last week of October Williams wrote to Fitzmaurice, "My bedroom floors—I have three bedrooms, one with a large double window for reading and writing—are of shelfing from Chiseldon Camp —well-seasoned material; my kitchen and scullery floors will be of concrete, cement, and gravel, upon six inches of broken stone. Alto-

gether we shall have used about 350 tons of stones and bricks and
70 tons of mortar. I have made my own door-sills in cement, and
shall do the floors, lathing, etc.: the pointing I also did and shall
do my painting, too." The District Surveyor had now visited to see
how the work was proceeding and had told Williams he considered
he was building a most beautiful house. The Swindon W.E.A. had
also journeyed out, and Williams addressed the gathering in the shadow
of the premises.

He had not been idle either in his garden, and by October had tilled
about 40 perch of new land. Though all his bush fruit failed he had
made £25 from the sale of vegetables, mainly potatoes. Yet at this
time he wrote to a friend in Australia, "For my part I have no real joy
outside the intellectual."

One thought was now uppermost in both their minds. Would they
be out of Dryden Cottage and in their very own house by Christmas ?
The goal was indeed in sight, and feverishly they sought it. During
November both floors were finished, partitions were up, windows in,
and the lower ceilings and walls plastered. Then the frost came.
Williams advised waiting before plastering the upstairs ceilings.
But the plasterers waved them aside and said the frost would make
no difference. They went on with the work and finished it in one day;
on the next every ceiling fell in. There was more delay. It now looked
as if the house would not be finished that year.

On the last day of the year the District Surveyor visited for the
second time and handed Williams Certificate B, which was then lodged
with the Ministry of Health. To Henry Byett Williams wrote,
" . . . we are waiting for the cheque. I am up to my eyes in painting—
next week for ceilings and walls, then finishing with paint, and after
that the 'trek'. I can assure you I am feeling more cheerful."

The house was all but ready to receive them. This was their child,
born of love and belief in each other's powers of endurance and abiding
purpose. There it nestled, brave and snug in the White Horse valley,
with the Wiltshire hills as palisades about it. And they named it
"Ranikhet". In the front of the house Alfred had inserted a stone and
himself incised the magic name upon it. On the north wall he had
inserted a weather-beaten tablet which he had discovered among the
ruins of Mark Titcombe's cottage. And this bore the date, 1671.
"Ranikhet" was indeed a palingenesis.

Early in January the government subsidy arrived and they were able
to pay all their bills. "Ranikhet" had cost £500; of this amount timber
with hauling amounted to £54, bricks to £34; the plans, prepared by
the village carpenter under Alfred's direction, had cost £5. The hauling of bricks and stone alone had cost nearly £20 in spite of the fact that
they had done much of this work themselves.

On the 15th January, 1921, Alfred and Mary Williams came into their inheritance and slept in "Ranikhet". Fitzmaurice's photograph was the first thing they placed upon the walls.

Then it was that Alfred wrote, "If I had only been a bricklayer and plasterer, instead of interesting myself in literature, I should never have worked half as hard." But the house was up, their pride and joy, the wonder and admiration of their friends. Alfred peered into the future, "I hope soon to get on with some new publication or other when I can find time to put things in order." This to Fitzmaurice.

"Ranikhet" dreamed in the shadows, of the far-off Indian hill station whence came its name. "Cambria Cottage" and "Rose Cottage", both built on "The Hook" years before to house Alfred's forbears, smiled approvingly as they welcomed the newcomer with the strange name. And did not old Sarah Bourton who had once given that piece of the meadow on which "Ranikhet" now stood to Ann and Joshua Hughes for their use, consider, too, how well her bounty had been blessed by their grandchild?

CHAPTER NINETEEN

ROUND ABOUT THE UPPER THAMES

THE two had been in such haste to quit Dryden Cottage and take possession of "Ranikhet" that they had not allowed the new house to dry out thoroughly. Consequently, before the end of January, Alfred was ill for several days with dyspepsia, while Mary had an attack of rheumatism. On recovery, they turned their thoughts once again to the future. Alfred believed that now they were in "Ranikhet" he would be able to earn enough money to keep them both going, from the sale of garden produce and from his writings. He thought the time was ripe for the publication of another book.

He had by him the manuscript of *Round about the Upper Thames* which he had written before enlistment and which had been serialised in 1915 in *The Wilts and Gloucester Standard*. It had taken him then about ten months to write, and instalments had appeared weekly in the newspaper for nine months. He had been paid twenty guineas for the serial rights, though the editor's original offer had been for six guineas. Williams now considerably revised this book, and in January and February submitted it to eight publishers before Duckworth accepted it. He was also anxious to follow up *Round about the Upper Thames* with his collection of folk songs as soon as possible. Writing to Fitzmaurice about this he said, "If I had not obtained the materials when I did, the work could not have been done now, for nearly all the aged men have died during the past six years, especially those who knew the songs." During those early months of 1922 Williams read widely about Hinduism and had already had several lengthy conversations with Henry Byett about Eastern matters.

On one occasion he had explained the basic principles of Brahminism to Byett, and had said that the Vedas were not only the basis of, but were much superior to, the writings of the Egyptians, Greeks, Romans and to the books of the Bible. The Brahmin idea of immortality was much more subtle than the "ego" or "soul" theory of Christianity. "The Rig Veda means very much to me; I live by it, spend what time I can in reading it, and am not happy when away from it."

Then, in the spring, his former fellow employee, C. H. Hollick of Swindon, who had introduced him to the writings of Max Müller as far back as 1910, knowing of his growing interest in and passion for Hinduism and eastern literature generally, lent him Müller's *Sanskrit Literature*. The book made a great impression upon him and the reading of it and of others by the same author, was to colour his philosophy for the rest of his days.

From now onwards Alfred Williams was certain in his mind of the exact nature of his attitude to life and immortality. Circumstances over the years had slowly driven him within himself so that he had become introspective and detached. He was in short a practical mystic who retired to unorthodoxy as a means of escape from the knocks and disappointments of the world. To Hollick he wrote on 25th May, "It is impossible for one to remain orthodox after reading Müller, and studying the history of religion with an open mind." Again on 16th June, "Müller believed the *essentials* of all the great religions to have been *revealed*, and to be equally true generally. But he believed the teachings of Christ to be the purest and most humanitarian. The Christian world, society and laws demonstrate this, but you will see Müller takes care to add this qualification which Christ taught to his disciples, free as yet from all ecclesiastical fences and entrenchments. Müller did not accept any miracles. It's the miracles that the modernists are up against, and they have to go; that ecclesiastical Christianity with its authority that Müller mentions, is emphatically founded on miracles, but Christ's own teaching, proven by his words—and not related to tradition—contains nothing but what is natural, true and good. You will see again what Max Müller says after mentioning the theosophic wealth of the Christian religion. But in doing this we must treat it simply as one of the historical religions of the world. Exactly, not as the only true religion of the orthodox, but as *one* of the historical . . . We have been ridden to death, and almost eaten up by the clergy of all sorts and sects——"

Alfred Williams was dissatisfied about other things, too. He spoke out boldly and bitingly to his friends about the prevailing conditions in England. He condemned the cuts in education which were then being made in the name of economy. He despised those he called "the crowd of new, inexperienced, and unthinking men, who, pretending to be filled with rage at the condition of the country's finances, had been rushed or pushed into offices for which they had no reasonable qualifications." He told Fitzmaurice that if the English wished to be a great people, the provision of education for the masses must not in any way be grudged. If the old conservative element in England refused to do this, or neglected to do it, such a policy would render it all the more easy for the younger generation to be influenced by objectionable propaganda, which it would be to the traditionalists' advantage to counteract.

Williams railed bitterly against the Government of the day for permitting the high price of food to continue, saying that there was not the slightest reason under a sound economic system for the basic foods, like butter, bread, cheese, bacon and sugar, to be so costly. Of our Indian policy he affirmed that the Indians would always be a trouble until they were given *all* the benefits of the many improvements brought about in their own country; the English still expected and looked for large profits from Indian enterprises. Indian sugar growing ought to be further developed and more agricultural colleges and experimental farms founded. Indian politics and the plight of the Indian people were always subjects close to his heart.

Owing to lack of rain, the summer was a disastrous one for Williams as far as his gardening work was concerned. In spite of long hours and intensive culture, he only earned £25 that season; peas and strawberries were a miserable failure. He accepted his losses as philosophically as possible, for he really enjoyed and appreciated the outdoor labour in all weathers, and he believed that one day he would make profits from his growing stock of fruit trees.

In June he made final arrangements with Duckworth for the forthcoming publication of *Round about the Upper Thames*. He had expected a fifteen per cent royalty, as for his previous prose, but this time he was offered ten per cent, as the book was going to be an expensive one to produce. He anticipated a return of about £20. Williams was anxious that the book should have illustrations and had, even before the war, discussed the matter with an artist friend; but the sketches did not materialise. Then it was decided that there should be photographs instead, and local photographers submitted a number of views of the countryside described, from which the publishers made their selection. Williams had also revised certain of the chapters. "I have cut out yards of stuff which my later and sounder judgment stamps as unsuitable—all good stuff in its way, and perfectly true, every word, but experience has taught me that it weakens the book" he wrote to Henry Byett. "I forced things rather. I expressed views; and experience has taught me that it is better to record facts, and allow the reader to formulate his own views based on these facts. Now, if I had a chance to revise the earlier volumes, there is much that I should delete."

Eagerly he waited for the appearance of the book, quietly occupying himself with gardening and reading. In August he read *Ramakrishna* which contained a valuable résumé of the Vedantic tenets. Then at last on 15th September, 1922, *Round about the Upper Thames* was on sale in the Swindon bookshops at 12/6, which Williams thought too prohibitive for people to pay. He wrote to the publishers and asked them to reduce the price to not more than 10/6, but they were unable to accede to his request because of the then high expenses of publishing. Duckworth also pointed out that the work was much better produced than his earlier books and contained photogravures, which were always costly to reproduce.

Alfred Williams was proud of having written *Round about the Upper Thames.* Of it he wrote to Fitzmaurice, "The book has little political or economical value, perhaps, but it aims rather at a picturesque yet actual representation of what was till recently the standard conditions —as regards 'life'—in the neighbouring locality of the Upper Thames." And to Henry Byett "The book is a good one—one, with no excrescences, no superfluity of description, etc., which abounded in my earlier works."

Round about the Upper Thames carried one stage further Williams' comprehensive plan of describing step by step, book by book, the pattern of the Wiltshire and Thames countryside. As each book unfolded itself and formed within him, so the actual labour of research increased. *A Wiltshire Village* and *Life in a Railway Factory* were familiar and concentrated units. *Villages of the White Horse* had entailed much travel into less familiar parts. In *Round about the Upper Thames* the net was thrown even wider and the new ground covered was "roughly speaking, that line between the Thames head and Radcot Bridge, i.e., the first twenty-five miles of the river's course, and it embraces portions of three counties—Wiltshire, Berkshire, and Gloucestershire". Williams visited nearly fifty villages and small townships in order to get his information. The book deals in some detail with some twenty of these. He wrote much about Highworth, Shrivenham, Watchfield, Inglesham, Buscot, Lechlade, Northleach, Fairford, Cricklade and Bibury. His theme, as ever, but now underlined and more passionate, was the decay of village life. He aimed at the re-creation of a past age, using as his means to that end, straightforward descriptions of country manners and customs, with traditional stories and incidents to fill in the general framework. Much of that former age he knew remained with a kind of reflected glory, but he was not blind to the obvious fact that the Thames countryside of his grand-parents' day had passed with the tides and winds, and for ever. Williams himself was entirely out of sympathy with the spirit of the twentieth century; he would have been more at home in the eighteenth, or sixteenth.

Round about the Upper Thames is dedicated

TO

REUBEN AND LOU
in memory of
many pleasant evenings
spent together in the village
with the flowers and the birds
and the old folks.

He had long felt that he owed some such gesture to these two old friends who had, over the years, given him their support and encourage-ment. And Reuben George and Llewellyn Robins were like him, in that they were of the earth, earthy. It is a pleasant story, this, the story of the Thames villages and their flowers, birds and old folks. These mellow and comely little places sleep untroubled in the valleys, breathing out their soft histories, and giving back to the downland winds the distant echoes of homely sounds that had once been heard in them. Their white streets and gabled cottages smile wistfully at us where they huddle under spire and tower, and their windows invite welcome. And the merry crowd, the self-same crowd of country folk of *A Wiltshire Village* and *Villages of the White Horse,* jostle each other afresh in these new and fragrant pages. Alfred Williams met them on the hills with their sheep, in the inns and inglenooks, by mill and by lock, in field and copse, driving horses, piling waggons, all living and rich with their broad Cotswold speech and traditions, and rounded as apples, with quaint and kindly humour. We step into the realistic world of "Ratcatcher" Joe, old Betty the Witch, Squire Akerman, Poll Packer, Lord Craven, Jeremiah Ewer and Giles Draper. And for the first time in all his writing, Williams has unconsciously given this book a hero in the person of Elijah Iles, better known as "Gramp".

Was there ever a more fascinating and unusual hero than "Gramp"— the grand old man of Inglesham? Aged ninety-five, he lived with his widowed daughter in a house overlooking the Thames and opposite Kempsford church. "Gramp" wrote Williams "is really a splendid figure—a delightful and congenial soul. He is of medium height, is broad and well made, and as erect as many a man at sixty. His head is massive and his features are typically English, with heavy brows, expressive eyes, aristocratic nose, and clean-shaven lips and chin. His long, silky, snow-white hair hangs nearly to his shoulders and adds reverence to his appearance. Every day, when it is dry and fine, with his feet inside a pair of large slippers, and gripping a stout stick in his hand, Gramp walks down the road to the old pound and chats with his neighbour. When it is wet and cold he sits by the fire, hat on head, and smokes his pipe, or hums over the airs he learned as a youth. Until he was over ninety, Gramp gathered flags and bulrushes from the river and made baskets, chair-bottoms, and other articles."

Round about the Upper Thames is rich in descriptions of wild flowers, bird and animal life, and the rolling English acres. Few nature writers have succeeded better that Williams in capturing, and then sealing in words, the whole pregnant atmosphere of a Cotswold ploughing match, the interior of a cottage, the river in flood, a bygone fair. And this was possible largely because of the attitude of mind and overwhelming love which he bore towards the upper Thames country. He came to it as no tourist, suddenly enthralled by the fleeting picture of a sturdy church or odd village character, nor as a journalist, who with rapid and generalising pen could fasten upon the outstanding features of the area for a few moments. Williams knew the scenes and people he wrote about; they were his Wiltshire inheritance. He was no stranger to the villages; every winding road to them welcomed his feet. The villagers were never odd nor uncouth to him but just part of an everlasting pattern into which he himself very easily fitted. That is why all his nature writing is charged with such truth and vitality.

This picture of an English hayfield—what memories of his childhood?—for instance, bears his stamp:—"The hayfield was situated about half-way between Lushill and Castle Eaton, in the valley of the Upper Thames, near to where the four counties of Wiltshire, Berkshire, Gloucestershire, and Oxfordshire come into conjunction. A hard road ran through the field, bordered by a high hedge on one side. Here the beautiful wild rose, shell pink and creamy-white, with sweet crimson-pointed buds and wax-like petals, enfolded, or curved outwards underneath, expanded like a saucer, or depressed like an umbrella, hung in luxuriant trusses and clusters from the top of the hedge down to the ground, shedding a soft radiance, and emitting a faint tea perfume. Between the rose boughs, along the shallow ditch, crept the dewberry with occasional blossoms and exquisite bluish fruit; here a teazel, light green in foliage, with prickly buds and thin rings of purple flowers growing from tiny cells like honeycomb, stood boldly up alongside a stately thistle, to the large head of which a drowsy humble-bee was clinging, though all her companions had long ago departed homewards to their nest in the mossy bank. . . . On one side the tall taper top of the rick, nearly completed, was visible in the farmyard; on the other the stately tower of Kempsford Church rose above the elm-trees and peered majestically over all the valley round about. Now a large dark cloud, like a bat, with head distinct and wings outstretched, rose slowly out of the west, covering the sky, and causing the interiors of the elms to show blue-black. The moist night wind, laden with the warm scents of the hay and the stronger smell of the ricks heating in the farmyard, came puffing up from the river, and the haymakers hung their rakes on the hedge and left the field, the rumbling of the heavy wagon echoing loudly down the road in the twilight."

Williams could not resist the appeal of water; a pool, a waterfall, or a hidden tinkling stream were ever a passion and delight. These seemed —with Liddington—to find a corresponding rhythm in him which ran joyfully through his whole being and stayed with him all his life. The River Coln must have been an enduring and ecstatic inspiration to him. "It is like a lovely laughing bride, crowned with flowers on her marriage morning, fresh, sweet, and pure, radiant with happiness, whose face, kissed with the morning sunshine, sends a gleam through the world and rejuvenates everything, shedding a new glory—'the light that never was'—on all around her, and adding an unspeakable gift—a moment of immortality. And how lightly and gaily she trips along, with feet that seem not to tread the ground, moving half on earth and half in the air, with a graceful, jaunty, bird-like motion that only blithe-hearted youth could execute, bewitching in her exquisite ease and simple natural loveliness! Even so beautiful is the Coln, swimming along over her stony bed through the fields, laughing aloud in the sunlight, flowing, flowing, ever flowing, clear and pure as though composed of nothing but freshest dew-drops, each one resplendent with the morning, twinkling in the glorious light of the unutterable dawn hours. The smile on her face, the musical ripple of her voice, the sweet pouting of her lips where the stones oppose her passage, the shadow no sooner received than dispelled, the snow-white foam flakes, borne like bunches of lilies on her breast, her long flowing hair streaming in the crystal, the graceful and voluptuous sweep of her skirts at yonder curve, the silver sandals of her restless gliding feet, her gauze-like garments of the summer fields, green and gold, white, opal, and purple, the flash of multicoloured light reflected from the plumage of her attendant kingfishers, her joy and bloom and perfect beauty are all-powerful and irresistible. Heaven is in her eyes; laughter is in her soul; the spirit of eternal Youth is about her and within her, and she has no secrets. She is a symbol of Life at its earliest and holiest hours, when the earth is newly awake and full of sunshine and song, and all things are freely and easily fathomable, before Sorrow's fruit hangs on the bough, the heavens are overcast, and we draw near to the depths that conceal who knows how many pains and afflictions, filled as they are with the doom of ourselves and all other earthly things."

So the Thames ran on through the gamut of the seasons. Its colours changed with its birds, its flowers bloomed, nodded and perished, the woods on its banks moved like a miracle from greenery to barrenness, and the summer days dulled into winter. And Alfred Williams saw the long valley spread out beneath him, and marked the huge storm clouds looming and threatening on the horizon. The river now carried another and more fatalistic music. The Thames was in flood. "Adown the hills a hundred torrents ran splashing, shouting, and leaping in headlong haste, as though eager to see which should come first to the lowlands. As the hatches were not yet removed, the streams overflowed their banks and covered the meadows in the upper parts of the valley. It took twenty-four hours incessant rain to cause the flood, with ten hours added in which to allow the water to be carried down by the brooks and streamlets. Then thousands of acres on both sides of the river were covered a yard deep or more; the hedgerows were submerged, and only the tops of the hawthorn clumps and withies were visible. The merry Cole leapt over the top of the hatches and roared and foamed below like a mad bull; but the Thames was silent, and rolled his torrent along steadily, though with tremendous power. In less than three days the flood subsided. Then crowds of wild-fowl sailed over the meadows, circling for small fish, and the great chubs that came out of the river went wriggling home again with their backs and tails half out of the water. A week afterwards the storm repeated and the river rose again, and so on several times until the wind finally sank and the pale moon shone in a calm, cloudless sky."

Few things gave Williams more pleasure than to get into conversation with the Cotswold people and to be invited by them into their cottages, for a cup of tea beneath the busy thatch. In *Round about the Upper Thames* he has reproduced for us in words an interior which has the same ring of authenticity and the same range of colour and intensity as a painting by Vermeer or de Hooch. "The carter's cottage may be held as a fair type of the average home of the Cotswold labourer. The house is of moderate size, with two rooms downstairs and two above. One of the downstairs rooms is set aside as a summer apartment, for when the sun shines hot against the front of the house the temperature within is raised to an uncomfortable pitch. The other is the general 'living-room', constituting dining-and-sitting-room and kitchen together.   The furniture of the room consists of a large deal table, an ancient sofa covered with faded red cloth, a chest of drawers, and half a dozen chairs, including the arm-chair by the fireside in which no one else must presume to sit when the carter is at home. . . . There are no less than fifty ornaments on the mantlepiece.   They are of all sorts and dimensions, but are chiefly 'old-fashioned' stone figures and pieces of quaint chinaware, many of them interesting, and some highly valuable. . . . As with ornaments, so with pictures and photographs; there are nearly a hundred hanging upon the walls of the living-room.   Of these the most conspicuous are a reproduction of "The Stolen Duchess" in colours, and two old Scriptural prints— "The Finding of Moses" and "Moses in the Land of Midian".   The mirror, before which the carter has his weekly shave, is marked with the name of a certain embrocation, warranted 'Good for Cattle', and the covering over the back of the good-wife's chair is a piece of hand-wrought embroidery depicting Joseph's flight with the infant Christ into Egypt.   Hanging up are a hempen halter and a great horn lantern for use in the stables; upon the floor are a long brass-handled whip and a flag dinner basket."

As a nature writer, Williams has found for himself a high place in literature because of his powers of selectivity.   He generally succeeded in his prose in seizing upon the essential characteristics of each individual country figure.   He had not the specialised nature knowledge nor the polished detail of Gilbert White, for he was not a naturalist of that *genre*.   Neither did his writing bear the same type of lofty philosophy nor the minute observation of Richard Jefferies, nor had it the vivid colouring and luscious imagination of William Hudson. Williams did not as a general rule identify himself so personally with bird, fish and beast as Henry Williamson does.   But no writer has excelled him in his altruism and forthrightness; his supreme ability was in the realism, understanding, and faithful depiction of the everyday people of his piece of the English countryside.

There once lived in the upper Thames valley "Ratcatcher Joe— overfond of liquor."   One Sunday, the Squire of Joe's village had had him placed in the stocks for drunk and disorderly conduct.   "But Joseph proved to be a greater nuisance in the stocks than as if he had been at liberty, for he did nothing but sing and shout and speak rudely to all who passed that way.   In the evening when the people were going to church, and the Squire's wife and daughters were passing, he made more noise than before and shocked them with his rude and irreverent expressions.   Then the squire, for very shame, set him free, and no one was afterwards put in the stocks there.   This is one of 'Ratcatcher Joe's' feats.   First he drank a pint of shoe-oil.   Next he ate one pound of tallow candles, two pounds of boiled fat bacon, hot, and a large cow cabbage cooked with it that when cut would not go into a peck measure. Then he swallowed the greasy pot liquor, and afterwards drank a quart of beer, completing the whole within half an hour . . . In sharp, cold weather, Joe used to wrap the newly caught rats round his body, next the skin, in order to keep himself warm."

Then we are told of the three witches, Betsy Hyde, Moll Wilkins and Poll Packer, the latter especially, "greatly dreaded by the carters and cowmen whose horses and herds she tampered with, stopping the teams on the road and causing the cows to get loose in the night and jump over the highest gates and fences. She was able to bewitch plates and saucers, knives, forks, and spoons, and even the very innocent slices of bread and butter, and to make them dance upon the tea-table. Her greatest feat was to make a wagon-line stand straight up in the air in the hayfield and so tease the farmer half out of his wits, who wanted to bind the hay on the wain and get it down to the rickyard before the rain came on."

Giles Draper could cut two acres of grass in a day and go on so doing for a week at a stretch; Whistling Joe the blacksmith made nails out of scrap iron and then sold them at fourpence a pound. What of Jack Hughes and Tom Bailey who dug a dead pig up "plunged it into a large tub of hot water, dressed it, and then carried it off and sold it as prime pork in the town?" Jeremiah Ewer of Crouch used to stand on his head and clap his knee with his hand so frequently that he wore a hole in his new smock within a week.

This then is the flavour of *Round about the Upper Thames*. The book received commendatory notices, every reviewer paying tribute to Williams' research, and acknowledging that he had saved for the future the story of the past. The four published prose works of Alfred Williams will remain the best monument to his industry and ideals.

But the book sold slowly in the first few months; by the end of November its author had himself sold 120 copies "in the corner of Wilts and Berks between Cricklade, Swindon and Faringdon". He was tramping the countryside again with a 12/6 book for sale, calling on his friends, knocking at lonely and wayside houses and getting into conversation with likely buyers; five copies only had been sold in Swindon. All that winter he peddled his book, for his income was negligible; his royalties were no more than £5 yearly and for the rest he had to rely on the sale of garden produce. He had heard no more from Kyle about the publication of a selection of his poems.

Williams was now anxious to complete the sequence of his books about the villages and their peoples by the immediate publication of the folk songs. To Dowsing he wrote, and not without some chagrin, "For the amount of work I put into this, in order to save some very interesting and valuable materials from perishing, I ought to get support; but a new spirit is abroad, in all ranks; really, the only people who do me any good or show me consideration and respect, are those ordinarily who are looked upon as the 'parasites'. This I do find more and more; the democratic classes, in the south at any rate, have no use for poets and writers of *belles-lettres*: the prevention of these would prove the extinction of art, to a large extent, and the death to poets especially of such as ourselves. . . . If I had not left the Swindon works before I joined the Army I should have been all right. Well, it doesn't matter much: there are only us two, and my plot of land, my peas and strawberries, will go some way towards keeping us together, and I find time for a read now and, then."

In January, 1923, to his intense delight, Duckworth accepted *Folk Songs of the Upper Thames*, the collection to include an essay on the folk song in its particular relation to the Thames area. He began to write this essay at once, and with a great deal of enthusiasm. He was offered a ten per cent royalty on all copies sold after the first thousand, an arrangement with which he was satisfied, since he considered he was very fortunate at that period to have found a publisher at all, for a work with such limited appeal. He always expected that he would have had to publish at his own expense.

In February Williams began the last major project of his life. He decided to teach himself Sanskrit so that he could read Hindu literature in the original and obtain first-hand information about the Vedantic philosophy. From the beginning he was enamoured of the language, and told J. B. Jones that his affinities in blood, intellect, and sympathy were Aryan, and that Sanskrit was his language to a greater extent than Greek or Latin ever had been or could be. One little book of Sanskrit tales in translation he read four times that month, besides a lengthy *History of India* to give him a background. His greatest need was for a Sanskrit grammar which he was finding difficult to obtain. He made a special journey to Oxford to buy one in the bookshops there but, to his amazement, found that there was nothing to suit him. Mary then began to make enquiries, and ascertained entirely by chance that Harvard University published a reader containing thirty original hymns from the Rig Veda intended to last the elementary Sanskrit student for fifty weeks. Though the book was expensive, she ordered it, paid for it out of her slender housekeeping money, and presented it with pride to Alfred on his birthday that April.

So his life flowered and developed. There were still the same pressing needs and constant problems to face and combat. They were so poor that they could not afford to buy a newspaper regularly, and Alfred had to borrow money in order to purchase distemper for the walls and ceilings of "Ranikhet". Owing to wet weather no work was done in the garden until March, when, with a burst of desperate energy, he trenched every yard of land he had, planted twenty-four rows of peas and prepared the ground for another twenty rows.

The proofs of the folk song book had now arrived and he was spending the greater part of each day on a most intricate piece of correction. His essay ran into twenty pages, and there were 250 songs with which to deal, each carrying a brief note as to its origin and history. To Fitzmaurice he wrote "I have a certain amount of faith in myself yet—a diminutive fraction—" and in April he heard that *Round about the Upper Thames* had sold 1,000 copies and was still selling. Their monetary position was still, however, their greatest trial.

He wrote to Henry Byett that month, "A farmer has offered me a couple of baby foxes. They were very friendly creatures, but how could I hope to find them breakfast and supper?" Alfred and Mary were themselves existing on two small meals each day.

CHAPTER TWENTY

THE FOLK SONGS

DUCKWORTH published *Folk Songs of the Upper Thames* on 3rd May, 1923. This was a memorable occasion for Alfred Williams and a great relief to him, too, for he knew that at last the songs were secure for all time, though the singers of them had long since died. He would have dearly liked Elijah Iles to see a copy of the book, and only a few days after it appeared, William Bridges, a very old friend and an exquisite singer of folk songs, died in his 97th year.

Williams always privately considered the collection to be the one really important piece of work he had done, because, though he did not consider himself to be an expert, he was the first man to make any thorough attempt at collecting the folk lore of the neighbourhood. Yet with his accustomed modesty he said to J. B. Jones who reviewed the book in the local press, that he looked upon the work as "nothing more than a friendly collection of home songs, neither scientifically treated, nor intended to appeal to the cold specialist of such things."

Folk Songs of the Upper Thames was the last country book which Williams published. He dedicated it to his mother, who had had such a lasting influence upon his character, and from whose lips he must have first heard many of the old songs in his childhood days. The songs were, with her, an indelible record of a vanished past, conjuring up in his imagination, a pleasant vision of an age of sound values and inward repose. For the fullest appreciation of the work it must be read alongside its companion *Round about the Upper Thames* which supplies a necessary and all-embracing atmosphere and background.

The essay which forms the lengthy introduction to this collection is a masterly treatise on the origins and scope of folk songs. It is so informative and scholarly that it would be difficult to find any more outstanding example of the peculiar genius of Alfred Williams, in the whole range of his writing. In it he reveals in the simplest language how he obtained the majority of the folk songs. He began, in nearly every instance, by winning the confidence and esteem of the oldest inhabitants of the Thames villages, and having achieved this, they were generally prevailed upon to open their hearts to him and hand over the treasures he was seeking. If unable to sing a song themselves the old people would pass him on to others who could do so. Williams spent long, though not unprofitable hours, interviewing and cajoling those who were rather chary of giving away their secrets to a stranger from another village. On more than one occasion Williams would have obtained no song had he not been prepared to buy it outright. A glass of beer at the local inn, sometimes more than one, a packet of tobacco here, some tea there, or a few sweets elsewhere, seldom failed in the end to produce a response. He soon discovered that only a dozen or so of the songs had been actually composed in the Thames valley, though all of them had been sung in the area for many years, having been left behind on sheets by the travelling ballad singers who visited the district, particularly at fair times, with the latest product of the music hall or drawing room. This discovery led him to believe that his task of preserving the songs had been begun twenty-five years too late at least; the best and most authentic folk songs had been irretrievably lost. He was well aware of the pseudo nature of many of the songs which were called folk songs. Few of them were in dialect though about twenty of them dated back to the Tudors.

The essay enumerated some of the occasions on which the songs were sung by the villagers. When labour in the fields was at a standstill owing to inclement weather, the men would gather round in the farmhouses and great resounding tithe barns, and go unflinchingly through long repertoires of songs until they could get back to their ploughing, reaping or sowing. The rustics also met in the inns where they held gargantuan singing matches, flinging up to the rafters and thatch the old rolling choruses with their quaint words and irresistible rhythms, until the very walls echoed with the tumult and heartiness of their voices. In *Villages of the White Horse* Williams had once written of "the crowd of cheerful rustics that assembled in the big room at the 'Blue Lion' shouting to the landlord for better beer and singing snatches of songs, some of them well worth remembering, such as the poaching song of 'Thornymoor Fields'."

And there were the grandams who sang the wistful songs to their wondering grandchildren, the mothers who whispered lullabies to their babes at the hour of sundown, and the hoary shepherds who hummed them to themselves and their flocks in the long silences of the listening hills and fields.

Alfred Williams was fortunate in finding so many people who were willing to supply him with folk song material. Besides those who actually sang or said the words of songs to him, there were many who, though he did not actually meet them, sent him copies of folk songs which had been handed down in their families. In addition, he was able to rely on about ten reliable stand-bys who, because of the number of songs they remembered, were able to provide him with many rare and beautiful examples of their decaying art. His chief singer was Elijah Iles, the evergreen and buoyant "Gramp" of Inglesham. When "Gramp" first met Williams in the spring of 1915 he mistook him for a new curate who had come to pay him a courtesy visit. Ripe with the wisdom and innocence of a nonagenarian, Elijah in order to put his visitor at ease, knowingly quoted a short passage from the Scriptures; on discovering his mistake he laughed heartily and offered as a recompense, a lengthy and somewhat bawdy folk song. From this time onward "Gramp" and Alfred were firm friends.

Then there was "Wassail" Harvey of Cricklade who for several weeks refused to open his mouth, until, fortunately for Williams, the toothless ancient developed a severe cold. A small dose of rum, however, warded off the cold and loosened his tongue at the same time, so that he proceeded to deliver a large number of interesting songs; Williams found it difficult to stop him once he got going.

Daniel Morgan, a general dealer, was a sparkling singer, and a character into the bargain, with a strange and fascinating family history. He and his crone lived in a remote cottage in the depths of the woods near Braydon. Williams visited Daniel on several occasions during 1915 and 1916, cycling over from South Marston in order to join the couple around their log fire. On long winter nights the three of them would sit in silence in the glow, Daniel deftly cutting clothes pegs from green withy, while his dame made potato nets—all to be sold at cottages in the neighbourhood or at the next market. Williams would bask contentedly in the firelight waiting for Daniel to open out. In due time the songs would come, one after another, and Williams would hastily note down the words, and then, leaving the pair to their tasks, would ride away into the darkness with the songs still running round in his head.

Other regular singers were David Sawyer of Ogbourne, a downland shepherd and a special favourite of Alfred Williams, John Pillinger of Lechlade, Shadrach Haydon of Hatford, Mrs. Hancock of Blunsdon, William Warren of South Marston, Thomas Smart of Stratton St. Margaret and Charles Tanner of Bampton, the latter a famed exponent of the morris dance. Several of these country people were over ninety years old; one aged 99, sang a delicate and winsome love song to Williams a few hours before his death, while another, 94 years old, had, as a young man, worked in the fields with soldiers who had fought at Waterloo, and whose greatest delight was to tell stories of "The Duke" and "Boney". Finally there was that titan, Gabriel Zillard from Hannington. "Of Zillard it is said that he would unbutton his shirt-collar at six in the morning and sing for twelve or even eighteen hours, if necessary, with the perspiration streaming down his cheeks".

Williams has much to say concerning the various kinds of songs he discovered, and of their range and choice of subject, writes, "no thing and no person escaped a composition. The king, the nobleman, the knight, the admiral and general, the squire, the soldier and sailor, the farmer, the miller, the mower, the reaper, the waggoner, the dairy-maid, the shepherd, the ploughman, the cobbler, down to the barber, sweep, and ragman were honoured in song." Williams praised the impeccable taste of the rural folk for everything that was natural, simple and beautiful.

The introduction concludes on a personal note, taking us behind the scenes of his experiences in the years when he was travelling around the Thames countryside. "The work of collecting the songs is laborious and tedious, though it is also interesting and pleasurable. I have everywhere met with much kindness and hospitality, especially among the cottagers. . . . They are always anxious to provide me with hospitable entertainment. This one will have me stay to dinner or tea; that presses me to partake of supper, or offers me a night's lodging. Another invites me and my household to spend the week with him. One crams my pockets with fruits; this offers me a peck of potatoes. Another begs me to accept the gift of an overcoat. This has knitted me a pair of socks, or gloves, and that one would make me a present of a nice warm pair of trousers ! . . . I have several times been taken for a tramp, and also for a German spy. . . . The greater part of the work of collecting the songs must be done at night, and winter is the best time, as the men are then free from their labours after tea. This necessitates some amount of hardship, for one must be prepared to face all kinds of weather, and to go long distances. . . . In frost and snow, fogs, rain, and on sultry summer nights I have journeyed along the dark roads, and climbed the steep hills bordering the valley, with the bats, the owls, the hares, and the foxes. I have faced the Thames's floods in almost inky blackness upon unknown roads and lanes, and shivered in the numbing cold of the damp nights exhaled by the river in the late autumn and winter months. Once, during a severe flood, following an extraordinarily rapid rise of water, I found myself immersed to the waist, in Stygian darkness, and miles from any town or village; I have often scrambled along the banks in the blackness above the roaring brooks to escape a wetting. In the spring I have loitered on my return, evening after evening, till past midnight, listening to the nightingale under the pure air and clear skies of the Cotswolds. Later in the summer, at the same hour I have sat in the grass by the roadside amid the beautiful glow-worms, while the air was warm and fragrant with the delicious scents of the newly-made hay. I have watched the late moon rise, now from behind the Cotswolds, and now above the rolling chalk downs of Berkshire, south of the White Horse; and I have looked upon its reflection at midnight in the calm river, now from Swinford, now from New Bridge or Radcot, and again from the Ha'penny Bridge at Lechlade, or at Castle Eaton."

This book is then, in spite of being, in the words of *The Times* reviewer, somewhat in the nature of a "hotch-potch", a valuable addition to folk literature. It will remain, even with its obvious blemishes, a permanent record of "that which amused, cheered, consoled, and so profoundly affected the lives of the people of an age that has for ever passed away". The songs themselves have considerable charm, especially the love and nature ballads.

On the whole, *Folk Songs of the Upper Thames* was well received, though sales again were slow. Bailey told Williams that he considered it to be "one more proof of your astonishing audacity of energy— all that going round by night in dark and discomfort to collect these things." In June, 1923, Frank Kitson wrote to Williams on behalf of the English Folk Dance and Song Society offering to give assistance in the publication of the remainder of the 800 songs which had been collected. Oddly enough, Williams declined, being under the mistaken impression that Kitson merely wanted to choose two or three of the rarer examples for the Society's collection. As a matter of fact Williams was not greatly in sympathy with the aims of the Society, for he believed that the old songs should not be revived merely to become the fashion of the moment and the innocent victims of commercialism. He stated on several occasions that the desire and need for folk songs had passed; the singing of them had been the chief and often the only pleasure of the old people, but modern times had brought other interests and delights to them. His collection he regarded as a piece of reconstruction rather than propaganda.

There still remains one of the notebooks used by Williams while he was making his survey. This a small, well-bound, black clothed specimen, was begun on 19th May, 1916. It contains the names of many of the singers and of the villages visited, there are hurriedly pencilled songs, lists of people from whom he hoped to obtain material, and other miscellaneous information about the songs themselves. For months on end he carried this particular notebook in his pocket.

During the spring and summer of 1923, Williams continued to work with energy in his garden and at Sanskrit. To Hollick he wrote on 18th May: "I have had some pleasant hours over Müller's *Chips from a German Workshop* and my learning Sanskrit has, of course, intensified the interest I take in the whole subject. I feel convinced that it is a great and useful study, most delightful, though difficult and tedious; but I suppose I may be a little *abnormal* in my love for it. It's doubtless a matter of temperament . . ."

But the inspiration which he was receiving from his reading, writing, and publishing, was considerably damped down by the disasters which continued to fall upon his gardening efforts. His monetary position was more precarious than ever, and he told Henry Byett in June that he had come to another parting of the ways. He had to decide whether he and Mary could possibly continue any longer under starvation conditions, or whether he would abandon his writing and gardening and seek employment once more in the factory or on the land. For several months they had been living on a diet of bread, lard, tea and cheap bacon; they badly needed new clothes and boots. He could look forward to no more than £8 in royalties the following November. That spring he had had to borrow £5 in order to buy seeds and manure for his garden. The uncertain weather, now too wet, now too dry, and the continual plague of pests, had succeeded in ruining all his efforts, so that he was anticipating a total loss of about £30 on his fruit and peas.

Disaster followed upon disaster, undermining his confidence and shattering his spiritual energy. Of the birds which regularly visited his garden he had once written, "The robins are my constant attendants, sitting on the same bush, sometimes on the very branch I wish to prune, so that I have to drive them away, but they return very quickly, and with them the silent inquisitive wren, the little whitethroat or the flycatcher. If I have laboured to construct a fence, or have set stakes or poles, I feel amply rewarded if a blackbird comes and sits upon any part of the work, whether he sings or not; and to see forty or fifty martins perched in a row upon the wire line that will one day support my gooseberries affords me more pleasure than as though every fruit thereafter grown were of pure gold, or of more value than costly pearl or glittering diamond." Poor disillusioned man! By 1923 he, the poet of "The Blackbird's Canticle" was threatening death and destruction to every thrush and blackbird he could lay hands on.

"It's no good", he said to J. B. Jones, "they will ruin my strawberries. I'll destroy every one of them; old ones, young ones, and eggs".

Mary Williams, now nearly at the end of her tether, turned to Henry Byett for advice as to their future; the latter has described the heart-breaking occasion. "Her face was sad and careworn; her voice told of a tiredness of the eternal struggle to live. . . . She was indeed a pathetic figure. I sensed that she would welcome advice to give up that mode of life and return to labouring for a wage. I cravenly shirked the responsibility of a definite reply. I knew I ought to have counselled surrender, with its concomitant of comfort and health, but I thought of the loss to the world of letters. I also hated to figure in the role of a defeatist, so found refuge in some sort of noncommital reply which left them to decide for themselves unassisted."

But what Byett *did* do, and immediately, was to write to Fitzmaurice and inform him of the tragedy which was being enacted at "Ranikhet". When Williams heard through Fitzmaurice's solicitor of Byett's gesture, he was on his mettle in a moment and said that he wished his friends would consult him before any move was made on his behalf; they did not understand the true position nor his particular temperament. The whole matter was distasteful to him. Nevertheless, an application was forwarded by Fitzmaurice to the Royal Literary Fund, and in August Williams was voted a grant of £75 intended to cover a period of three years. The Trustees were greatly impressed with *Round About the Upper Thames* and *Folk Songs of the Upper Thames*, copies of which Williams had been asked to send to them. It was suggested that he might consider the possibility of writing another country book in the near future.

Needless to say the money came as a godsend and saved the situation at "Ranikhet" for the time being. Some of the strawberry plants recovered, too, and Williams eventually sold nearly 300 lbs. of fruit for £12, which partial success decided him to concentrate the main of his gardening energies for the future on the production of straw-berries and peas. He thought that with any kind of luck he might reckon on recovering 10/- a perch from his strawberry beds. So that autumn he bought thousands of new plants, setting them out in long rows, and each containing several different types in order to ensure a complete succession. Quite a lot of the money received from the Royal Literary Fund was used for these purchases. In September a wholesale merchant offered to buy all his strawberry crop until 1934.

Determined not to be thwarted by failure, Williams tried his hand at journalism again. The *Cornhill* praised an Indian article, the *Bristol Times and Mirror* did likewise, but neither editor was willing to print. The whole business of trying to convince editors to accept work which he knew they did not need was depressing and degrading to him and not calculated to keep the true literary spirit alive in him. All the same he declared in September, "I would rather die than find myself suddenly well-off as regards material needs, but exiled from my most cherished pursuits, friends and associations." And to Fitzmaurice, "I can still enjoy the Latin 'Odes' and the little books of Sallust; take a new interest in the rather rude style of Herodotus; appreciate Shakespeare and his plays as I never did before, and look forward with great pleasure to the time when I can read the Sanskrit text of the most charming fables of the 'Hitopadesa', which I hope to begin next year." Though life was hard, and difficulties pressed upon him, Williams refused to surrender his faith, and, as he wrote to a friend in Australia, "There are compensations of the evening, with book and slate, and cheerful fire, and my wife to keep me company—the finest friend of all."

He forged ahead with Sanskrit, reaching out to maturity in scholarship. One day in September he cycled over to Boar's Hill to meet Robert Bridges. The two conducted a long enquiry into the origins of language with particular reference to Sanskrit, and Williams was amazed and rather shocked to learn that Bridges, who was President of the Pure English Society, did not know a single word of Sanskrit, a pure language which had given many words to English. But the meeting was as ever a balm and inspiration to him, for the Laureate was always helpful and never patronising.

During October, Williams read and fully mastered 250 lines of the "Mahabharata" which comprised the immortal story of the Nala and Damayanti. He found this work very hard going for a novice but the fable was so lovely and compelling with its rich and melodious lines that he did not consider he was labouring at all. He had recently been told that out of twenty universities in Germany, Sanskrit was taught at nineteen, which drew from him the following, in a letter to Fitzmaurice, "And here we are trying to get rid of Greek, because it is tedious to learn. . . . By putting aside everything that is *laborious*, and choosing only that which is utilitarian, in the material sense, we shall be taking tremendous risks. We are changing rapidly, and we progress too, materially; but I cannot seem to get away from the obsession that there is something of infinitely more value in life than mere riches and the comforts they bring; something that is never grasped by the hand, but felt and lived, and the joy of which can never fade nor perish."

That November, Williams decided to revise *Sardanapalus*, the five-act lyrical drama which he had written twenty years before. He also rewrote much of *Round the Cape to India* and renamed it *Artillerymen Afloat*. Work poured from him during the winter of 1923. By the end of the year he had read close on a thousand lines of Sanskrit poetry and prose, the Vedic hymns making an especial appeal to him.

He had already been told by Sir James Currie, and received the information with some amusement, that a man was either mad when he
began to learn Sanskrit, or mad at the end of it.   He certainly had never
experienced anything more exciting and spellbinding.

Williams' last decision of the year was to write yet another book on
the Thames district, to follow on naturally from *Round about the Upper
Thames*.   He now intended to deal with the lower half of the river,
fron Faringdon to Oxford, and to call the new book *Round about the
Middle Thames* or *Villages of the Middle Thames*.   He thought that it
would take him until 1925 in order to amass his material but he looked
forward to his new task because of the relief it would give him from
his indoor studies.

Fitzmaurice had not been idle in Williams' interest all this time for,
though he had succeeded in obtaining the grant from the Royal Literary
Fund, he now wrote to the Prime Minister and suggested that Alfred
Williams' name should be included in the next Civil List.   Sir Thomas
Davies, the Member for Cirencester, also backed this application,
reminding the Prime Minister that some years before he had told him
about Alfred Williams and his struggles.   Mr. Baldwin was greatly
impressed with the claims made for Williams but, after careful consideration, he decided that he could not include his name in the Civil
List because he was too young.   Williams was nearing his forty-seventh
year.   But just before Christmas Day, Williams received from the
Royal Bounty Fund a cheque for £150 in appreciation of his literary
work.

So, secure in the knowledge that their physical needs would be satisfied for some time, Alfred and Mary were hopeful once more.   Alfred's
spirits rose on a daring crescendo as he felt new springs of energy and
enthusiasm within him.   Mary, relieved and thankful, but so often
on the edge of precipices, waited.

CHAPTER TWENTY-ONE

STRUGGLING YEARS

SO Williams persevered, earnestly striving to combat depression
and to resist defeatism.   He spent the whole of January, 1924, in
reading the Sanskrit *Hitopadesa*, finding freedom of spirit and exaltation
in these ancient fables, whose supreme elegance, priceless wisdom
and affectionate quality, greatly attracted him.   His chief labour was
to acquire a large enough working vocabulary; he had had to look up
nearly every word of the *Hitopadesa*.   But he carefully followed his

direct methods of learning a language. "I have never spent an hour in trying to write Latin, or Greek, or Sanskrit", he wrote to Fitzmaurice in February, "but I read all I can, and attempt to make myself proficient in construing. I found with Sanskrit that if I looked after the grammar merely, I should spend a couple of years upon it, and then have done no more than make myself familiar with a great mass of rules, etc. But by getting a Reader and pushing forward, I remembered the rules better because I saw them *applied* and I remembered the nouns and verbs, too, and became used to the Compounds and conjunct consonants."

He had now completed his revision of the Artillery book and of *Sardanapalus*, being helped a great deal by Fitzmaurice with the latter. He had also made a collection of his factory poems under the title *Factory Rhymes*. Between the middle of February and the end of March, Williams submitted the three manuscripts to several publishers but was unsuccessful in placing any of them. He told Duckworth that if he would take *Sardanapalus,* he himself would dispose of 200 copies, but the publisher pointed out that there was no paying public for such a work.

Williams now turned his thoughts to the new book on the Thames, affirming that he would not be disturbed from this for two or three plays; his country books, he said, were the only things he could write which possessed any permanent value. Besides, he was reasonably sure of getting this type of book published. He planned for it to have twenty chapters and to deal in detail with the Thames country from Coxwell to Wytham and back again along the north bank of the river. By 30th March three chapters had been written; a dozen were ready by June and, "if, after 50 miles of cycling, and much interrogation, I discover a quaint custom, or a curious item of information, or see a new bird by the river, it gives me no end of pleasure. . . . I am so occupied with my writing that I have no time for the ordinary business of the world."

But he had to attend to his "ordinary business" all the same. There was the garden to claim his regular attentions. In the spring there had been a heat wave when his seedlings perished and withered. Then followed cold winds and frost so that he lost 150 crowns of his best strawberry plants. But those which withstood the weather, ripened well and he sold 220 lbs. of the fruit that season, besides 200 lbs. of blackcurrants, which brought him in £30.

On the last day of August he had written the last chapter of the Thames book. He spent the best part of September at Sanskrit, reading 300 lines from *The Great Tale* and the whole of *The Dharma Castra* which was the canonical law book of the Hindus. Not often did he break away from his study or his garden, but one day in that month he and Mary dropped everything and made for the Thames. They cycled to Radcot Bridge and fished there all day, catching a fine eel and a small bag of roach. "I hold that nobody knows the Thames who has not fished in its waters: and one who writes of the river who has not angled in it, is at a palpable disadvantage. Yet I reckon angling to be among the sins of lazy people", he wrote to Fitzmaurice.

With the Thames book out of the way, and little to do in the garden, Alfred Williams concentrated upon general reading for some weeks. He delved into Kant and Bishop Berkeley, and spent some enjoyable days with Pope's *Life and Letters* and J. H. Morgan's new *Life of Viscount Morley*. Fitzmaurice gave him the run of his library, which drew from Williams the remark, "When I open books I have a desire to forget the present, and plunge into the discussions, controversies, and entertainments of a past day." The Sanskrit work went on—he still read long into the night—and he was making great use of Fitzmaurice's copy of Skeats' *Dictionary*. The Vedic Wedding Service was translated that year.

Williams concerned himself a great deal with Indian politics towards the end of 1924. He condemned in strong terms to several friends, European ignorance of Hindu culture. He believed that Anglo-Indians were jealous of the Indians, largely because the general standard of European culture was low, and lacking in a desire to get beyond a certain point in the quest for knowledge. He deprecated British commercial enterprise in India. Yet he did not think that the country was yet ready for Home Rule because of the political incompetence of the people as a whole. The majority of them wanted no change, but resented short-sighted attempts to westernize them. It was the duty of the British to restore the old India to the people, to present them with their own art and literature and to see that they had colleges and universities which could teach them about Indian culture. As with Egypt, we were making the fatal mistake of taking too much out of India, instead of helping her peoples more.

Williams had now decided to call the Thames book *The Banks of Isis* and to dedicate it to Fitzmaurice. In November he submitted the work to Duckworth but to his intense disappointment the firm was unwilling to publish, pointing out that *Folk Songs of the Upper Thames* had had poor sales. *The Banks of Isis* now went to Basil Blackwell of Oxford who was also not prepared to publish the book. When it was returned for the second time, Williams accepted the position philosophically; he went into his garden and planted a dozen new bush plum trees and half a dozen Bramley seedling apples. "At least" he said, "those who do not read my books think highly of my strawberries. "

Before 1924 was over he had started thinking about another book. Acting on a suggestion made by John Bailey to him, he had in mind a book of semi-political letters to workers, opposed to Socialism, to be called *Letters from a Working Man to Working Men.*

The new year began badly for the couple, for they were in bed for some weeks with influenza, due, according to Williams, to the low and damp situation of South Marston. As soon as they had recovered he was back at his writing again. To Fitzmaurice he wrote in February, 1925: "There is no doubt but that interest in countryside books is waning: witness the melancholy fact that I cannot sell a copy in Swindon. . . . I am getting ahead with the "letters" and have written more than half the book. They deal with Unions, the Railways, Farm Workers, Town and Country, Work and Wages, Political Parties, History, Education, Hobbies, Poses, Smallholders, Learning Languages, The British Empire, Ireland, Egypt, India, etc." When not at work on the book he read the Vedic Funeral Hymn, and *Sutra*, which dealt with the ritual of funeral ceremonies. The "letters" were finished in April. There were 100 of them, addressed to a number of imaginary people, though it is more than likely that Williams had actual people in mind. The wide field covered by the letters gives an indication of how intimate and detailed his knowledge was of labour conditions. They display keen observation and there is much forceful writing, but, as a whole, they lack a really effective style, never rising above average journalese. They aim at satire, but often are merely destructive. The best letters are those which deal with the lot of the factory worker and farm labourer, which is not surprising, since here he was able to write with conviction and from first hand knowledge. The value of *Letters from a Working Man* lies in the information they give of Williams' own life, and of the way in which he had been thinking for some time. They show to a marked degree how some of his political opinions were formed and then developed.

But Williams could find no publisher for the book, which he now put into the hands of a literary agent. He always said that if he had been writing on the Labour side he could easily have found a publisher. He had now by him six works in manuscript, and though he tried publisher after publisher, he was told over and over again that there was no market for his work. He could get no-one to take a risk. "You see how very precarious this work is and must be", he wrote to his Australian friend, "Richard Jefferies found the same: that was the cause of his poverty. . . . Swindon doesn't buy a book, which disheartens publishers, as they carefully reckon with local sales." His only success was in persuading the *North Berks Herald* to accept *The Banks of Isis* for serialisation at a fee of 20 guineas.

Bitterness and grief ate into him. It was not so much the fact that he and Mary had so little to live on—it was no new thing for them to be in want—as the growing knowledge within Alfred that his recent books were receiving no recognition. He believed that the world had never accepted h m as an authentic poet and author, and that now, in spite of all that had been published, people were forgetting his very existence. No one could shake him from the belief that greater trials were to come to him, that he was a back number, and that "Ranikhet" would have to be sold.

"I have had heaps of promises" he wrote to a friend in June 1925, "and was always told that I should reap a little recognition for my literary efforts: I fear I have been fooled; but it's the way of the world." He was also despondent because he could not buy all the Sanskrit books he needed; he had recently cycled to Oxford and examined the Sanskrit literature in the Bodleian. And the garden, too, had given him its annual fright. Because of severe blight he had lost £20 worth of apples, plums and blackcurrants; luckily for them both, the strawberries produced a bumper crop, and by the end of July he had disposed of six hundred pounds for £28. They could both breathe again.

Then, in the midst of all his worries, Kyle informed him he was now in a position to publish *Selected Poems*, three-quarters of which had been in type since 1920. Williams' spirits rose. Had the tide turned ? John Bailey had already agreed to write an Introduction, and Robert Bridges to accept the Dedication. *The Banks of Isis* was now appearing weekly in the *North Berks Herald* and attracting considerable local interest because of the power and fascination of its nature writing. This work is very much a saga of the Thames, which runs serenely through every chapter. We never lose sight of its plashing waters, and its quiet voices echo within us, as, with Williams, we move along its banks and leisurely explore each backstream village. Though the country characters of the earlier books are not so often encountered, we are introduced to a new and more delicate company—the wild animals, birds, fishes, butterflies and flowers of this mid-Thames hinterland. Before, Williams had used the natural scenery of the ground covered, as a backcloth to the ancient stage upon which the village peoples moved in all the drama of their native wisdom and grace. It was this glowing backcloth which created the whole atmosphere of the rural England he depicted. In *The Banks of Isis* there is the same kind of natural background, but it is painted with even more vivid colours; the stage is here too, though less obvious, but across it fly, dart and swim the shy-eyed creatures of the banks, meadows, pools and streamlets which lie near to a dozen or more villages from Great Coxwell to Cumnor and Wytham. These, the untamed ones, are the heroes and heroines of Williams' last country book. But the villagers are here, also. The waggoners and ploughmen, the innkeeper haranguing with the blacksmith, parson, squire and sexton, witches and woodmen, watermen of every type, the ageless shepherds of the White Horse, the gypsies of Harrow Down Hill, weave their untroubled ways through the warp of an ever changing pattern. Williams treats the whole district as if it were a huge and busy turntable which swings in some new character from chapter to chapter, while we are watching from the Windrush or waiting idly for a ferry boat at Bablock Hythe or Evenlode. It is in *The Banks of Isis* that we meet and lose our hearts to Linny the gypsy queen, dark skinned as an Indian, who died when she was 101 years old, and then was able to assemble mourners to keep up her wake for a week, from all over the South Country. "She smoked a short black clay pipe and made her own medicines of the marshmallow or other wild herbs, and she carried besides, a store of badgers' fat or that of the viper for anointing sores and wounds, in the treatment of which she was considered to be eminently successful".

On 16th December, 1925, *Selected Poems* was published by Erskine Macdonald. Williams had promised to guarantee £62 10s. od. worth of sales, so he immediately set out on his travels as before, to dispose of as many copies of his book as possible. The published price was 6/-. Neither he nor Mary were in really good health at the time— he had dyspepsia again and she, a troublesome cold. During that winter their income was slightly augmented by the returns from sales of potatoes grown in "Ranikhet" garden—18/- for a two hundredweight sack, 8/6 for half a sack, and carriage paid. And three weeks after the appearance of *Selected Poems*, Williams was able to hand Kyle £50. To Henry Byett he wrote: "I have the confidence to believe that this book will be permanent. Before, people hardly knew what to accept as my 'poetical canon', but now, with this volume, there will be no doubt. This isn't pretending too much, but one must have the courage of his work and convictions, and I ought by now to know where I stand. Of course, those who imagine that all artistic effort is wasted in this age (and my own among it) are wrong, and I've not been deceived or mistaken, in following the course upon which I started. . . . Swindon hasn't grasped the fact yet, which is, that A.W. is not in the making, but that his work is for the most part accomplished."

Selected Poems contained so many errors, owing to a printers' strike and because Williams was not given the opportunity of correcting all the proofs, that he wished to withdraw the book, but he was advised by the Authors' Society that he could not do this, as the legal position was that there must have been an implied agreement though no document had been actually signed. The book was well reviewed, especially by *The Times* and *The Times of India*. Critics stressed the strength, sanity and simplicity of the poems, and observed echoes of Whitman, Meredith and Shelley.

Bailey's "Introduction" gives point and purpose to the selection.

He outlines the main facts of the life of "a rare and interesting figure", in this phrase epitomising Alfred Williams' chief contribution to his own and future ages. "Here is a man who passes from a boyhood spent at a village school and in work on a farm, to years of exhausting labour in the heated atmosphere of a railway forge. And yet before middle life this man of little official education and, apparently, less leisure, has taught himself French, Latin, and Greek, and found time to acquire, in addition to all that, a remarkable knowledge both of the folk lore and the natural history of his native county. Obviously such a man is no ordinary man". Bailey mentions his friends, his soldiering ("the best limber-gunner of his battery"), the building of "Ranikhet", his learning of Sanskrit. He characterises Williams' attitude to life as brave, sincere, sympathetic and intelligent, these being the foundations upon which all his poetry had been built. He was, above everything else, a courageous man. Of the poems themselves, he says in quoting the last section of "The Hills"—"I am sure Cowper would have loved and praised their simplicity, sincerity and quiet beauty, the ever-ready sympathy of their poet's heart, and the ever watchful curiosity with which he notes the ways of nature and of man. . . . This book shows us a man, who, though the opposite of a favoured child of fortune, has known how to live in the present, and find in it abundance of things interesting and beautiful, lovable and good."

Selected Poems contains 114 poems, of which 23 are early poems, 29 are love lyrics, 10 are nature poems, 24 are about India, 23 are sonnets, and 15 are on miscellaneous topics. Naturally there is much overlapping. The book is divided into six sections, each containing several poems which had appeared in the earlier books.

Nature in every mood is reflected in nearly every poem. The whole of "The Hills" is here, and the "Ode to Morning", with the greater part of "Natural Thoughts and Surmises". Cowper might have indeed written "In my Garden". Williams naturally included a tribute to Richard Jefferies. There are five attractive bird poems and the two which were inspired by Liddington and the Downs. "The Shepherd's Song" and "The Reapers' Song" break again on our ears with their reminders of the country folk, while "Futurity" sums up in blank verse Williams' whole philosophy of life:—

> "Perfect trust,
> Obedience to the will, sincerity,
> White-handed Hope and close-grained Fellowship".

The love poems are seventeenth century in concept and atmosphere. Their imagery and subtle conceits, their disciplined emotions and clever rhythmic effects stand out as the hallmark of the accomplished craftsman. "Time Heals all Wounds but One" is the best poem in this section with its moving verse:—

> "Time heals all wounds but one,
>   And will not brave the worst;
> Hearts that are broken brokenly live on,
>   And darken till the prison-fetter burst.
> Time heals all wounds but one."

Williams also wisely included the haunting "Leave me not ever" and the almost flawless "All things delight in sleep".

The Indian section is made memorable by the long poem "India" which had been composed in the Himalayas and first published in *The Empress*. The passages describing the mountains are typical of his idiom:—

> "The sun
> Streams gentle, and the air invigorates.
> Aloft, on wing divine, the eagle soars;
> The lizard is asleep upon the stone;
> The sun-birds flash and glitter, while the dove
> Croons on the bough her ancient melody.
> And all the mountain-side is gay and glad."

"The Indian Herdsman's Song", "Leaving Ranikhet", "Evening" and "To the Himalayas" show Williams to be possessed of the keenest ear and eye for beauty. The lyric called "Afternoon" glitters with images:—

> "Only the butterflies
> Are patient of the sun.   The bee, that sips
> The dewy souls of flowers, and homeward fleets,
> Laden with golden joys and liquid sweets
> (Where toils the hive, and fragrant honey drops)
> Is fallen asleep within the lily's lips
>   Tired with his ecstasies.
>
>   Fainting, the rose
> In sweetest agony her spirit yields,
> Scattering her snowy image on the grass;
> The rhododendron blooms, a burning mass,
> Droop in the thicket of the chestnut shields;
> Now come the weary oxen down the fields,
>   And the mystic buffaloes."

Among the miscellaneous poems one renews acquaintance with the sonorous "Music in Salisbury Cathedral" and "About Wiltshire". It is interesting, too, to see "Aspirations" which contains the philosophical germ later expanded and developed in "Natural Thoughts and

Surmises". Finally, there are the two sonnet sequences on "Stonehenge" and "Salisbury Cathedral", the "Lord Fitzmaurice" sonnets, and the soliloquy on the Roman ruins at Chedworth, all of which had appeared in the earlier books.

The selection contains nearly all Williams' poems worthy of preservation; it is a pity that none of "The Testament" is included. The book will remain as a monument to his love for nature and mankind; it represents the positive creed of a man who, like the metaphysicals, completely achieved an escape of the spirit and who blended himself with something outside himself "which makes the new life a new creation". Williams could well claim that with his *Selected Poems*, the last book published in his lifetime, he had achieved fame enough to be ranked at least with George Herbert, Sidney, Crabbe, Thomson and those who had been the Wiltshire poets of a former generation.

So Alfred Williams neared his 50th year. In spite of the good notices and excellent sales of *Selected Poems*, his sense of frustration was not lessened as he moved into 1926. The months passed one by one but he was oblivious to them. On 6th March he very successfully lectured on "Folk-Lore Origins" to the Gloucestershire Historical Association at the Cheltenham Ladies' College, and on the following day to the Gloucestershire Literary Club in the Gloucester Guildhall on "Folk Songs". He owed both these engagements, for which he received fees amounting to five guineas, to the good offices of Henry Gee, Dean of Gloucester, who had been lent *Folk Songs of the Upper Thames* by the Dean of Winchester, an old friend of Alfred Williams.

At the end of March he was the guest of honour at the annual dinner of the Wiltshire Society in London. He had now struggled through a thousand lines of *Hitopadesa* and was more and more amazed by its practical truths and its challenging aphorisms and proverbs. And after reading *Tess of the D'Urbervilles*, which J. B. Jones lent him in April, he wrote: "No one could read it without feeling he was richer in experience. Hardy's mind is often too complex for me to penetrate, but I don't suppose there is another man in England who could write of the countryside as he has written; other books by other writers appear very poor beside his. I should like to read his other novels, but I cannot spare the time and keep my other interests going".

May 1926 was an unhappy month for Alfred and Mary Williams. His eyes were troubling him again, he had a chill on the spine, Mary was full of rheumatism, frost had ruined half his strawberry plants and all his bush apples. In addition, the General Strike had depressed him and called forth from him strong condemnation of the policy of the Trade Union leaders, and of the Government. He believed that the limit to post-war prosperity had been reached, and that there was a powerful move on the part of reactionaries to revive every sort of superstition that would re-enslave the spirit of the people. To his friend in Australia he wrote: "I think the general stoppage was a profound mistake; the pity is, or was, that the Union leaders did not nearly grasp the utter seriousness of the move, and the effect it would have on the wellbeing of the working classes." Williams was so concerned with the whole business that in July he wrote a letter to *The Times,* dealing with what he called "Terrorism in the Trade Unions."

In August, he walked in the rain on Liddington with John Bailey, who was on holiday at Hungerford, and talked mainly about William Dowsing and *his* struggle for recognition.

His strawberries had realised £20 and he had a fair potato crop, but by September he estimated that he had lost another £20 on the garden that season, which called from him the following remarks to Fitzmaurice: "At present, smallholders have too much land. They are not sufficiently instructed. They have no capital to work the holding. I advocate one-acre plots for the beginner. Put the spade into it. Subsoil the land. I hold that if a man is told what to do, and how to do it, he can average 15/- a perch, £120 an acre, but he could only do this *on one* acre. Immediately he goes beyond, he must hire labour and get machinery, etc., and away goes his cash." These ideas on smallholding Williams embodied in a further letter of 600 words to *The Times,* which appeared in September. He spent nearly the whole of that month subsoiling and trenching every inch of his land. He was still trying his hand at occasional journalism. An article on "Folk Songs" had been accepted by the Folk Press for their new magazine *Wood Lore;* others, which used the information of some of the *Letters to Working Men,* appeared in the local press. *The Yorkshire Times* paid him a guinea for "Rare Wiltshire Birds", *The Wiltshire Gazette* another for an article on "The Wiltshire Wassail" and "Mummers". By October, working at high pressure, Williams had written twenty articles on a variety of topics, a bare threequarters of which were marketed. A dozen of them, amounting to 22,000 words, realised £3 13s. 0d. To Dowsing he wrote, "You have learnt, long ago, that a man's power is *in himself*: if he hasn't the 'push in him' it is no good looking to others, especially in literature. Better men than you and I get 'turned down' every day by Publishers and Editors; victory is won when one has realised that it doesn't matter a damn ! I do a few articles . . . in the winter, perhaps, 10/- a time, 1,500 words! An editor asked me to do him one recently on cottage architecture, and it took me four days. I haven't got the 10/- yet".

This article on cottage architecture, which had been written for the *Wiltshire Times,* had a sequel. It was brought to the notice of Sir Frank Baines of H.M. Office of Works, who then wrote to Williams for advice on preserving folk architecture, and sent him a private copy of a scheme of organisation for so doing which was being submitted to the Royal Society of Arts. Williams' article had talked about the reconditioning of rural cottages where practicable. He thought that council houses were very good in everything but appearance. It was more sensible and economical to improve the amenities of the old cottages.

In November he was given an old Blick typewriter. "So I am now able to copy off my own scrawl", he wrote to Henry Byett. "It's an antique thing, but it is better than the pen for editorial work. As for articles, I've written them by the dozen this year, but there's nothing much in journalism." Also, in that month, owing to the Coal Strike, they were unable to have a fire; for days on end Alfred sat in his study, so cold that he could hardly grip a pen or hammer words out on the typewriter. He used to go and work in the garden for an hour or so in order to give himself sufficient warmth to get on with his writing indoors. He was still finding it difficult to get enough Sanskrit books, but eventually Fitzmaurice made it possible for him to borrow what he needed from the library of the India Office. For two years Williams had been trying to buy a secondhand Sanskrit dictionary but was unable to find one. In December he decided he could wait no longer, so, breaking into the small store of money which had been laid aside for extremest urgency, he bought a new dictionary published by O.U.P. Fortified with his new treasure (though its small print and huge size worried him) he was ready to meet another year and all its disappointments, with all the courage and faith remaining to him. And to Fitzmaurice, now over 80 years old, he wrote at the turn of the year: "The Hindu *Hitopadesa* closes with these words—"day by day may great joy be to all"—but what is the good if we do not try to grasp it ?"

But the struggling years were souring Alfred Williams.

CHAPTER TWENTY-TWO

TRAGEDY

HIS first decision in 1927 was to finish the railway novel which he had started in India. He had always held out strongly against the writing of fiction, though several of his friends had suggested, on more than one occasion, that he had the power to write a really outstanding story based upon his own life experiences and intimate knowledge of railway conditions. J. B. Jones has told of how whenever he broached the question of a novel with Williams, "the conversation inevitably drifted again into his favourite topics; botanical lore, strawberry culture, metrical experiments, classical

translation, or latterly, Hindu literature, Buddhism and the Himalayas."
By the end of February, however, three-quarters of the novel had been
written, and it was finished before March was out. It had nineteen
chapters and some 70,000 words, and Williams called it *The Steam-
hammer Shop—a Romance of the Forge.* Regarding the plot of the novel
Williams had outlined this once to Henry Byett, "Of course there
must be a villain, a hero and a heroine, and a love element. The
villain is a man who is a cruel tyrant to his employees, and I make him
take part in a murder, or attempted murder, by taking both hero and
heroine on the river at Lechlade, with the object of capsizing the boat,
drowning both. The ultimate result, however, is that the villain is
himself carried over the weir, and is the only fatality. Collaterally,
there runs another set of characters, and a story of railway life, with,
curiously enough, a motor smash, in which a railway official is involved." The story was largely autobiographical, with Williams as
the hero in the person of "Wilfred Weston", and Mary figuring as
"Grace Aldwyn" the heroine. South Marston becomes "Colebrook",
and Swindon "Winton". It is all rather melodramatic and it is not
surprising that no publisher would look at it. Its only interest lies
in the information it probably gives about Williams' life and habits:
he really had no gifts nor inclination for this kind of writing. The
novel was just hack work. He needed money. For the greater part
of that spring the couple were fighting influenza as well as low spirits.
The unequal struggle for mere existence never abated, and the two clave
desperately to each other, plumbing the wells of their love, but sad
at heart and ever wondering when release would come. Alfred
especially sank deeper and deeper into melancholy; Mary was at the
same time bewildered and resigned. He still had flashes of his old self
when he could tell Fitzmaurice with truth that though he could not
always create, he could always enjoy, for he knew that culture would
bring its own reward. "There are great times ahead. We shall not
see them, but others will see them. When we think of the New York
to Paris flight by 'plane, and the wonders of radioactivity, and the
electron, we are filled with a great hope, and a great enthusiasm.
People won't read Homer so much nor Ovid . . . but life will be
larger—more full and complete." The garden was a failure again.
Bad weather lost him over £20 worth of apples, and only half the
strawberries matured. He was still grinding out articles; six on
"Vanished Village Industries" in the *Wiltshire Times* brought him in
five shillings a column—a pittance indeed for the hours he had spent
on them. On 21st October, 1927, he realised he had been married
for twenty-four years, and he told Henry Byett that his life had been
a failure, and a disappointment to Mary, the very pattern of hope and
fidelity.

In December, Williams embarked upon the last great piece of work of his life with a decision to translate the Sanskrit "Panchatantra", for he had discovered that this mighty book contained much exquisite folk and nature lore, and thought it might appeal to English readers. It was at this juncture that he made the fortunate acquaintance of A. A. Macdonell, Boden Professor of Sanskrit in the University of Oxford. Macdonell had heard of Williams' work, and after meeting him in Oxford, told him how much he admired his brave efforts to learn Sanskrit and how much he would like to help him with the rendering of the "Panchatantra". He also told Sir Edgar Bonham Carter, Director of the School of Oriental Studies, about Williams, with the result that the latter was invited to meet Sir Edgar and his staff in the following year. Williams could not accept this invitation, however, because he could not afford the fare to London and back— and it was too far to cycle.

Williams now sacrificed every spare moment to the massive new task in hand. He lived very much to himself, rarely going far afield, and viewing the world at large, as it were, from behind a curtain of his own making. Not that he ever became a recluse—it was just that he needed every minute for what he was confident would be his final project. In February, 1925, he wrote to Fitzmaurice, "One by one the great players are passing off the scene. It is the fashion to say we have progressed—but we have our problems still. There is a 'higher standard of life', at least, most people say there is. My idea is a more highly developed intellect, a keener appreciation of the truth and a higher aesthetic sense. But we want to be practical, too, sane, and human. I am not satisfied with the present intellectual standard. . . . I sometimes feel out of touch 'really' with much that I see around me, and one cannot write what one would like to write, well—no one would print it. . . . It is my burning desire to see humanity free, physically, intellectually, spiritually. I cannot do much towards furthering this, beyond my personal example, if that is worth anything." By Easter, Williams had read the greater part of the "Bhagavad Gita" and had got through five books of the "Panchatantra". All this put a serious strain upon his eyesight which was a constant trouble to him. By June he had translated eighteen of the tales from the "Panchatantra", and was thinking of doing fifty of these for publication. Macdonnell gave him valuable advice, told him that the University would lend him books, and put him in touch with E. B. Nash of Roehampton, who was a renowned Sanskrit scholar. Williams' plan was to simplify the tales in such a way as to preserve the main story, without destroying the general atmosphere and idiom.

As the year wore on, it was clear that his garden again would not give him full return for his labours. He lost four-fifths of his strawberries, and two-thirds of his apples through frost; these were worth about £30 to him. Williams racked his brains in a despairing effort to solve the problem of how to prevent the frost from affecting *his* garden. He thought of covering his strawberry plants with cloches when they were in bloom, or of taking on another site: he dismissed the latter idea for the time being because he knew a plough would be needed, and he dared not risk the physical fatigue of such an arduous operation when he had the "Panchatantra" at his elbow. If only his plan to establish a connection with the editors of leading journals had succeeded he would have been saved the consequences of disastrous fruit seasons. He discovered too late how keen the competition was for the favours of editors. In December, largely upon the recommendation of Fitzmaurice, The Royal Literary Fund made Williams another grant of £75 to be spread over three years. The £25 sent was sufficient to see him and Mary through the winter and spring. Nevertheless, he bought with some of the money, Arthur Ryder's translation of the "Panchatantra" and the earlier text called "Tantrakhyayika", which he needed. And shortly before Christmas, 1928, after exactly a year's vigorously applied study, Alfred Williams completed his *Tales from the Panchatantra*. Macdonnell highly praised the translations and said they were very suitable for the general reader; he also offered to write an Introduction to the book. He suggested that the manuscript should be sent to the Indian Institute at Oxford for its opinion, which Williams did early in 1929. The Institute in congratulating him said that the work would be of great value to all future Sanskrit students, but advised him that he might have difficulty in finding a publisher. This unfortunately proved to be only too true, for Williams could persuade no publisher to take the translations.

To Henry Byett he wrote in 1929 (in January), "I shall not undertake another work of the kind, because I feel that I have found my *final satisfaction* in Sanskrit, as far as literature goes. In addition, the study is a long one, and the field to be covered is vast and varied." This then was resignation. It was certainly not defeat. But had Alfred Williams by now some other knowledge working within him? Did he realise, if only dimly, that he *had* written his last book and dug over his garden for the *last* time? Were his feet already set upon another and far darker road? "I have found my final satisfaction". All that year he felt everything personally and acutely, being under the impression at times that the villagers were ill-treating him. He grew morose, irritable and secretive. Only Mary's love and his own dour courage bore him up. He even seriously thought of raising a mortgage of £500 on "Ranikhet" and its land, and of leaving Wiltshire altogether. He harped on the theme that he had never received sufficient recognition. Writing to Australia at the close of the year he said:

"When I look back over the past eighteen months and see how few letters I have written to anyone, I am really half ashamed. What's the reason? Well, I've had many sad disappointments of all sorts. I've been always grinding away but don't seem to 'hit off' much."

He read some Greek that autumn, the whole of *The Canterbury Tales*, some philosophy and Buddhism. Ironically, his land yielded its best strawberry crop ever, realising £30 for him. Nevertheless, in spite of this success, he began to negotiate with one of the local farmers for another piece of land on the road to Highworth. He told his friends that he had now finally decided to get out of "Ranikhet", to buy the new land which lay in a much higher position, build another house, and go in for intensive strawberry culture. He felt confident that the site he had chosen would not be subjected to such severe and ruining frosts. Neither would Mary be so prone to rheumatism and he to colds, for which he always blamed the low situation of "Ranikhet" and the little stream which ran at the bottom of his garden. He was still planning for the future.

The negotiations, however, fell through. The farmer asked an exorbitant price for the land; besides, it was so situated that it had a very narrow frontage to the main road but ran so far back that the duty of hedging and ditching would fall upon Williams. The ground was in an impoverished state and Williams was advised that it would cost a great deal of money to make it fertile and always need much unprofitable labour to maintain. He remained in "Ranikhet", therefore, his only comment being, "Well, I suppose we must stay here and welcome the frosts next spring".

In the autumn of 1929, too, he began to sell many of the plants and trees in his garden, as he had insufficient money to see him and Mary through that winter. To a friend who had sent him 10/- for some of these he pathetically wrote: "I am sorry I have no roses, as I go in for fruits; and our flowers are perennials. I sent you a nice lot of Madonna lilies and Lily of the Valley, delphiniums, etc., etc., You must see what is in the bag when it arrives. I hope you will be satisfied: I think it is good value as you can't get a Madonna Lily bulb at less than a shilling each. If a friend would like a lot like it I could do one more lot: or if you would like several young apple trees I could sell you four for 10/——trees which I myself gave 3/6 each for."

He had also revised the whole of the *Tales* following the advice of a well-known publishing firm to whom he had submitted them. This was on the point of accepting the work but eventually decided against doing so on the grounds that its matter would only appeal to a limited public. Referring to this advice, Williams wrote to Fitzmaurice, "I swear the reader was either drunk or crazy. He attempted a scheme of recommendations and got himself in a fix, then chucked up. Since then I have re-written the tales. It's all tedious—very tedious; but it does not matter much." He was now considering the possibility of publishing the book himself, for, as he said to Henry Byett—" . . . it's a classical study, and that being so, one had better fail in that than succeed in a vulgar object. The best, the best, the best! Moral and mental satisfaction I call it".

In November he was in bed for several days with a chill, and as soon as Mary had nursed him back to some kind of health she took to her bed with what was thought to be an ulcerated stomach. She was only able to take Benger's Food—"So I have to do the nursing, and most of the housework. A good thing I'm feeling very well again." Mary did not improve: Alfred was worried and mystified. The local doctor was consulted and shook his head as he advised her to attend the Victoria Hospital in Swindon for specialist examination. This she did on 10th January, 1930. A large malignant growth was discovered at the bottom of the gut. The last blow had fallen. This then was the beginning of the end. "My dearest one has a cancer." The surgeon said he would operate and do his best for her but considered his chances of success were slender. Alfred was shattered; though he had been nursing Mary day and night since November, he had no idea that she was so seriously ill. Nothing could comfort him now. When Fitzmaurice heard the news and sent him ten guineas, Williams, in acknowledging the gift, said, "Your lordship has always been generous, and your kind letter this morning touched me deeply. Thank you very much, my lord, if ever I wanted a word of cheer I wanted one now." Mary entered hospital; Alfred remained in abject misery in the nightmare loneliness of "Ranikhet". He believed there was a curse on the house. None could comfort him. Bridges sent him an autographed copy of his *Testament of Beauty*, but Alfred was cold to beauty. The operation took place on the last day of January, 1939. It was unsuccessful. Nothing could be done to cure Mary, for the cancer could not be checked. Alfred realised, but would not accept the fact, that his beloved "Mim" was dying. "We must bear our misfortune as well as we can, which is always made lighter by the kindness and sympathy of a few faithful friends," he wrote to Fitzmaurice; and to another old friend, "I want to have her all I can, even in her sufferings. It is terrible to think of the separation: but I shall have to nerve myself to it. Why do we love each other so?"

On 4th February, John Bailey sent him £5 with which to buy Mary extra comforts. On the 11th, Williams wrote to Henry Byett, "I have yet to recover (if I ever shall) from this most terrible of sorrows—terrible to me, because I shall have no-one in the world when she is gone. I have known more and more how necessary she was to me, and to my efforts and aspirations. Without her, I see no value in any-

thing, but a life of emptiness. Many have suffered, however, and
I must remember that. But it is hard. This, after all, is the price
I have to pay for such success as I have won. My dear comrade has
to bear the expense with her own life. You know how we have worked,
wanting the bare necessities of life; at least, I could never give my
beloved girl any comforts. For 15 years I have been fooled by promises
and I believed them. See the result ! My dearest has to go the hard
way to death without seeing any of our hopes realised. The pity of
it quite overwhelms me." He never was to recover. Mary lingered on.
Twice she nearly died from haemorrhage. Her legs and thighs were
grotesquely swollen and she had wasted away almost beyond recognition. Sentence of death had been passed upon her by the cruellest of
Fates, yet they both hoped against hope that miraculously she might
improve. Alfred was visiting her twice daily, cycling in from the
village to Swindon along the bleak and merciless roads. "My house
and home is empty now and I am caring for myself as well as I can.
This comes of having no children, but your lordship has suffered the
pangs of loneliness and isolation. What I shall do later I have yet to
find out. My dear wife is more than my right hand: she was a great
part of my very life."

His garden lay chill and neglected, locked in its winter fastnesses.
He was not writing nor reading any book. His heart was ice as he
roamed dejectedly through the silent and dusty rooms of "Ranikhet".
Mary was dying. All was passing; nothing was real. Poetry, Greek,
Latin, Sanskrit had no significance for him. At last the great heart
had been broken and the uncrushable spirit shivered. "Vici" mocked
him from the past. To this had an ideal brought them. How soon
would be the end ?

He had sent the Sanskrit tales to Basil Blackwell at the beginning of
the year, who was impressed with the work and now invited Williams
to discuss publication with him in Oxford. He has described their one
and only meeting, "On the appointed day he arrived punctually, a man
seemingly in the fifties, and with a charming smile. As soon as he
entered my room I was aware that I was in the presence of a rare spirit,
but being slow, and often wrong, in my estimation of men, I could
not tell what lay behind the serenity, the cheerfulness and the gentle-
ness which both his face and manner revealed. Our discussion raised
no difficulties. He would revise his typescript according to my suggestions, and bring it to Oxford again in a week or two to meet the
artist in my room, and to complete the preliminary plans for publication. He courteously excused himself from lunching with me, for he
was anxious to be getting home. When was his train ? He had
bicycled. I thought that a meal between two rides of twenty-seven
miles could hardly be amiss, but let it go at that, and proposed a day

for the next meeting. A look of pain came into his eyes as he asked me, very gently, if the day after would be equally convenient, for his wife had just undergone a very serious operation of doubtful value, and the day I had offered was that on which he was to bring her home from Swindon hospital. So 'the day after' and the hour of 2.30 was agreed, and Alfred Williams went his way." Blackwell accepted the *Tales* for publication there and then and thought they might find a good market.

A number of Alfred's more influential friends, including Robert Bridges, Fitzmaurice and J. H. Morgan had for some time been petitioning the Prime Minister—the third who had had Williams' name brought to him—to include his name in the next Civil List. Mr. Ramsay Macdonald tentatively agreed to do so, and on 20th February Williams heard that he was to receive a grant of £50 from the Royal Bounty as an advance payment if a Civil List Pension was awarded. The arrival of the cheque (actually paid by Mr. Macdonald out of his own pocket in the first instance) a few days later was a mixed blessing, for though it would meet present needs, Williams was grieved that Mary would not be there to share in the benefit and security which were now probably coming to him. Mary had been discharged from hospital as incurable and spent a sad but short time with Alfred in their home. He gave her the best Burgundy as a daily tonic, which stimulated her circulation and helped her to eat, but it was a heart-breaking experience, watching the efforts of a dying woman to live; she was soon back in hospital. The devoted pair had lived together for the last time under the loved beams of "Ranikhet". Alfred reached his 53rd birthday during this agonising month. And so into March, with Alfred making a daily pilgrimage into Swindon. It was clear to all his friends that he had greatly changed. He was neglecting himself and obviously had no heart to take proper nourishment. Every day he took Mary in some medical comfort. He was making the supremest effort to keep going and to pass on to her all the remaining vigour of his spirit. He told J. B. Jones that the strain at times was more than he could bear. "It will break me, I'm afraid." On 17th March, Williams learned from the Prime Minister that he had been awarded a Civil List pension of £50 in recognition of his literary work, and that the first quarter's payment would be forwarded to him on 1st April. In this manner, recognition had at length come to him, but it was ashes in his mouth. In one of his last letters to Fitzmaurice he wrote, "Whatever honour may be attached to the grant fades into insignificance in the light of circumstances."

His old Swindon friends, "Lou", Henry, and J. B. Jones rallied round him, doing all they could to comfort him and to bring him some sort of calm. Hardly a day went by that did not bring him some message of condolence. The villagers watched with pity the tragic and broken figure with downcast looks and heavy black-ringed eyes, set out on his cycle each day, more often than not from a fireless house, or saw him as he returned in the darkening evening with no message of hope on his lips. "Like a maimed bird he was" said one of his neighbours. He was not now making a double journey into Swindon every day for he was physically exhausted from lack of sleep and food and the Victoria Hospital was situated in the highest part of the town, and necessitated cycling up a steep hill. But he still visited Mary twice daily, putting forth every ounce of courage in order to sit at her side with a bright face and a cheering word. He spent the periods between the visits either roaming leaden-footed and despondent around the comfortless streets of Swindon or staying in the homes of some of his friends; he was with "Lou" Robins and his wife in their little shop most days.

March dragged on. In its last week, J. B. Jones journeyed out to South Marston to see Alfred. He found him calmer but fighting rising emotion; all the while he talked of Mary and the blow which had fallen on them, blaming himself that he had not realised what was wrong with her earlier. The two friends communed with each other until the evening, and then, "It was dark as we left the house, he accompanying me to the gate, but not, as often, a considerable distance down the road. We had a few moments together, the last, and I pressed a few Bradburys into his hand as I wished him goodnight. 'Notes!' he hoarsely exclaimed, and did not refuse them. As I walked into Swindon I felt appalled. This granite man was shivered at last. Alfred Williams was a broken man. I had witnessed a worse tragedy than death."

The days moved to 9th April. On the evening of that day, Alfred called to see "Lou" before proceeding to the hospital. On entering the house he sank dizzily into a chair, quivering with nervous strain and exhaustion. Mrs. Robins gave him tea and this revived him, but there was a wild and unnatural look about him as he began to talk about his "dear Mim". All his thoughts and conversation were about her as his speech grew louder and more incoherent. Suddenly he sprang from his chair, and like a tortured animal, beat the air with outstretched hands, calling piteously on her name, moaning hopelessly and brokenly, trembling and gesticulating as the tide of unrestrained passion swept over him. His friends looked on, hardly daring to interfere with what they had never seen from him before. After several minutes the mad fit passed as both heart and strength failed him; he fell back in the chair to find relief in tears that now streamed down his cheeks unchecked. When he had sufficiently recovered and was still, he apologised to "Lou" and his wife who were very distressed at his outburst, and then left their house for the hospital. He was never to enter it again. He had said good-bye to "Lou". He found Mary much worse than she had been earlier in the day. Seeing the poor shrunken body lying there in pain and considering the possibility of her lasting out for some time with him unable to do the best for her, with perhaps the workhouse looming ahead, he said, "My dear! This is going to be a tragedy for us both." Mary, not realising what thoughts were passing through his mind, whispered slowly in reply, "You don't mean that, Alf? If you say that, I shall wish I had died under the anaesthetic." He made no answer, but gently kissing her good-bye, stumbled tear-blinded out of the ward and to his bicycle. The journey back to Marston was only accomplished by the greatest will power. Many times he had to stop and rest because there was such a frightening pain over his heart, but eventually he was back home. He felt so ill that he immediately went to bed, but was in such pain that he was unable to take off his boots. He rubbed some Sloan's liniment over his heart and then probably lay down for a while. Feeling the need for an aspirin tablet he reached out and extracted one from a new packet of five which was on the dresser near his bed. He rose to get some water, and in so doing, collapsed over the bed and died. It was just after midnight.

The next day the neighbours were surprised at not seeing him about, or getting ready to cycle into Swindon. One, Miss Jennie Maisey, who had known his habits all her life, observed the uncollected morning letters under the front door of "Ranikhet". Suspecting that something was amiss, she knocked repeatedly at the door, but receiving no answer, called a neighbour; together they examined the key holes both back and front and found the keys were in the locks on the inside. As there was no movement from within by the early afternoon, Miss Maisey put a ladder up to the bedroom window, and looking in, saw to her horror, Alfred Williams lying dead across his unslept-in bed. She now got her nephew to ascend the ladder, and he, breaking the glass of the window, opened the catch inside, entered, went downstairs, and let in his aunt and other neighbours.

A single aspirin tablet rested on the pillow to the left of Alfred Williams, with the remaining four still in their packet on the other pillow. The bottle of Sloan's liniment lay dripping on its side on the nearby dresser having been knocked over him by as he fell over the bed. His shirt front was open, and his right arm was extended in the direction of the dresser.

A doctor was summoned from Highworth who, on arrival, reported the facts to the Coroner, who ordered a post mortem. This revealed that death had been due to heart failure; no inquest was deemed necessary.

Two days later, Mary, at her own request, was brought home to "Ranikhet", the dying to the dead. Her courage did not fail, for she wanted to be with Alfred in the home which had crowned their endeavours, until his burial. And she had many things to attend to for him before she herself followed him to the grave. Her only concern now was to live long enough to put everything in order. "I am grateful he went first" she said, "for I can bear the pain of parting better than he could have." "Lou" and Mrs. Robins more or less lived in "Ranikhet" during these days, and J. B. Jones and Henry Byett, with several of the neighbours, were ready to help when needed. None shirked responsibility in that house.

On 15th April, 1930, when the downland spring began to light up the Wiltshire village with its first sunshine, and bluebells and violets were starring the White Horse hedgerows where they stretched along the immemorial hills, Mary watched, from "Ranikhet", a slow procession move to the church. They were burying him, then. She had got them to prop her up, with pillows, in her bed, and in direct line with the window, so that she could follow him with her dimming eyes as far as possible. She asked for a Prayer Book, and they placed one in her slender and lovely hands, and she read the Burial Service while they were laying him in earth.

Four of the villagers who had known him from boyhood bore him to his grave. Reuben George was there with twelve members of the Swindon W.E.A., there were workmen from the G.W.R. stamping shop, Henry Byett, counsellor and intimate comrade for 34 years, "Lou" Robins who had loved him like a brother for 30 years and had been almost the first to hear him read his poems while in manuscript, and J. B. Jones who had championed and befriended him for 22 years. The little church was filled with silent mourners, for there were neither hymns, psalms nor sermon. And one who stooped to lay flowers upon his coffin had attached to them Alfred Williams' own words from *The Testament*.:

"I will sing my song triumphantly,
I will finish my race,
I will work my task.
Be strong, O my soul, for another."

CHAPTER TWENTY-THREE

FULFILMENT

SO was Mary left behind in that quiet room of "Ranikhet". "Lou" Robins and J. B. Jones were constantly by her side attending to her correspondence, for letters poured in from every county of England. Alfred's will, unsigned, unwitnessed, was found in a drawer. This left everything to Mary's niece, for he had obviously thought Mary would die before him, and he knew her wishes as to the disposal of their estate. In his writing desk, "Lou" came across money carefully wrapped in separate pieces of paper, each labelled and earmarked for various purposes. It appeared that he had put aside £23 for the purchase of seeds and other items for his garden during the coming season, but, in order to buy comforts for Mary while she was in hospital, he had broken into this sum. His bank book showed a balance of £62 5s. 0d., of which £50 represented the cheque received from the Prime Minister; the rest was all that remained of the seed money.

Mary immediately made a new will. This stated that "Ranikhet" should be sold and the money realised invested for three of Alfred's nephews, that his books and letters should be left to "Lou" Robins and J. H. Morgan to be disposed of at their discretion, that the royalties on all his books should pass to the Swindon Victoria Hospital and that a piece of land which was theirs should be sold and the proceeds given to the blind of Swindon. This particular plot of land faced "Ranikhet" and had been bought by Alfred and Mary some years before, at cost of great privation to themselves, so that their view of the hills should not be obstructed. Mary wanted to give the land to "Lou" Robins, but he declined it, and it was only when she pressed him that he suggested she should will it to the Swindon Blind Committee.

Her next concern was for Alfred's books and manuscripts. "Lou", at her request, had these packed in five cases and conveyed to his home. Only the Sanskrit books remained behind in "Ranikhet". Mary had special plans for these. Eventually those in Swindon were sorted out and many given to various friends. The remainder were offered by "Lou" to the Swindon Education Committee for the "Richard Jefferies' Club" and were later placed in the Commonweal School. Many of the manuscripts were also accepted by the Education Committee and housed in the Technical College. Others were burned by those who thought they were merely useless scrap paper, not realising that Williams had often written new works on the backs of old ones because of his inability to buy clean paper.

"Lou" now went to Oxford to meet Basil Blackwell, who has described the occasion. "He was stone blind. He told me that he had been Alfred Williams' closest friend and that he felt I ought to be told the whole story. He had, I gathered, chosen the first early closing day in Swindon to leave his tobacconist's shop and make his journey to Oxford. He felt it was due to his friend and due to me, and as he sat before me with the strange stillness and slow speech of the blind, this honest man spoke words which made my ears tingle." "Lou" then proceeded to tell Blackwell the story of Alfred Williams' life and of the tragedy which had come to him. "And now his wife's one care was that his Sanskrit books, the great Lexicon, Grammars, etc., should be given to the University library. Could I help her there? I asked if it would comfort her if I went to see her ('It would indeed'), and arranged to meet the blind man at the house in South Marston a day or two later.

I found the little house built with their own hands and entered the sitting room. Small, clean, furnished with the bare needs for sitting at table for food or work, austere as a cell, it contained Alfred Williams' books. They stood on a small desk by the window, eight or ten books, the nucleus of a Sanskrit scholar's working library. . . .

I went upstairs. The bedroom was as bare as the room below. In the bed, the clothes pulled up to her chin, lay the dying woman. The ivory skin was drawn tight on her face, and her neck was wasted almost to the bone. Only her eyes moved. Beside the bed sat the blind man, and between them on the floor was a case containing all Mary Williams' earthly treasure. I was asked to open it, and there was the revised typescript which Alfred Williams had promised to bring to Oxford. There was nothing else in the case save discarded sheets of the same work. It was all of a piece with the sense of finality which possessed that house.

Mary Williams' first care was for the Sanskrit books, and I promised to see that they were well bestowed. We then spoke about the typescript, briefly, for it was clear that words were costly in that room, and I said I would lose no time in producing the book."

A few days later, "Lou" Robins made a second journey to Oxford. This time he took with him the huge Sanskrit tomes and handed them over to the Bodleian Library. Amongst them was the lexicon and grammar books, *Selected Works of Sri Sakaracharya*, *The Bahgavadgita*, and Arthur Ryder's translation of *The Panchatantra*.

Mary's tasks had now been completed. She lay calmly happy, waiting in patience for the end, with her breathing so quiet at times, that the watchers often thought she had slipped away from them. Alfred had been buried, his library had been disposed of, all his friends and acquaintances had been written to, *Tales from the Panchatantra* was in

the publishers' hands, her will had been made. Nothing now remained
for her but to say her own goodbyes.

On 9th May, Blackwell forwarded £20 for the copyright of the
Tales and told her the proofs would soon be in her hands. On the
15th, Mary received a personal letter from Mr. Ramsay Macdonald
which stated that he hoped she would be willing to receive assistance
in the form of a Grant from the Royal Bounty. In view of her husband's services to literature and because he had been awarded a Civil
List Pension, a grant of £100 was to be made to her immediately.
The Prime Minister suggested that "Lou" Robins and W. D. Bavin
should act as trustees. It was "Lou" who actually opened this letter
and had it read to him, for Mary was almost unconscious and beyond
hope; he there and then decided to keep its contents to himself, for
it was clear that Mary would never need the money. The same day
"Lou" wrote to the Prime Minister and informed him of the circumstances, with the result that the £100 was never sent.

An appeal was now launched by the Mayor of Swindon on behalf of
Mary, and trustees were appointed to administer any funds which might
be so raised. But all was too late. Mary was long past the things of
life. For a few more days she hovered on the threshhold of death.
And then in the slow sad hours of the early dawn of 29th May, 1930,
she slipped away at last to join her waiting lover. And none were
there who would deny her. Alfred and Mary Williams were united
again, locked in earth but free and all-glorious in spirit, in sight of
Liddington and "Ranikhet". The wheel had, in truth, turned full
circle. And all was fulfilled.

APPENDIX I

TALES FROM THE PANCHATANTRA

SHORTLY after the death of Mary Williams, the proofs of *Tales from the Panchatantra* arrived from Basil Blackwell. "Lou" Robins took charge of them and, relying largely on the assistance of friends, first corrected and then personally conveyed them to Oxford. The book was published in the summer of 1930.

Alfred Williams had dedicated the *Tales*

TO MY BELOVED
M. M. W.
TO HER
who shared my labours and vigils
my joys and sorrows
and by her sweetness of spirit
self-sacrifice, and tireless devotion
cheered and encouraged me
in my studies
and especially
in the translation of these fables
I DEDICATE THESE FABLES.

The work, strikingly illustrated by Peggy Whistler, includes besides A. A. Macdonell's "Introductory Note", the tributes to Alfred and Mary Williams written by J. H. Morgan for *The Times*. Macdonell's note briefly traces the history of previous *Panchatantra* translations, and says regarding Williams' particular contribution, "I have read all his translations through, and the impression they produce is one of fidelity to the text, making allowance for his simplifications, which do not affect the narrative".

There is also a scholarly "Translator's Preface" which refers to the *Panchatantra* as one of the most famous books of all time, since it had had a powerful and lasting influence upon the literatures of western Asia and mediæval Europe. An explanation is advanced for the pruning of the tales of "unnecessary ornament", Williams' main aim being to introduce them to the average English reader. "One feature of the tales" he writes "is the universality of their sentiment. We are constantly reminded that human nature has not changed very considerably during the past twenty, or twenty-five centuries."

This preface calls to mind Williams' brilliant Introduction to *Folk Songs of the Upper Thames*. In point of fact, *Tales from the Panchatantra* is in direct line with all his country books; they are pure folk lore. The tales also show how deep seated was his delight and belief in natural philosophy, for the speech put into the mouths of the animals, fishes, birds and reptiles, who are the personages of these stories, is rich with eternal wisdom, and full of a wide understanding of human thoughts and emotions. These ancient Hindu creatures, wiser and more subtle in their generation than those which move across the pages of Aesop, are the legitimate forerunners of that legion created for another art in our own day by Disney. They concern themselves with nearly every facet of everyday life. Here we have discourses on "religion, polity, education, love and marriage, joy and sorrow, friendship and treachery, victory and defeat, making money and losing it, and everything else of ordinary interest."

The tales are therefore authentic Parables containing profound religious truths. It had been the purpose of their first editor, the ascetic and saintly Vishnusharman, to lead his fellows to the wells of true wisdom, beauty and happiness, by presenting them with these stories.

Tales from the Panchatantra is undoubtedly a masterpiece of its kind. It is worthy of survival because, not only is it a remarkable study into the origins of language and literature by one whose patient research and devoted concentration ranged him alongside the Sanskrit scholars of his day, but also it is valuable evidence of the kind of ethics which have concerned the souls of men in every generation. There is no shade of escapism here, mysticism perhaps, and certainly complete release of the spirit. The poet of *The Testament* and *Natural Thoughts and Surmises* was better qualified than most to understand and effectively deal with these stories from the dawn of history. Although their themes are lofty, real and noble, Williams succeeded in clothing them in the same simple and beguiling prose which was his special artistic gift.

Tales from the Panchatantra was treated by most reviewers as a children's book; the only intelligent and discerning notice appeared in *The Johannesburg Star*. It had a poor market at the time but is now almost unobtainable.

In September, 1931, Blackwell issued a selection of the stories for school use under the title of *Tales from the East*. The editor of this little book, Michael Lynn, said in his foreword "were Mr. Williams alive nothing would give him greater pleasure than the knowledge that his work has been made a vehicle for the conveying of children to the very cradle of story-telling". And this was assuredly true of the South Marston villager who had so serenely loved and appreciated young children.

APPENDIX II

PUBLISHED WORKS BY ALFRED WILLIAMS

Songs in Wiltshire. 1909. Erskine Macdonald.
Poems in Wiltshire. 1911. Erskine Macdonald.
Nature and Other Poems. 1912. Erskine Macdonald.
A Wiltshire Village. 1912. Duckworth & Co., Ltd.
Cor Cordium. 1913. Erskine Macdonald.
Villages of the White Horse. 1913. Duckworth & Co., Ltd.
Life in a Railway Factory. 1915. Duckworth & Co., Ltd.
War Sonnets and Songs. 1915. Erskine Macdonald.
Round About the Upper Thames. 1922. Duckworth & Co., Ltd.
Folk Songs of the Upper Thames. 1923. Duckworth & Co., Ltd.
Selected Poems. 1925. Erskine Macdonald.
Tales from the Panchatantra. 1930. Basil Blackwell.
Tales from the East. 1931. Basil Blackwell.

APPENDIX III

UNPUBLISHED WORKS BY ALFRED WILLIAMS

Mark Titcombe: A Rhyme.
Rhymes of the Forge.
Aeneas: A Poem. Two extracts from this were published in *Nature and Other Poems.*
Indian Life and Scenery, or *Mid Palm and Pine.*
A Worker's Letters to Workers.
Sardanapalus: A Play (in verse).
Dudley Sansum: A Poem.
By the Fireside: A Poem.
Boys of the Battery.
Round the Cape to India.
The Steam Hammer Shop: A Novel.
Various Lectures, Newspaper Articles and other Prose fragments.
Various Sonnets, Translations and shorter poems.
Round About the Middle Thames, or *The Banks of the Isis.*

CHRONOLOGICAL TABLE

1849 Elias Lloyd Williams, 13th child of David Aust Williams and Ann Roberts, born Conway, North Wales.

1850 Elizabeth Hughes, 3rd child of Joshua Hughes and Ann Hayden, born South Marston, Wiltshire.

1868–9 Building of "Rose Cottage".

1870 Marriage of Elias Lloyd Williams and Elizabeth Hughes.

1871 Building of "Cambria Cottage".

1877 February 6th—birth of Owen Alfred Williams in "Cambria Cottage".

1880 Elias Lloyd Williams and Elizabeth Williams separate.

1885 Alfred Williams becomes a "half-timer" on local farms.

1889 Leaves school to work at Longleaze Farm, South Marston.

1890 Priory Farm, South Marston.

1892 Rivet hotter. Later Furnace Boy at G.W.R. Works, Swindon.

1893 Begins to paint. Drop Stamper in Works.

1897 Buys and reads Shakespeare's plays.

1899 Death of Elias Lloyd Williams at Colwyn Bay.

1900 Correspondence Course, Ruskin Hall, Oxford.

1901 Begins to learn Latin.

1903 October—marriage of Alfred Williams and Mary Maria Peck.
Begins to live in "Dryden Cottage".
Begins to learn Greek and French.

1904 Wins £100 newspaper prize.
Writes *Sardanapalus*.

1907 Two poems in *New Songs*.

1909 Two poems in *Garnered Grain*.
Meets Lord Fitzmaurice, Alfred Zimmern and Albert Mansbridge.
Reads complete works of Richard Jefferies.
Songs in Wiltshire.

1910 Meets John Bailey.
Reads works by Max Müller.

1911 Meets Edward Garnett.
Poems in Wiltshire.

1912 *A Wiltshire Village*.
Nature and Other Poems.
Meets Robert Bridges.

1913 *Cor Cordium*.
Villages of the White Horse.

1914   Leaves G.W.R. Works. Begins market gardening.
1915   *Life in a Railway Factory.*
       War Sonnets and Songs.
1916   Begins collecting Folk Songs.
       Gunner. Royal Field Artillery.
1917   Ireland.
       Scotland. Gunner. Royal Garrison Artillery.
       Winchester. Writes *Boys of the Battery.*
       Sails for India.
       Death of Elizabeth Williams.
1917–   India.
1919   Writes *Round the Cape to India* and *Indian Life and Scenery.*
1919   Leaves India.
       November—demobilised.
1920   Clerk and Assistant Overseer South Marston Parish Council.
1920–   Building of "Ranikhet".
1921   Resigns Clerkship.
1922   *Round About the Upper Thames.*
1923   *Folk Songs of the Upper Thames.*
       Begins to learn Sanskrit.
1924   *The Banks of Isis.*
1925   *Letters from a Working Man to Working Men.*
       Selected Poems.
1927   *The Steam Hammer Shop.*
       Begins to translate the *Panchatantra.*
1930   March—Civil List Pension.
       April 9th—Death of Alfred Williams in "Ranikhet," South
         Marston.
       May 29th—Death of Mary Williams in "Ranikhet," South
         Marston.
       Tales from the Panchatantra.
1931   *Tales from the East.*

GENEALOGICAL TABLE

John and Elizabeth Hughes   John and Elizabeth Hayden

David Aust Williams—Ann Roberts   Joshua Hughes—Ann Hayden

Elias Lloyd Williams—Elizabeth Hughes
(1849—1899)   (1850—1917)

Ernest Lloyd   Edgar David   Elizabeth Ann   Henry Oliver   Owen Alfred—Mary Maria Peck   Laura   Ellen   Ada Mary
(1877—1930)   (1880—1930)

Joshua Hughes born and died South Marston.
Elizabeth Hughes born and died South Marston.
David Aust Williams born and died Colwyn Bay.
Elias Lloyd Williams born Conway, died Colwyn Bay.
Alfred Williams born and died South Marston.
Mary Williams born Eddington, Berkshire, died South Marston.

INDEX